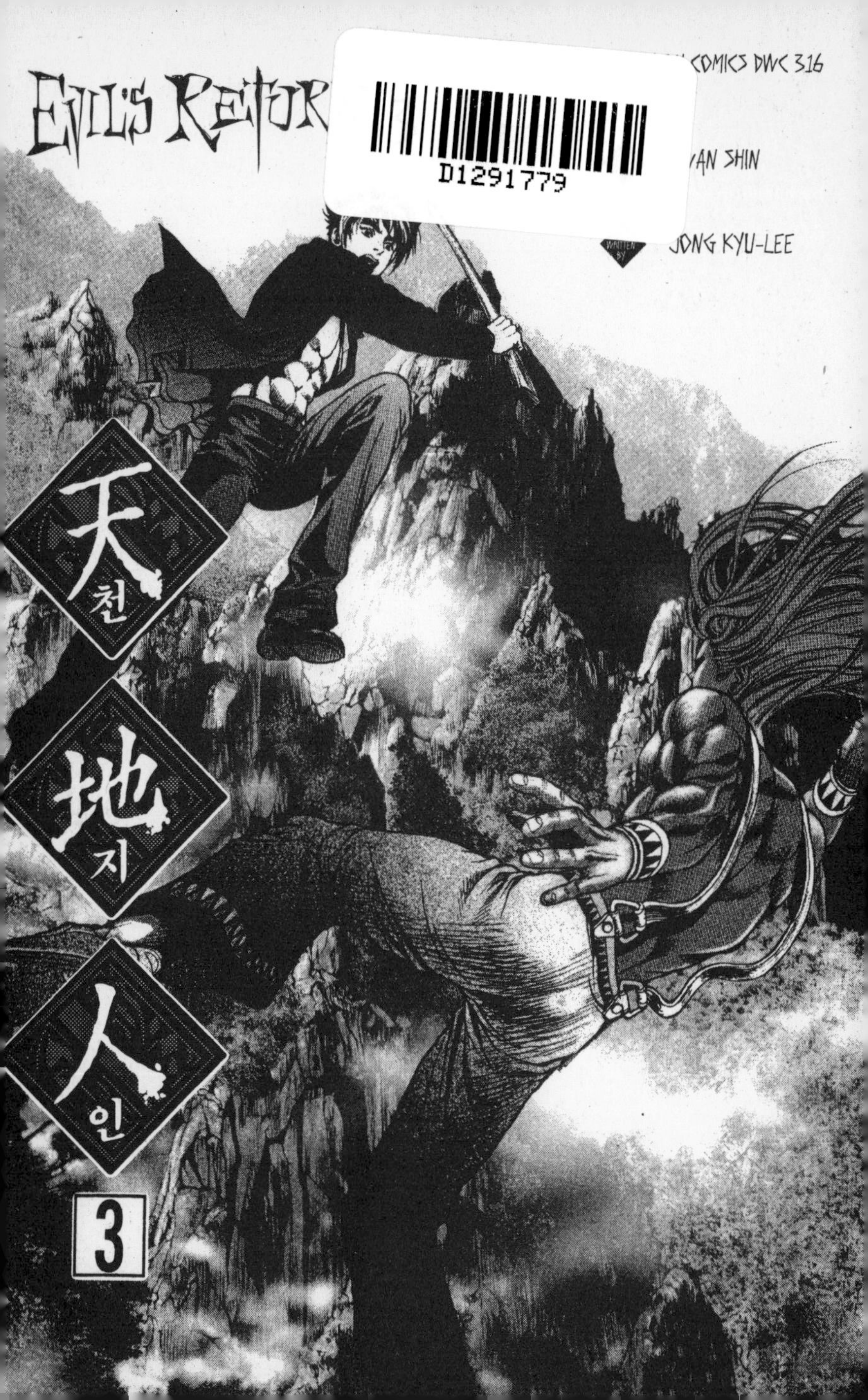

EVIL'S RETUR
COMICS DWC 316
YAN SHIN
WRITTEN BY
JONG KYU-LEE
天 천
地 지
人 인
3

Evil's Return Vol. 3

written by Jong Kyu-Lee
illustrated by Hwan Shin

Translation - Seung-Ah Lee
Associate Editor - Wendy Hunter
Retouch and Lettering - Jackie Del Monte
Production Artist - Louis Csontos
Cover Design - Patrick Hook

Editor - Luis Reyes
Digital Imaging Manager - Chris Buford
Pre-Press Manager - Antonio DePietro
Production Managers - Jennifer Miller and Mutsumi Miyazaki
Art Director - Matt Alford
Managing Editor - Jill Freshney
VP of Production - Ron Klamert
President and C.O.O. - John Parker
Publisher and C.E.O. - Stuart Levy

A  Manga

TOKYOPOP Inc.
5900 Wilshire Blvd. Suite 2000
Los Angeles, CA 90036

E-mail: info@TOKYOPOP.com
Come visit us online at www.TOKYOPOP.com

ISBN: 1-59182-967-4

First TOKYOPOP printing: Janary 2005

10 9 8 7 6 5 4 3 2 1

Printed in the USA

EVIL'S RETURN

VOLUME 3

ART BY: HWAN SHIN
WRITTEN BY: JONG KYU-LEE

HAMBURG // LONDON // LOS ANGELES // TOKYO

EVIL'S RETURN

STORY SO FAR...

SEO YUMI'S FIRST PERIOD SIGNALED TO LEGIONS OF DEMONS THAT SHE, THE PROPHESIED MOTHER OF HELL, WAS READY TO MOTHER THE HELLISH HORRORS OF ANY DEMON THAT COULD GET ITS HANDS ON HER. BUDDHIST DISCIPLE AND STUDENT BODY PRESIDENT SUNWOO HYUN WAS HER ONLY LINE OF DEFENSE AGAINST THE EVIL FORCES. BUT WHEN HOTHEADED AND HEAD-OVER-HEELS-IN-LOVE FRESHMAN TAE CHAIL CHALLENGED HYUN TO A DUEL OVER YUMI'S LOVE, THE FRIGHTENED YOUNG WOMAN WAS LEFT ALONE TO DEAL WITH A HORDE OF POSSESSED STUDENTS SWARMING THE SCHOOL GROUNDS. AFTER DEFEATING CHAIL, HYUN RUSHED TO HER SIDE, ONLY TO BE KNOCKED COLD. THINGS LOOKED BLEAK UNTIL CHAIL SHOWED UP SWINGING, READY TO DIE FOR YUMI. THE ENSUING BATTLE BROUGHT BLOODSHED AND BEDLAM TO THE SCHOOL, BUT IT ALSO REVEALED THAT THERE IS A HIDDEN SECRET DEEP WITHIN CHAIL'S SOUL...THE IMPRINT OF AN ANCIENT WARRIOR WHO MAY RIDE AGAIN.

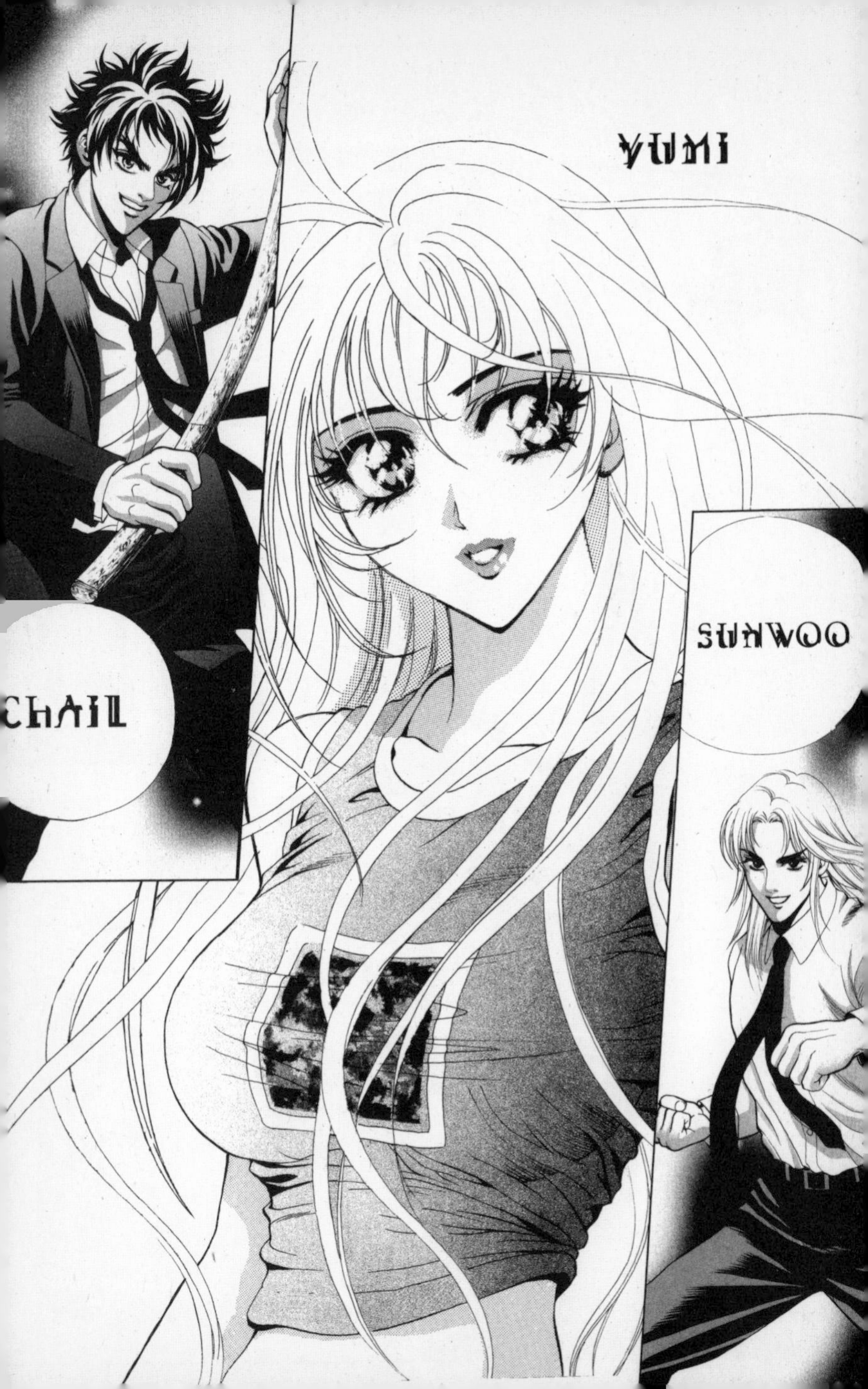
YUMI
CHAIL
SUNWOO

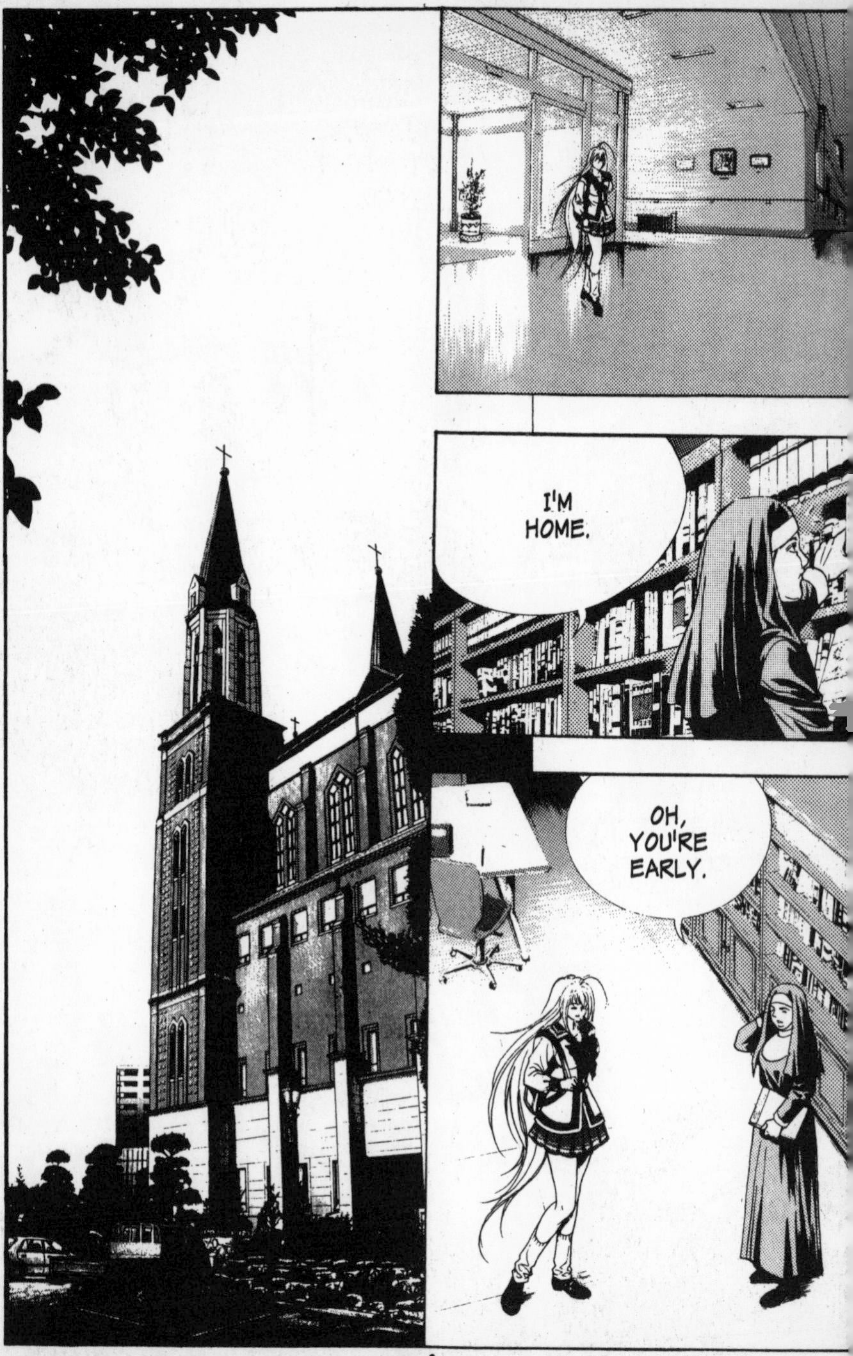
I'M HOME.
OH, YOU'RE EARLY.

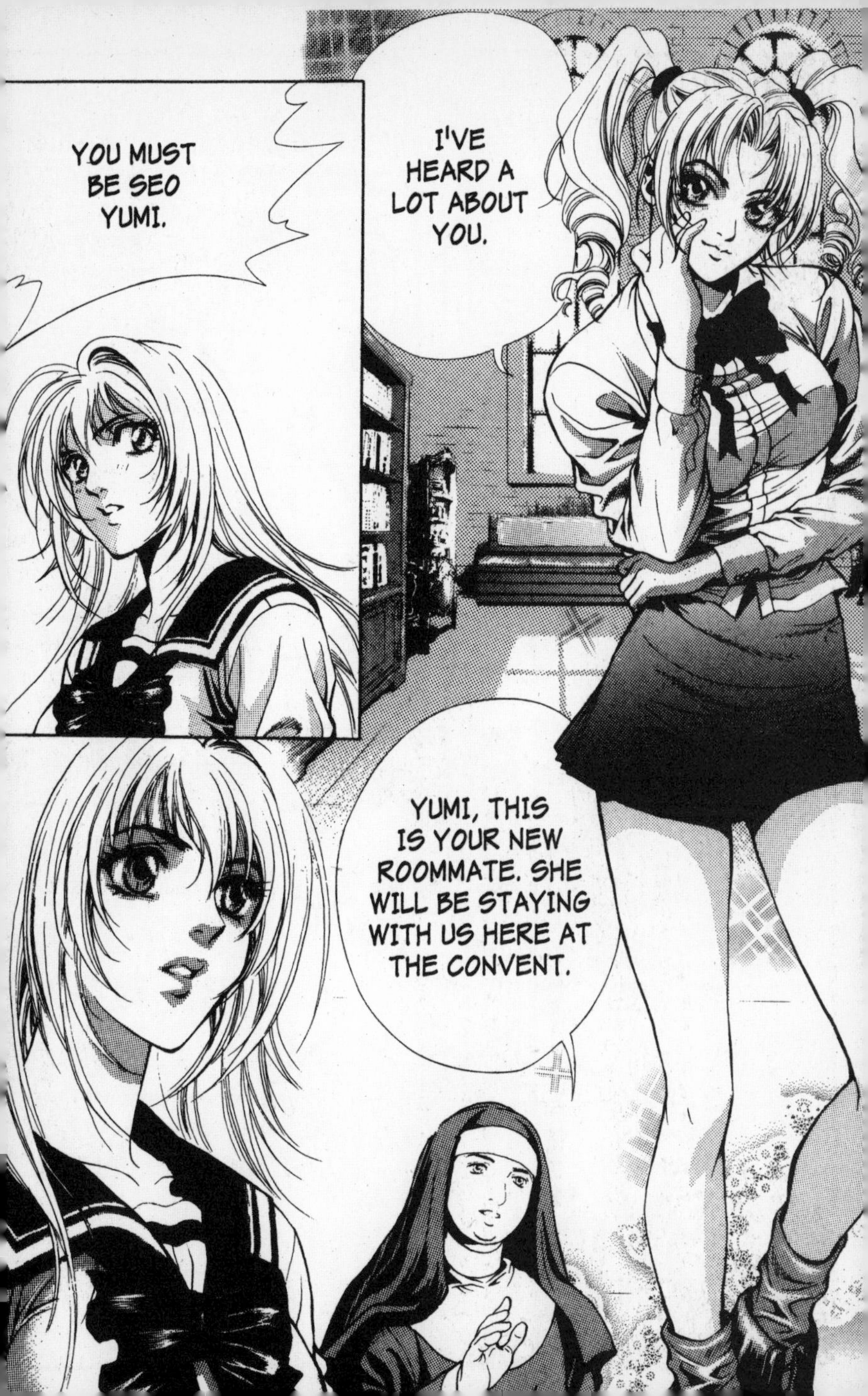
YOU MUST BE SEO YUMI.
I'VE HEARD A LOT ABOUT YOU.
YUMI, THIS IS YOUR NEW ROOMMATE. SHE WILL BE STAYING WITH US HERE AT THE CONVENT.

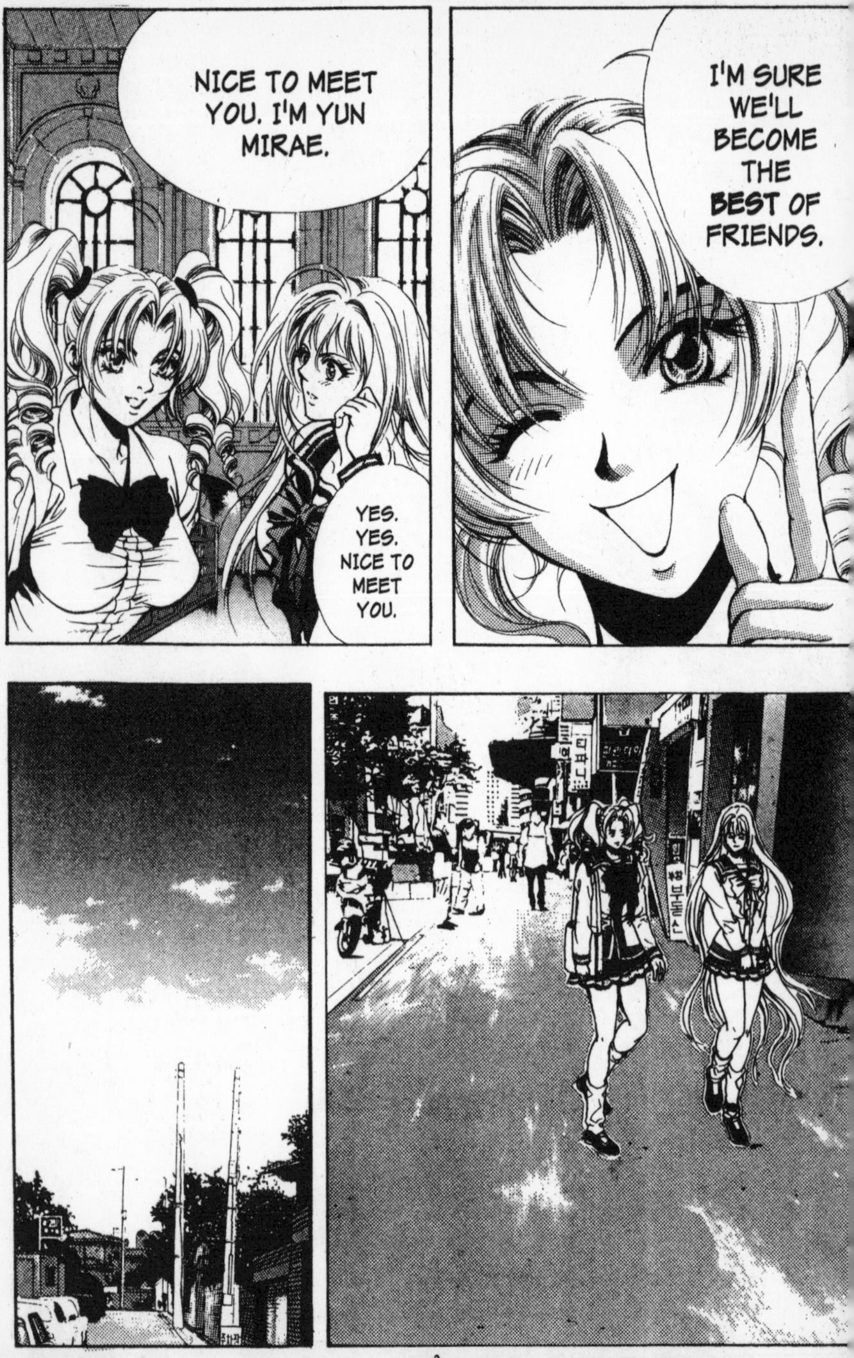
NICE TO MEET YOU. I'M YUN MIRAE.
YES. YES. NICE TO MEET YOU.
I'M SURE WE'LL BECOME THE BEST OF FRIENDS.

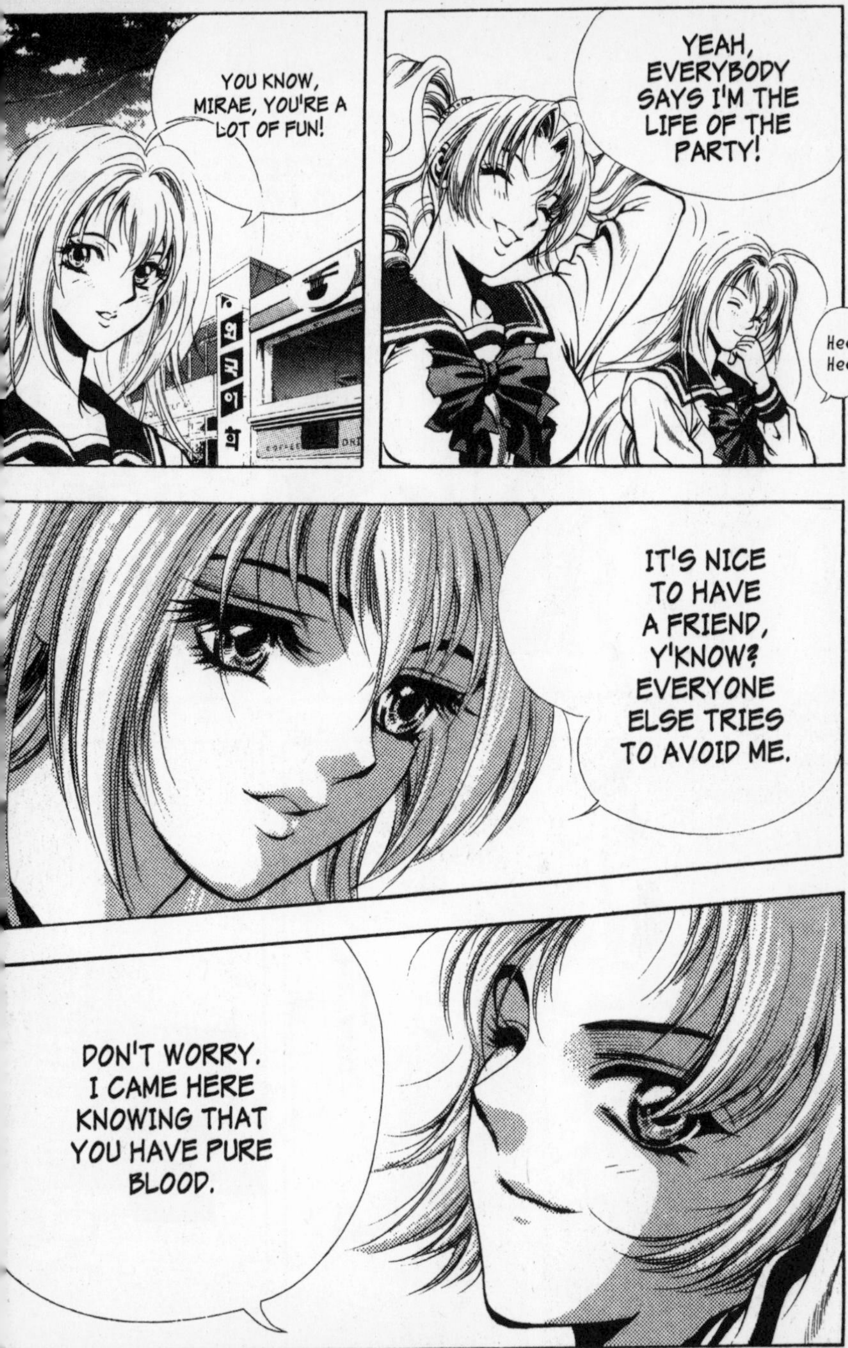
YOU KNOW, MIRAE, YOU'RE A LOT OF FUN!
YEAH, EVERYBODY SAYS I'M THE LIFE OF THE PARTY!
Hee Hee
IT'S NICE TO HAVE A FRIEND, Y'KNOW? EVERYONE ELSE TRIES TO AVOID ME.
DON'T WORRY. I CAME HERE KNOWING THAT YOU HAVE PURE BLOOD.

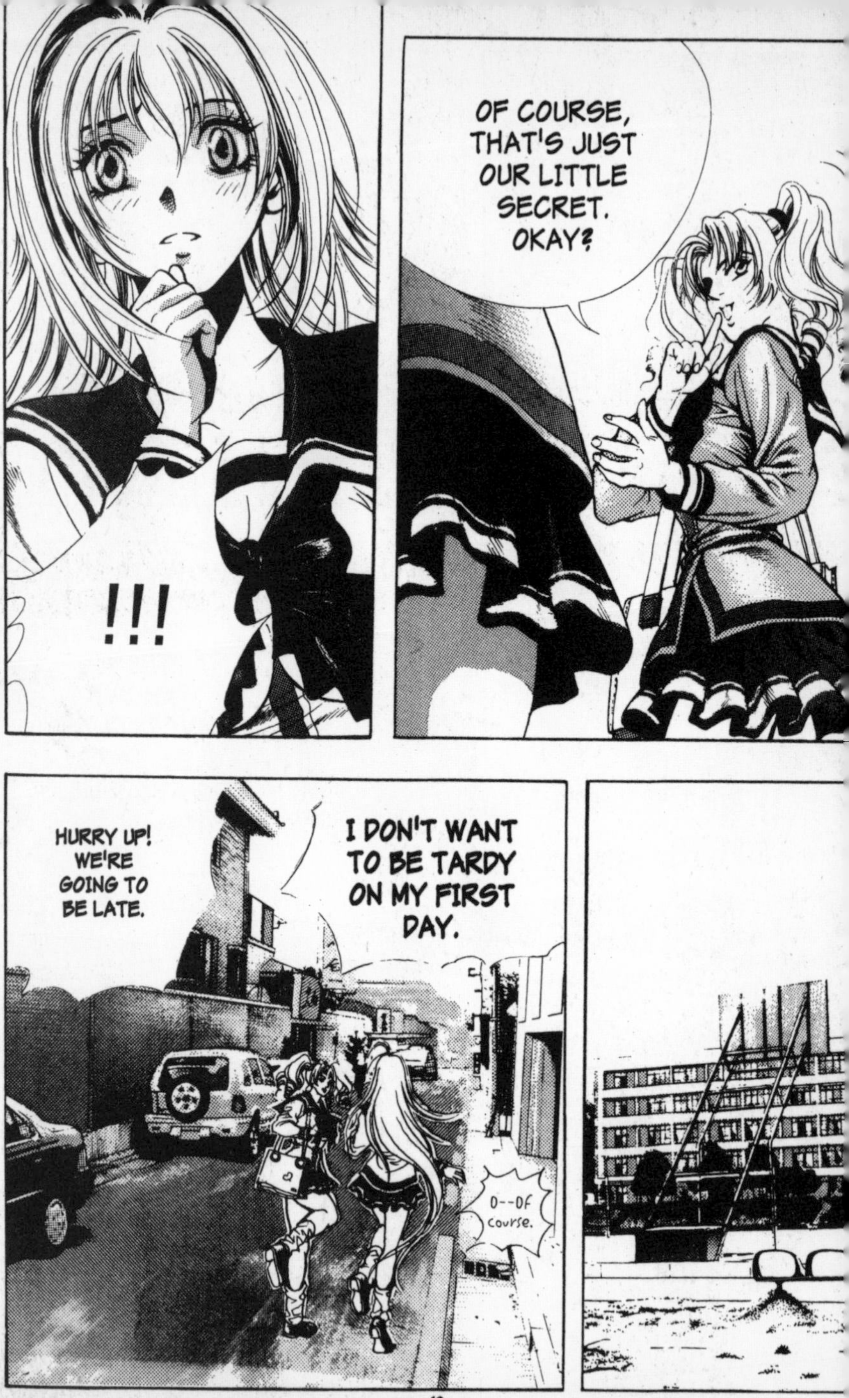
!!!
OF COURSE, THAT'S JUST OUR LITTLE SECRET. OKAY?
HURRY UP! WE'RE GOING TO BE LATE.
I DON'T WANT TO BE TARDY ON MY FIRST DAY.
D--Of course.

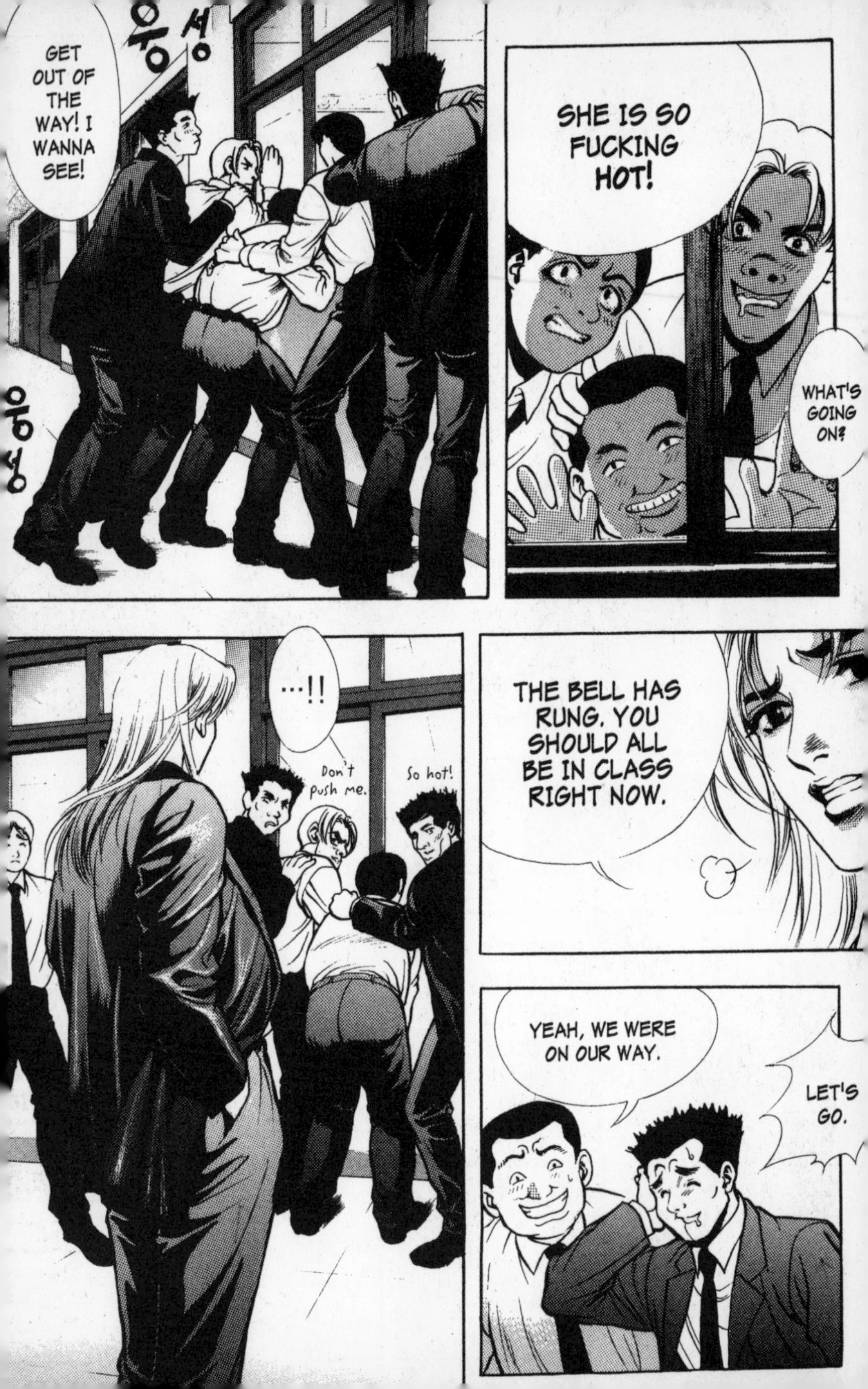
웅성
GET OUT OF THE WAY! I WANNA SEE!
웅성
SHE IS SO FUCKING HOT!
WHAT'S GOING ON?
...!!
Don't push me.
So hot!
THE BELL HAS RUNG. YOU SHOULD ALL BE IN CLASS RIGHT NOW.
YEAH, WE WERE ON OUR WAY.
LET'S GO.

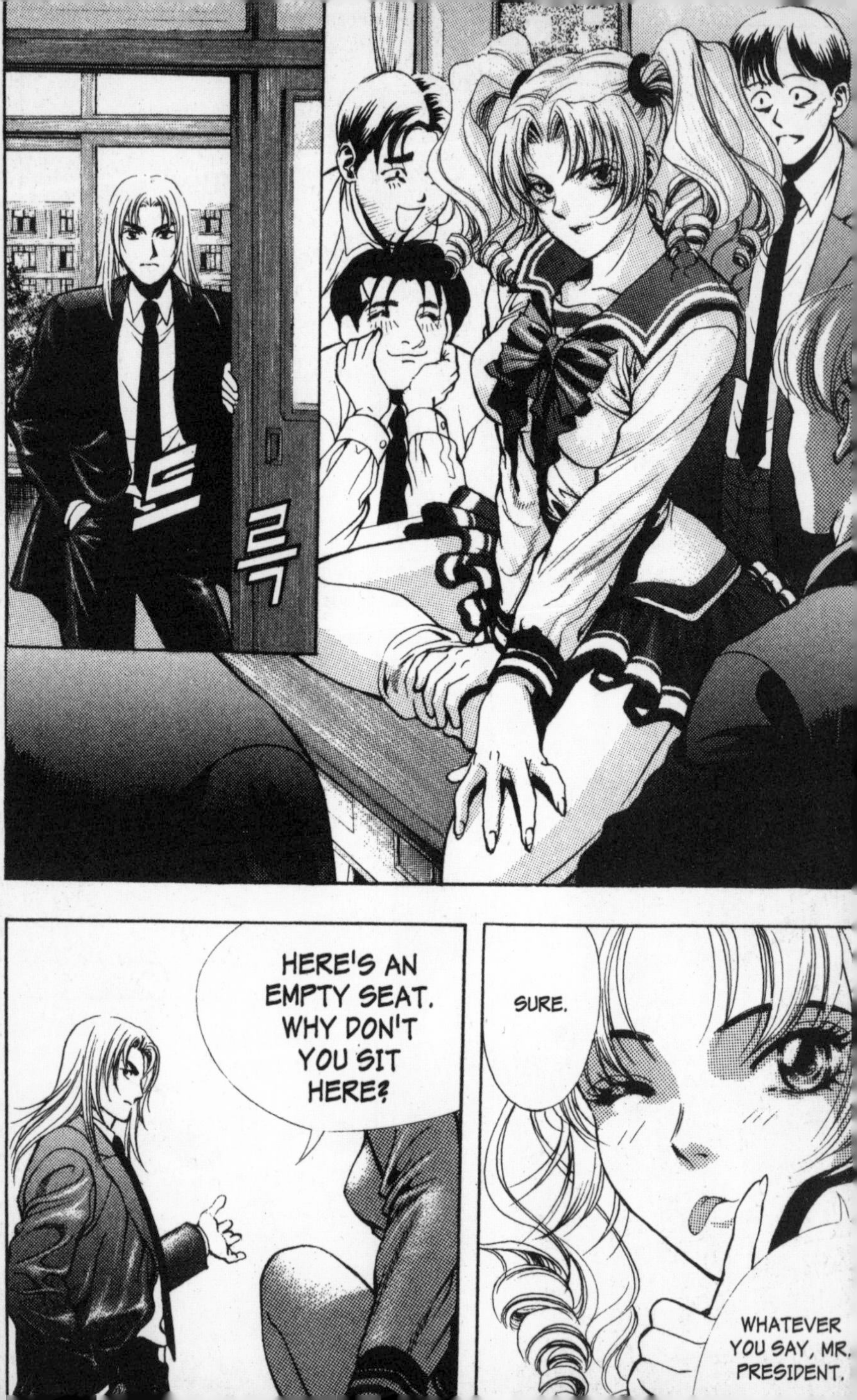

드륵
HERE'S AN EMPTY SEAT. WHY DON'T YOU SIT HERE?
SURE.
WHATEVER YOU SAY, MR. PRESIDENT.

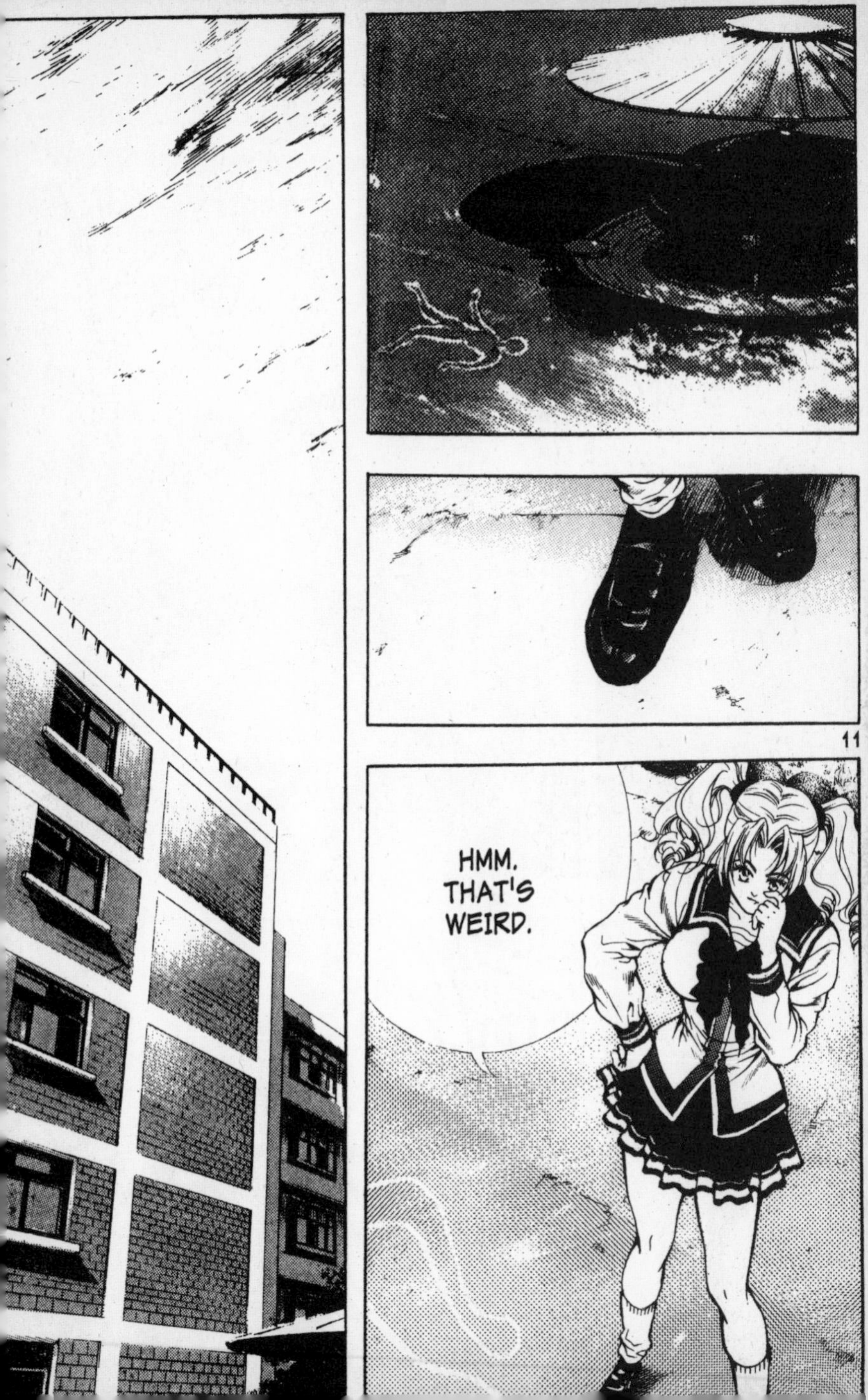
HMM. THAT'S WEIRD.

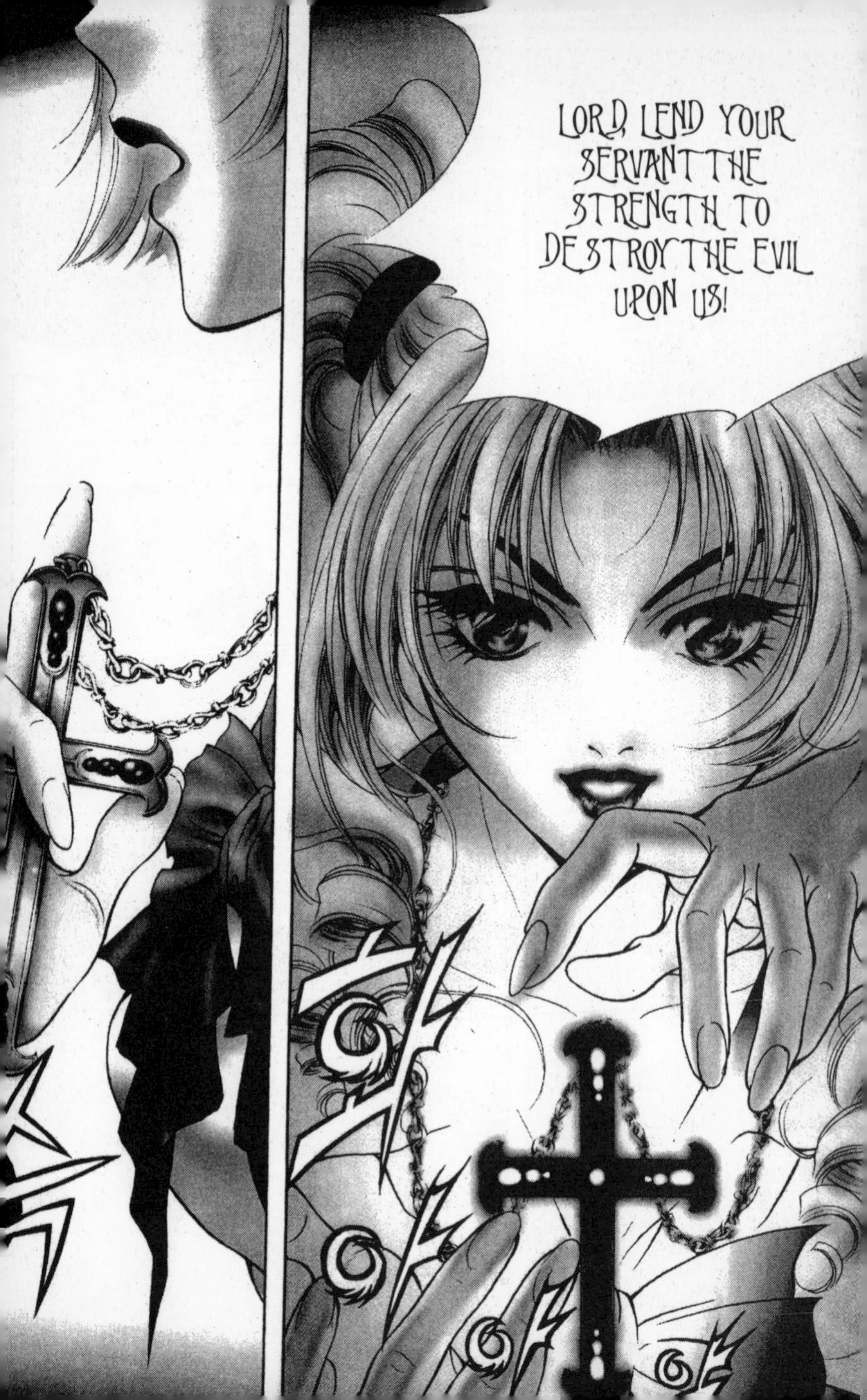
LORD, LEND YOUR SERVANT THE STRENGTH TO DESTROY THE EVIL UPON US!

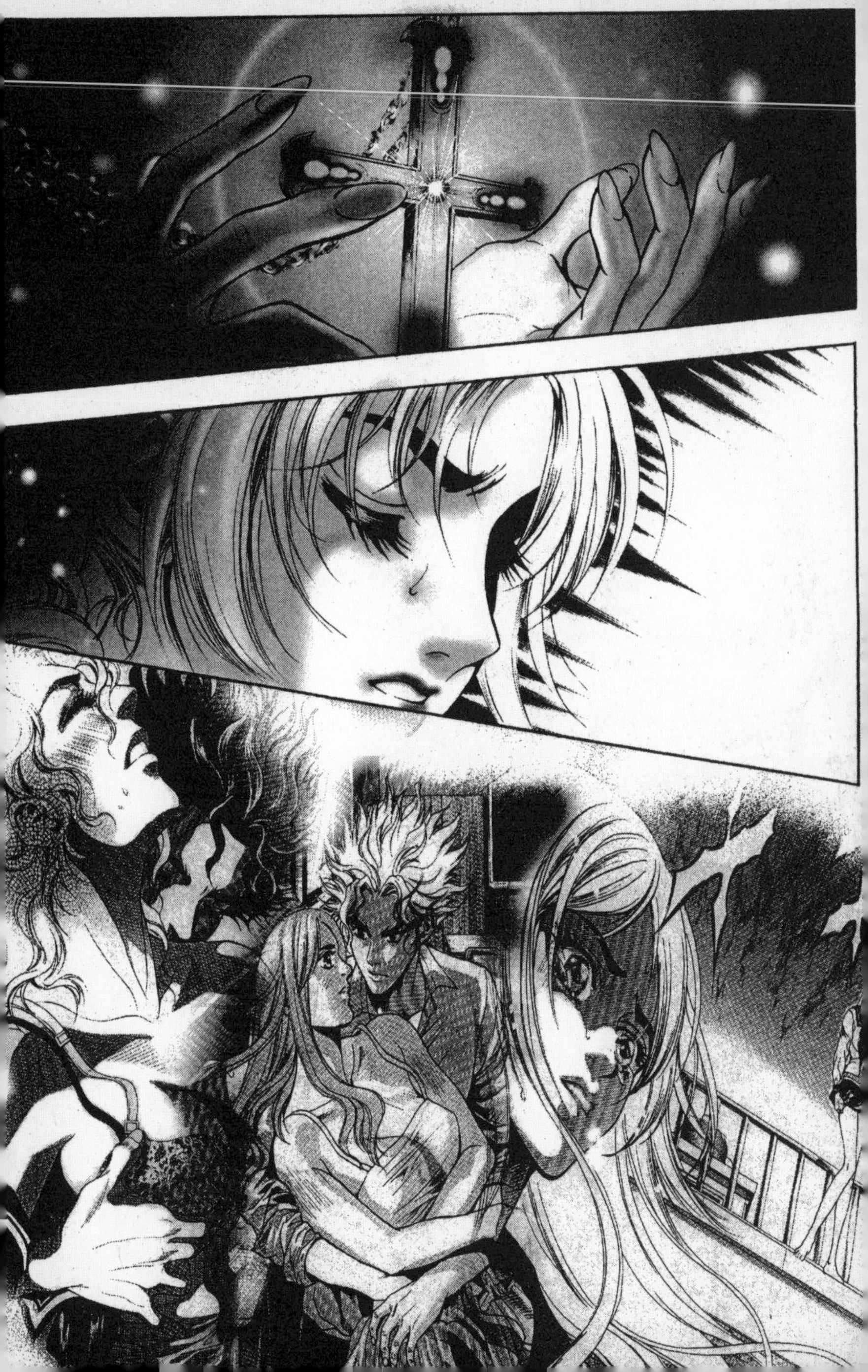

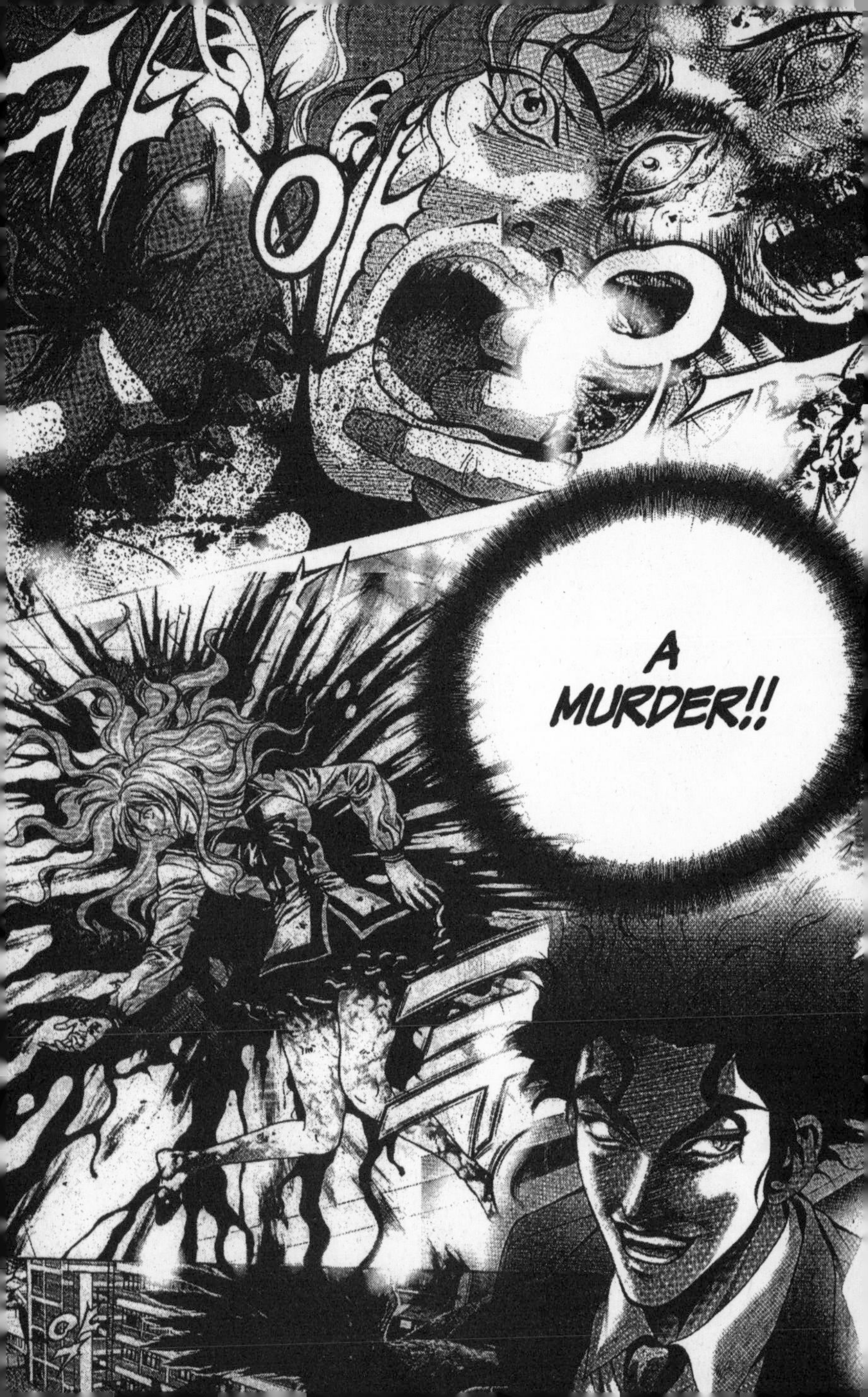
A
MURDER!!

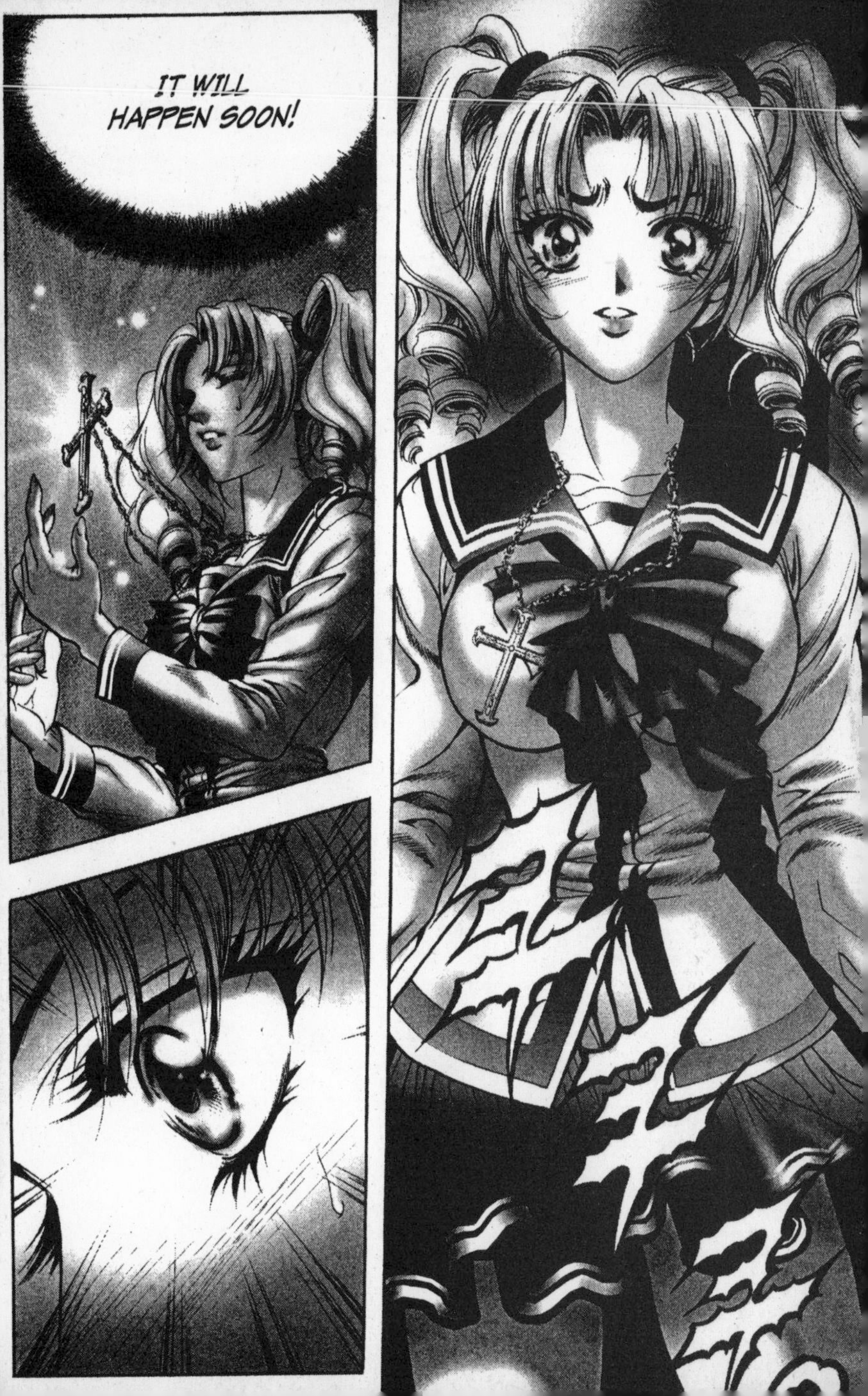
IT WILL HAPPEN SOON!

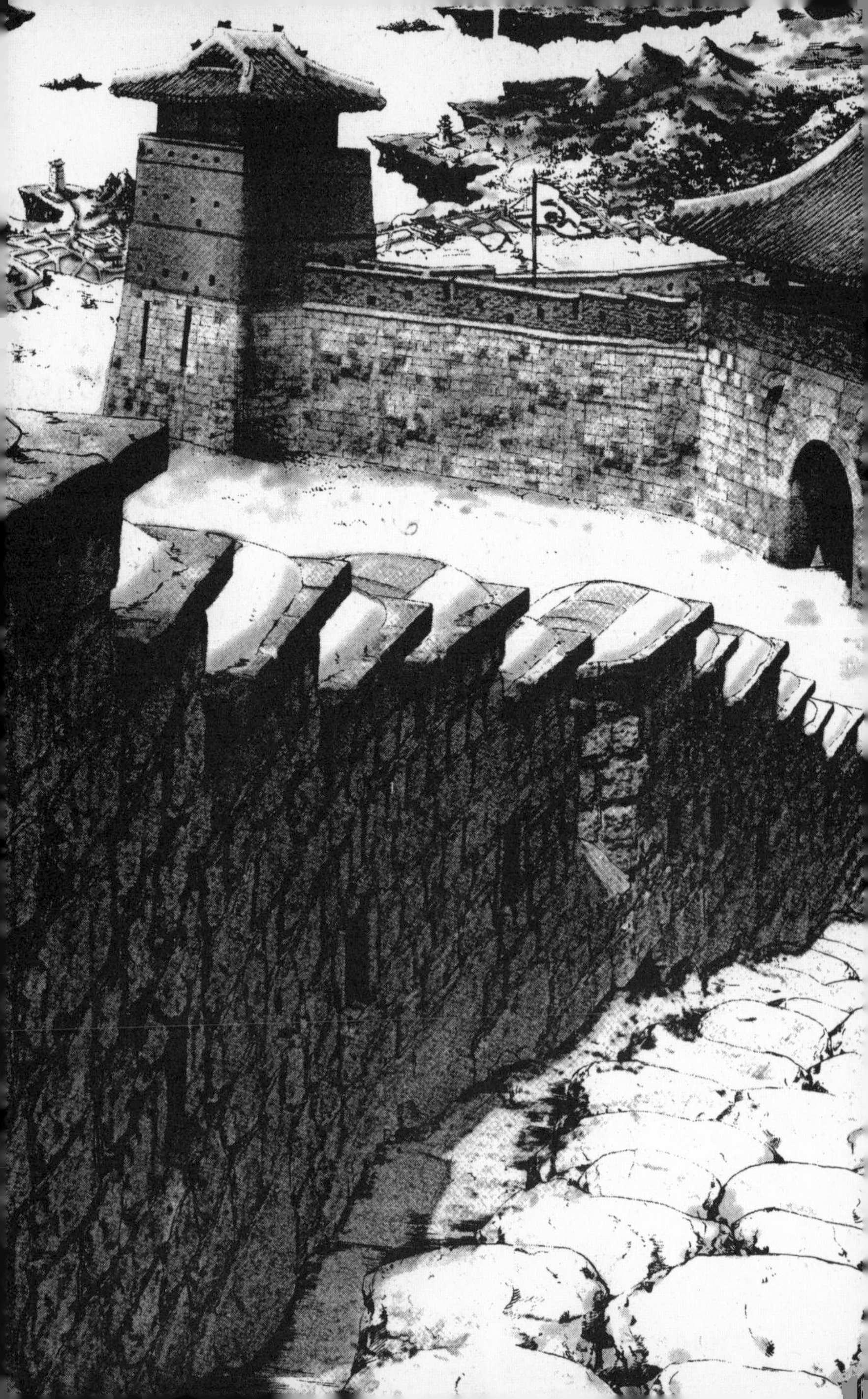

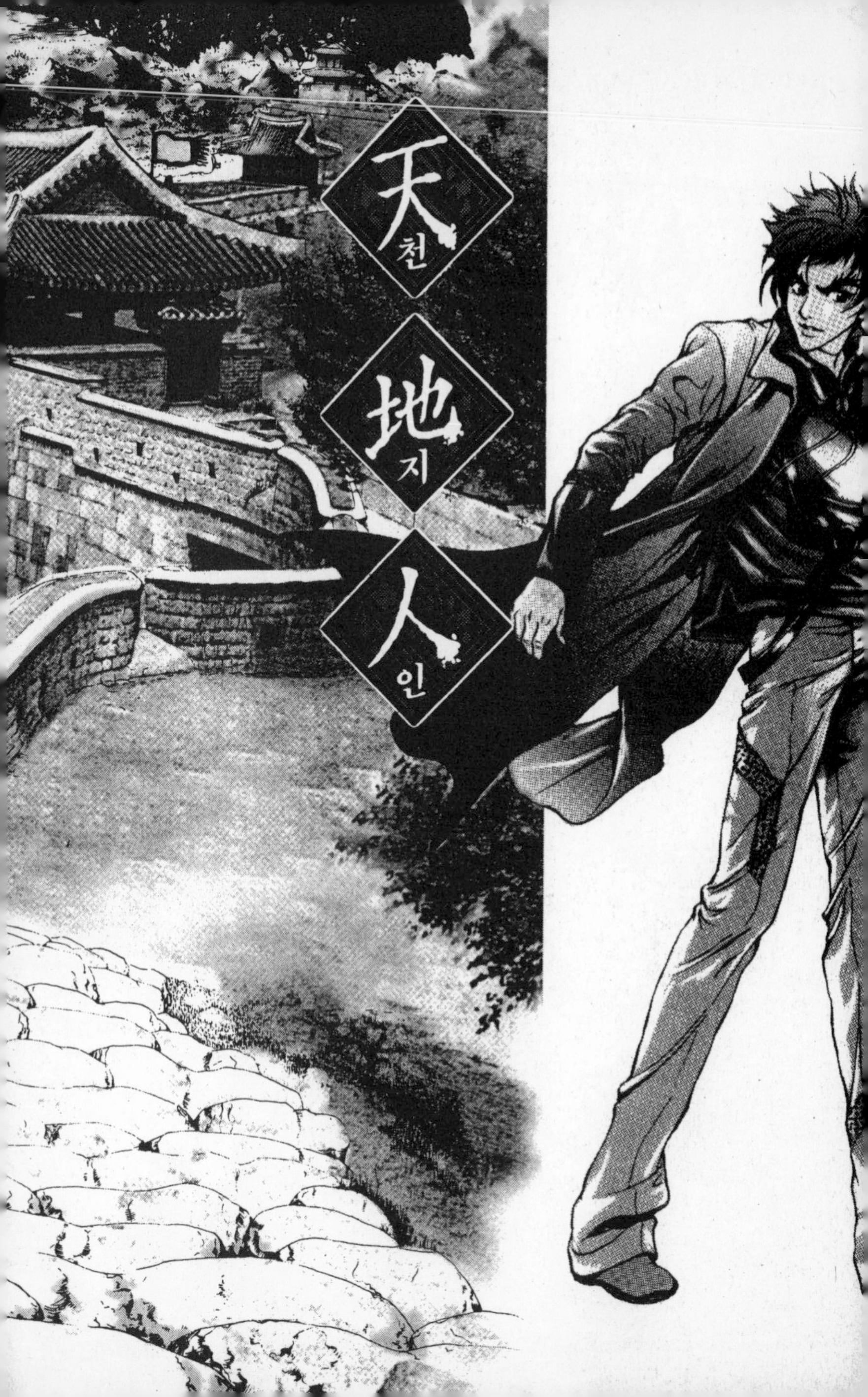
天 천
地 지
人 인

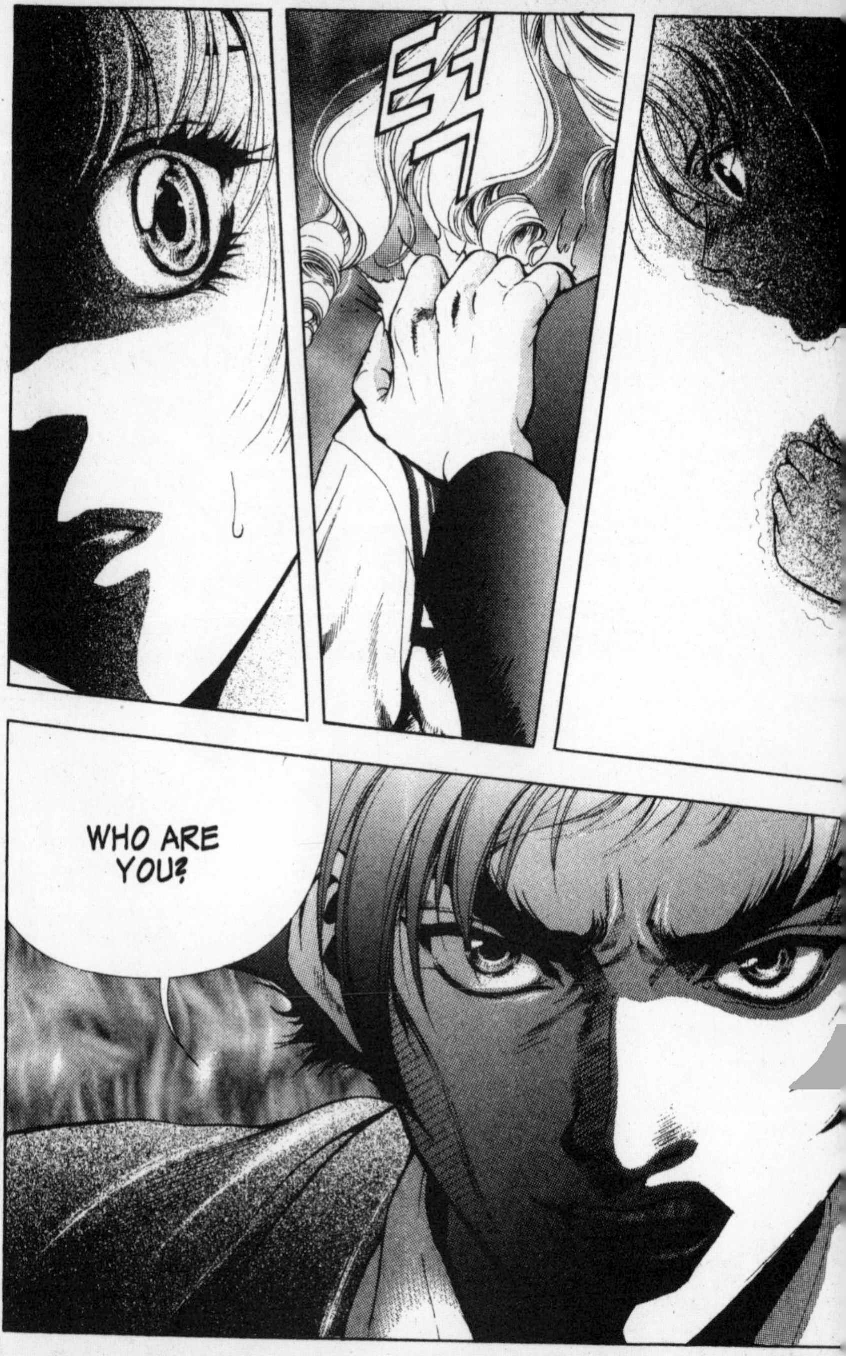
턱
WHO ARE YOU?

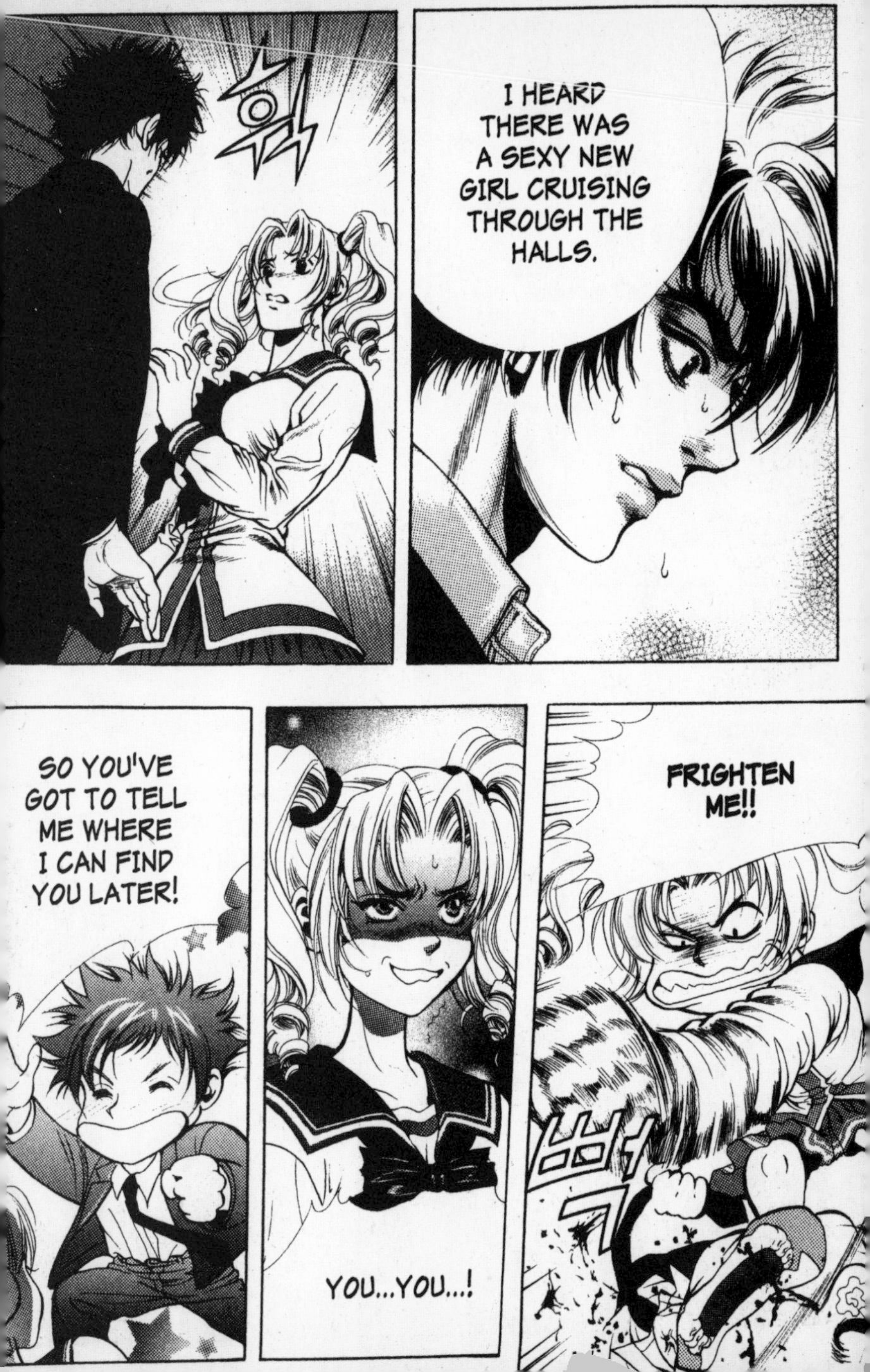
I HEARD THERE WAS A SEXY NEW GIRL CRUISING THROUGH THE HALLS.
FRIGHTEN ME!!
YOU...YOU...!
SO YOU'VE GOT TO TELL ME WHERE I CAN FIND YOU LATER!

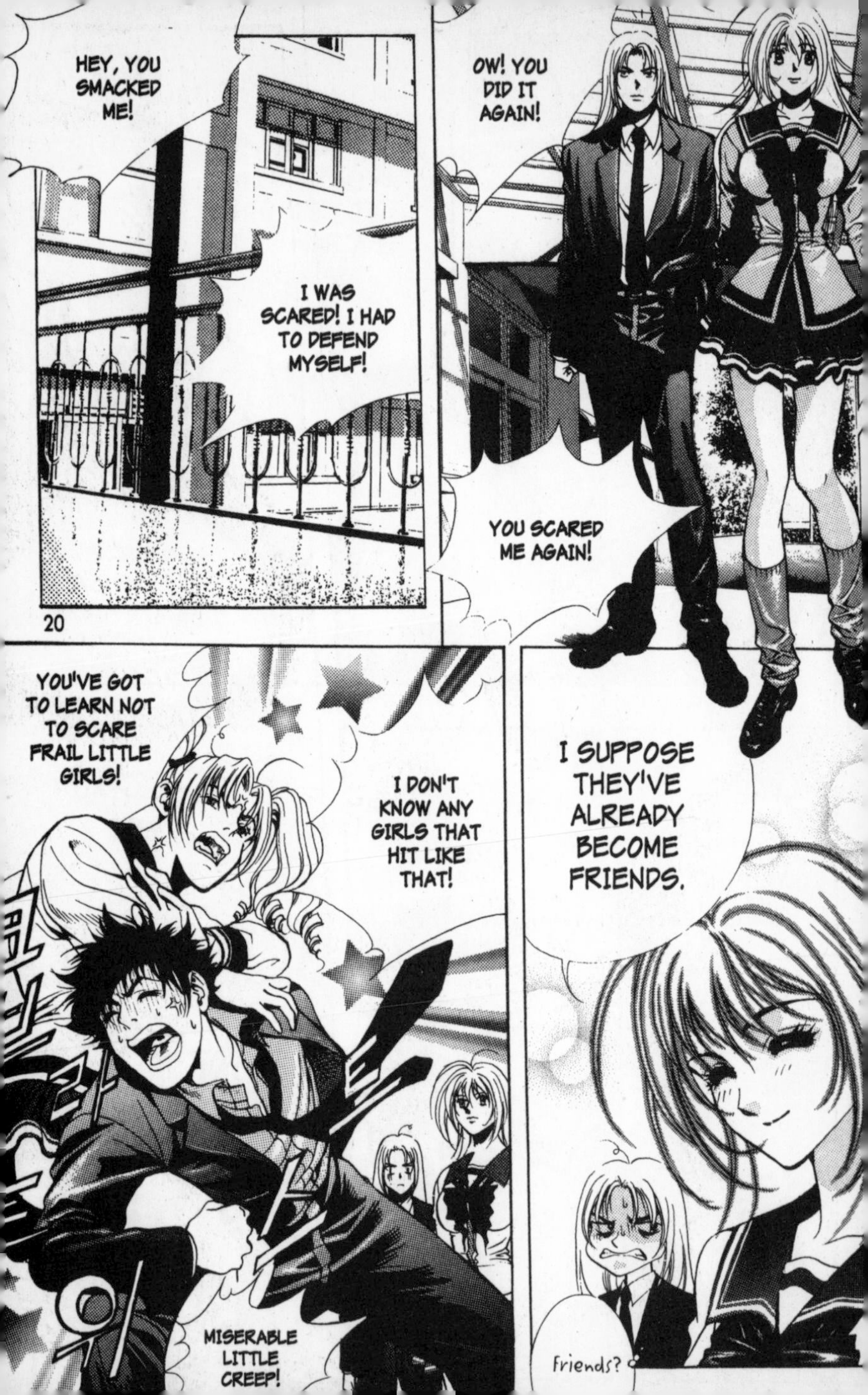
HEY, YOU SMACKED ME!
I WAS SCARED! I HAD TO DEFEND MYSELF!
OW! YOU DID IT AGAIN!
YOU SCARED ME AGAIN!
YOU'VE GOT TO LEARN NOT TO SCARE FRAIL LITTLE GIRLS!
I DON'T KNOW ANY GIRLS THAT HIT LIKE THAT!
MISERABLE LITTLE CREEP!
I SUPPOSE THEY'VE ALREADY BECOME FRIENDS.
Friends?

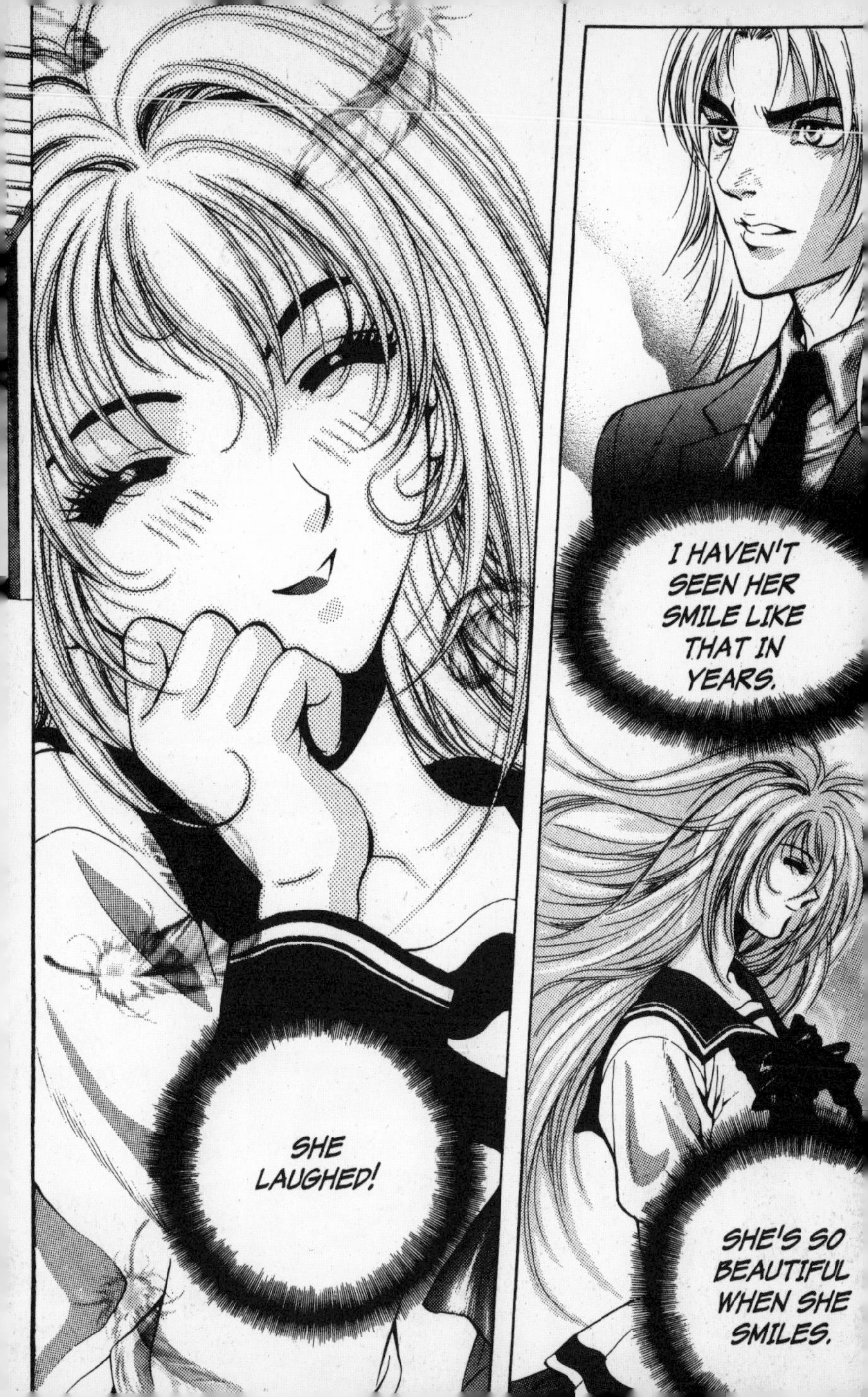
I HAVEN'T SEEN HER SMILE LIKE THAT IN YEARS.
SHE'S SO BEAUTIFUL WHEN SHE SMILES.
SHE LAUGHED!

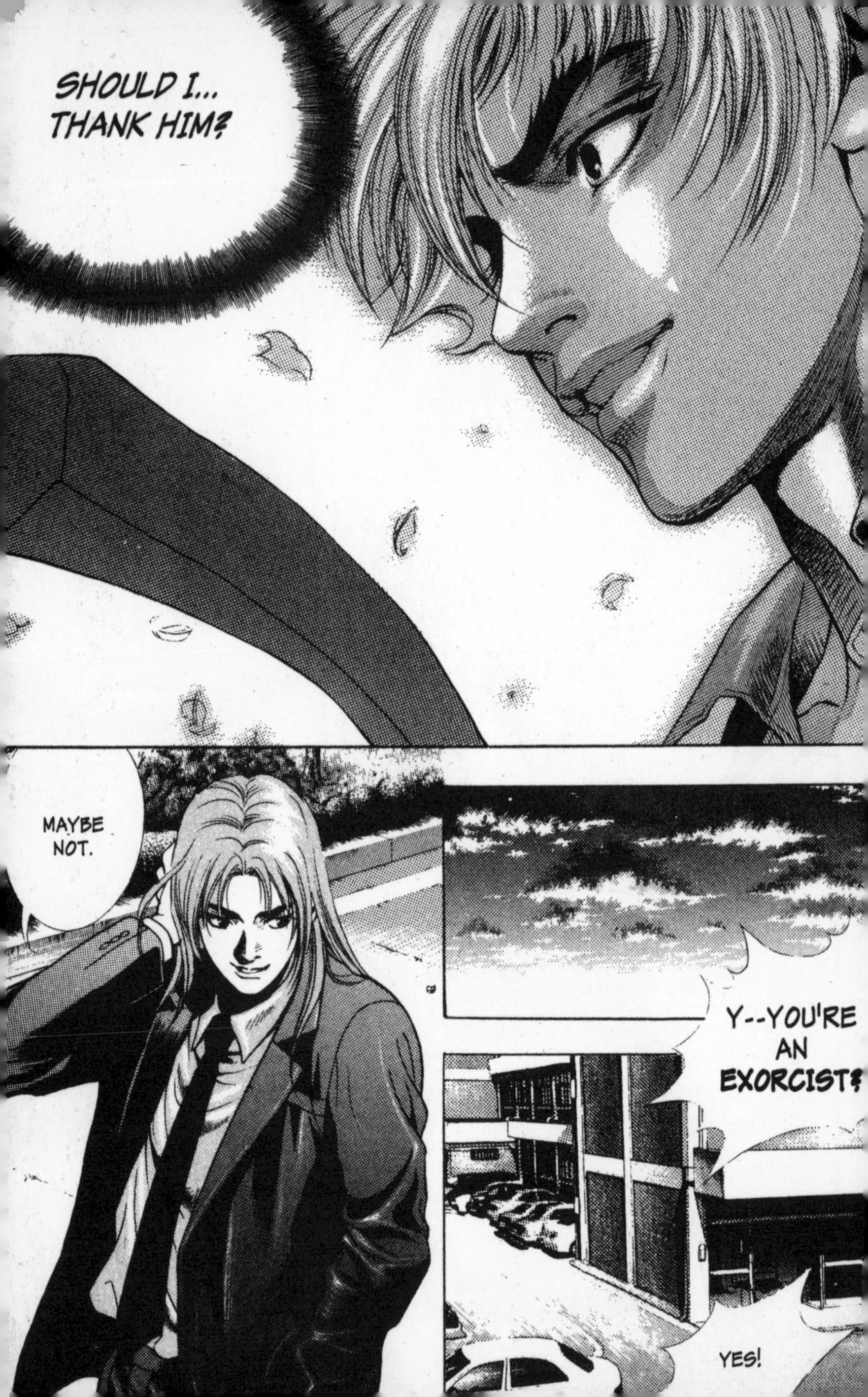
SHOULD I... THANK HIM?
MAYBE NOT.
Y--YOU'RE AN EXORCIST?
YES!

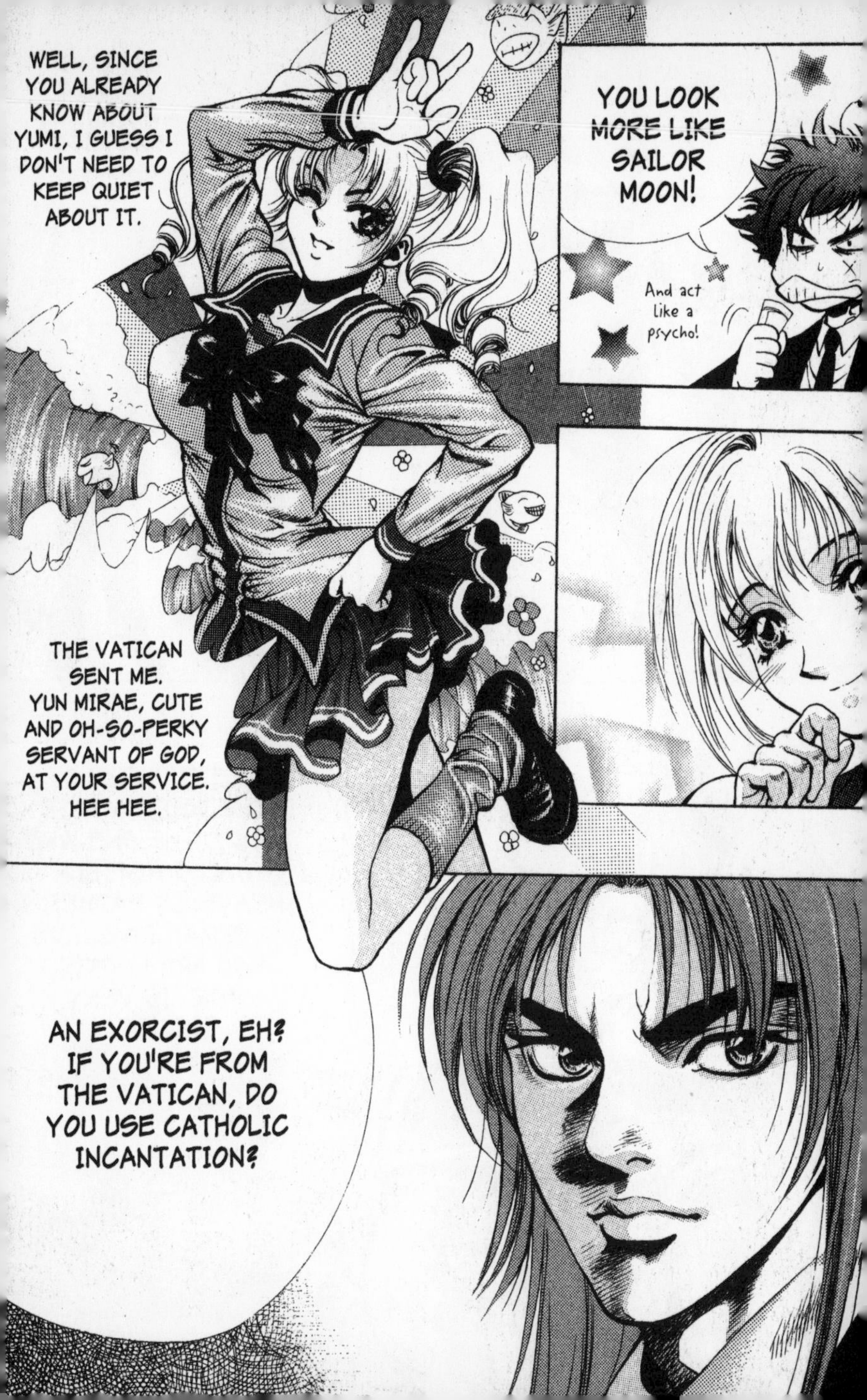
WELL, SINCE YOU ALREADY KNOW ABOUT YUMI, I GUESS I DON'T NEED TO KEEP QUIET ABOUT IT.
THE VATICAN SENT ME. YUN MIRAE, CUTE AND OH-SO-PERKY SERVANT OF GOD, AT YOUR SERVICE. HEE HEE.
YOU LOOK MORE LIKE SAILOR MOON!
And act like a psycho!
AN EXORCIST, EH? IF YOU'RE FROM THE VATICAN, DO YOU USE CATHOLIC INCANTATION?

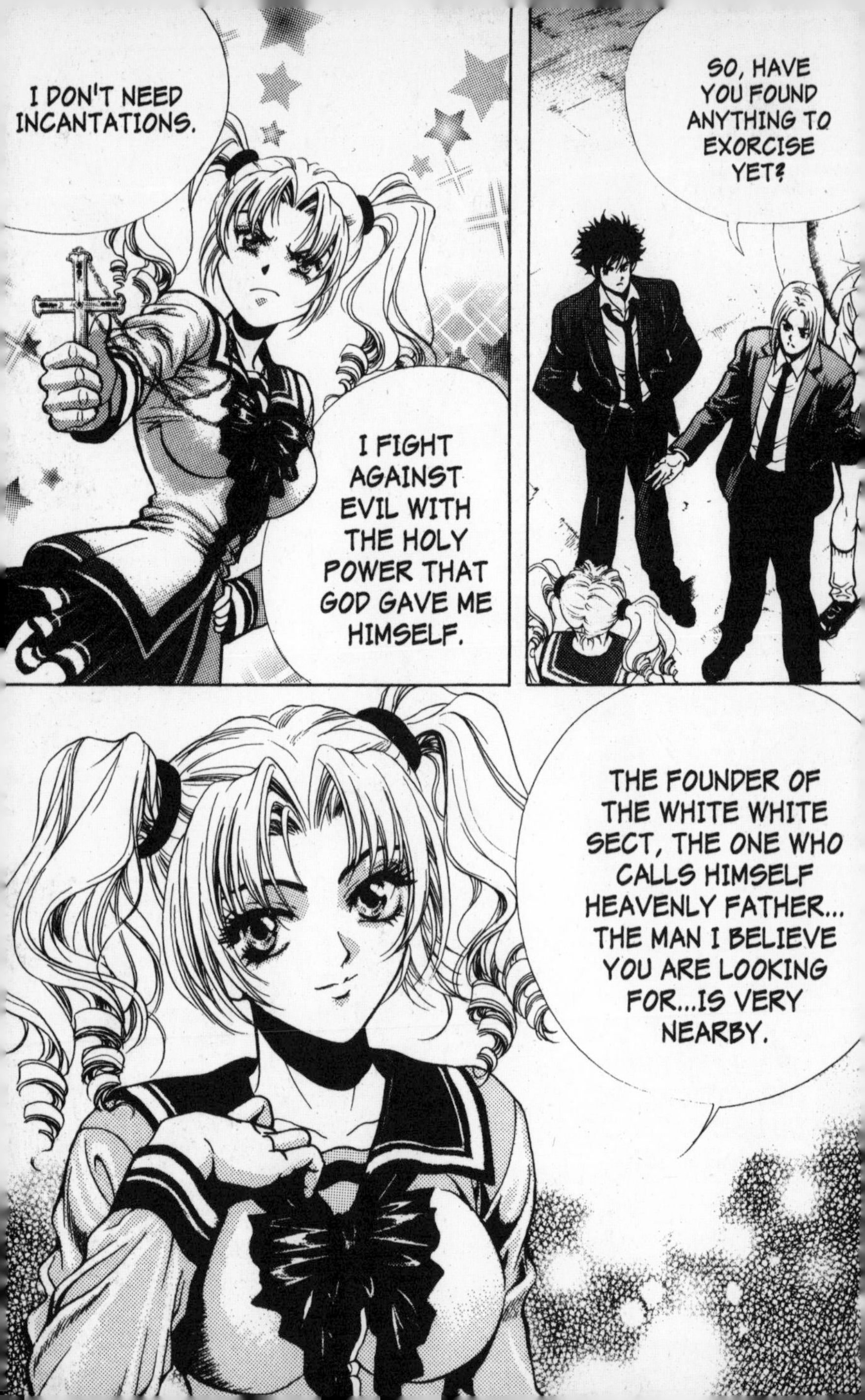
I DON'T NEED INCANTATIONS.
I FIGHT AGAINST EVIL WITH THE HOLY POWER THAT GOD GAVE ME HIMSELF.
SO, HAVE YOU FOUND ANYTHING TO EXORCISE YET?
THE FOUNDER OF THE WHITE WHITE SECT, THE ONE WHO CALLS HIMSELF HEAVENLY FATHER... THE MAN I BELIEVE YOU ARE LOOKING FOR...IS VERY NEARBY.

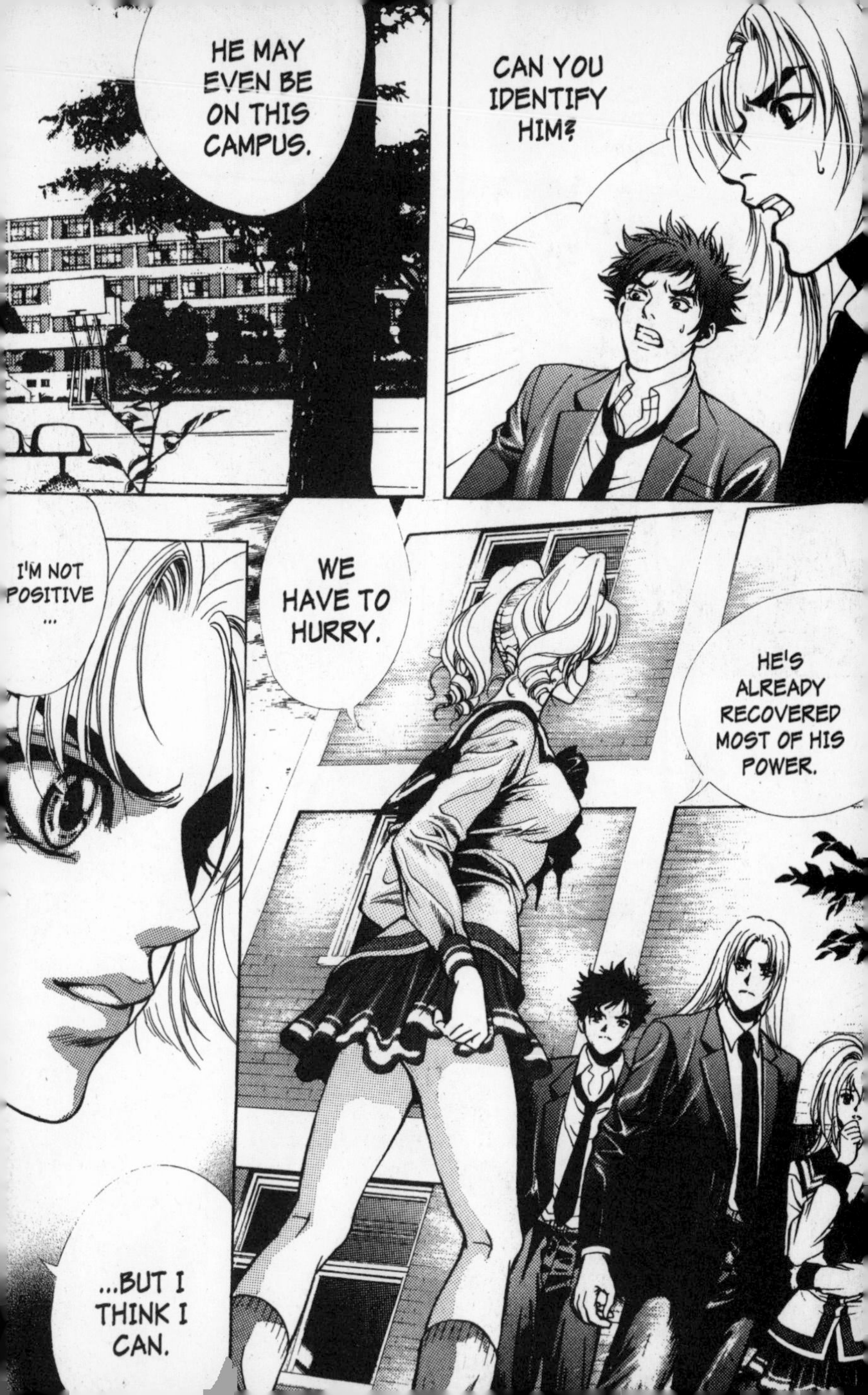
HE MAY EVEN BE ON THIS CAMPUS.
CAN YOU IDENTIFY HIM?
I'M NOT POSITIVE ...
...BUT I THINK I CAN.
WE HAVE TO HURRY.
HE'S ALREADY RECOVERED MOST OF HIS POWER.

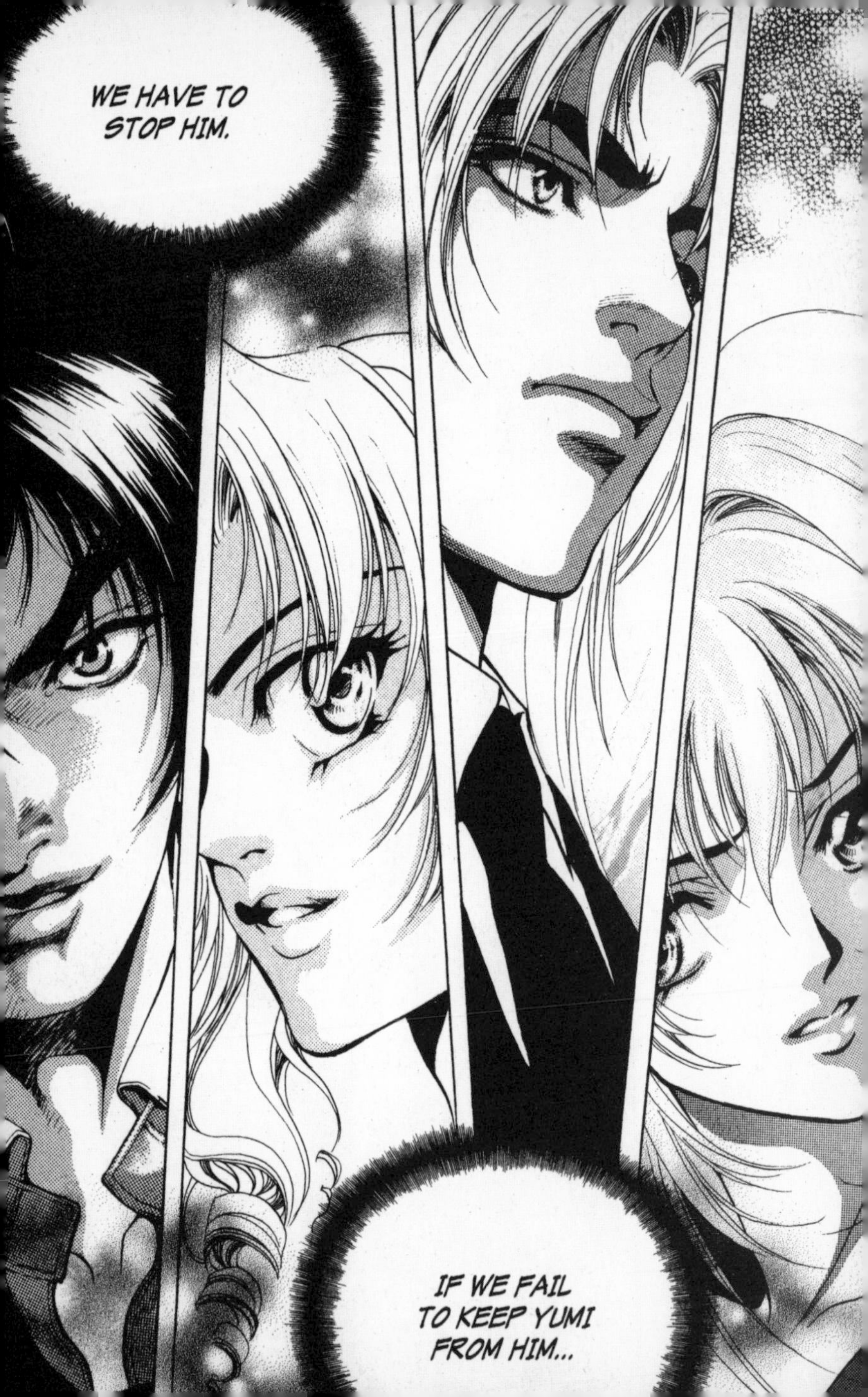
WE HAVE TO STOP HIM.
IF WE FAIL TO KEEP YUMI FROM HIM...

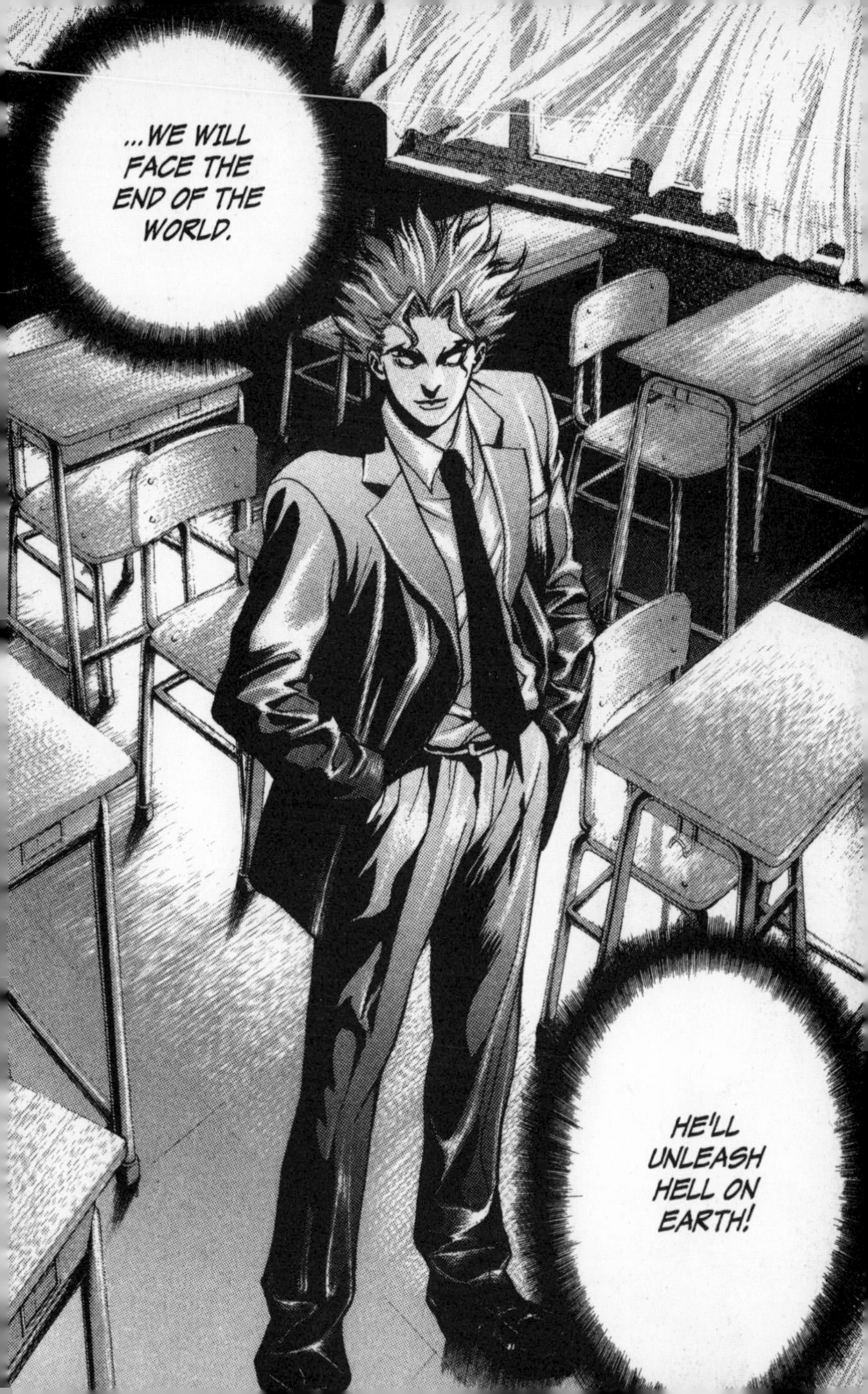
...WE WILL FACE THE END OF THE WORLD.
HE'LL UNLEASH HELL ON EARTH!

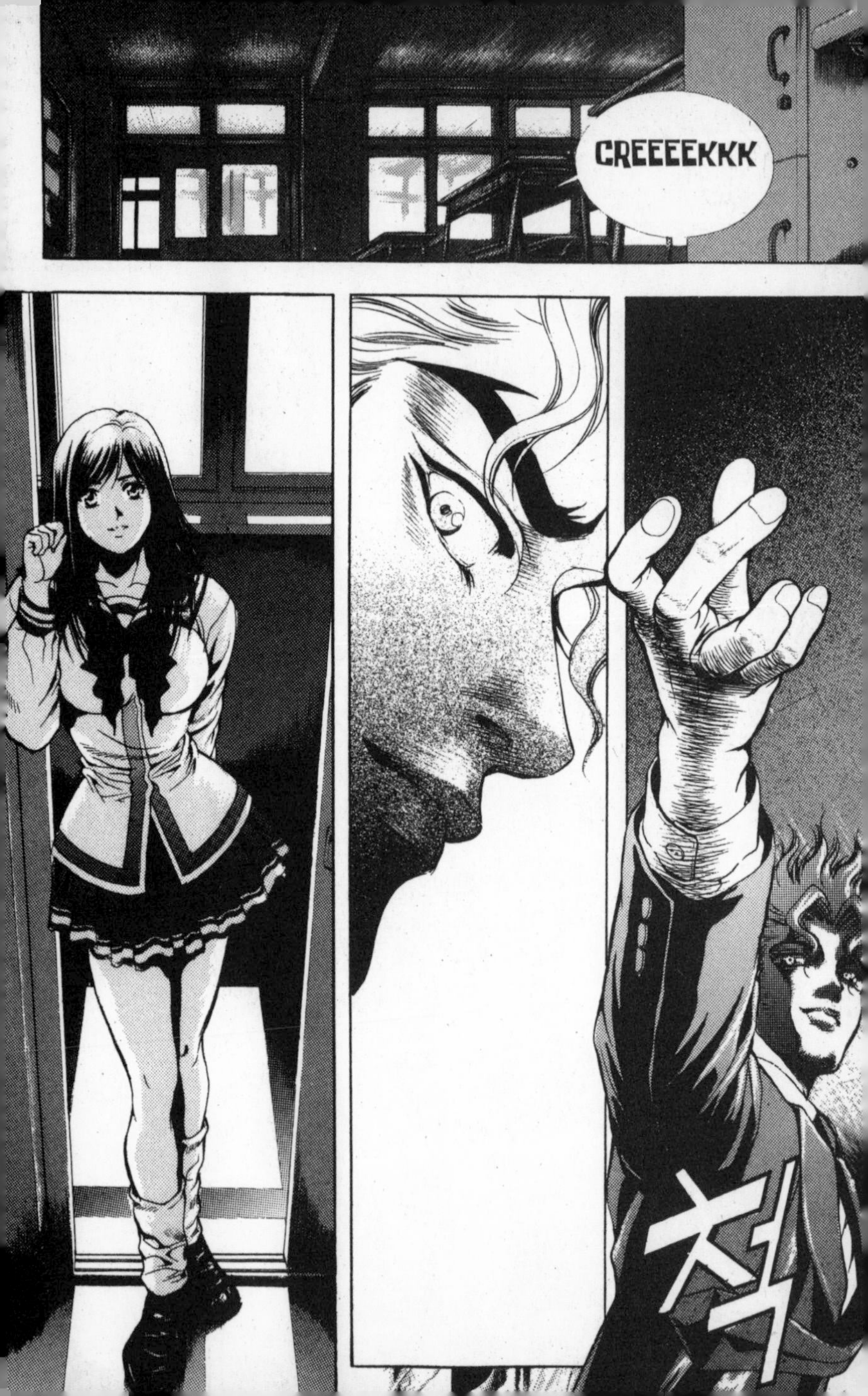
CREEEEKKK

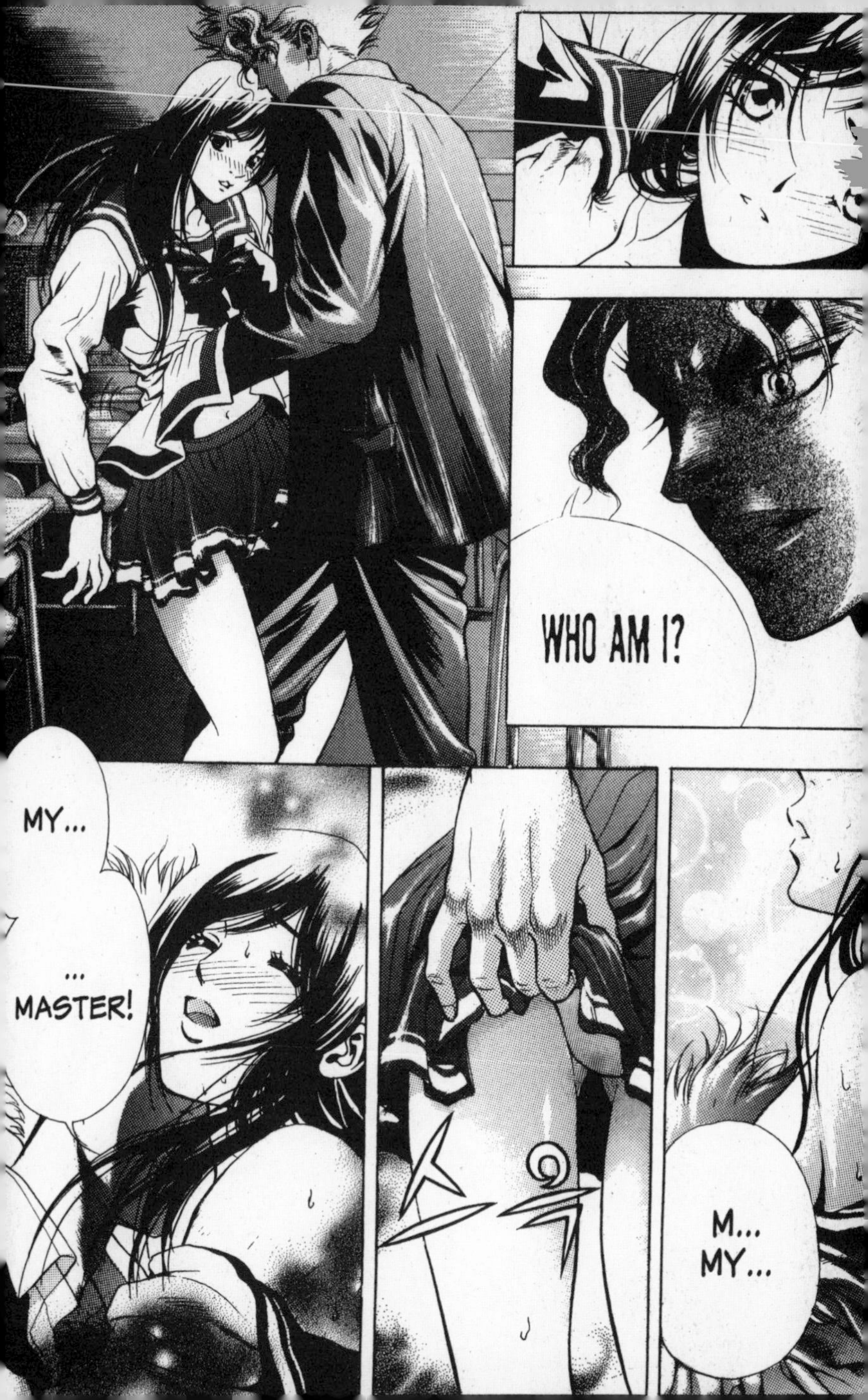
WHO AM I?
M...
MY...
MY...
...
MASTER!

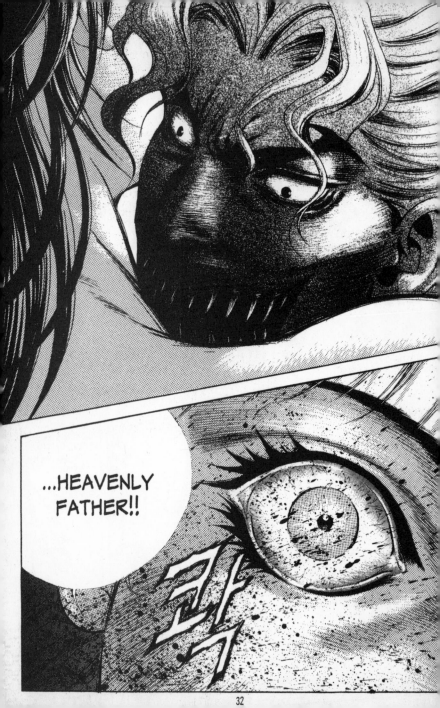

...HEAVENLY
FATHER!!

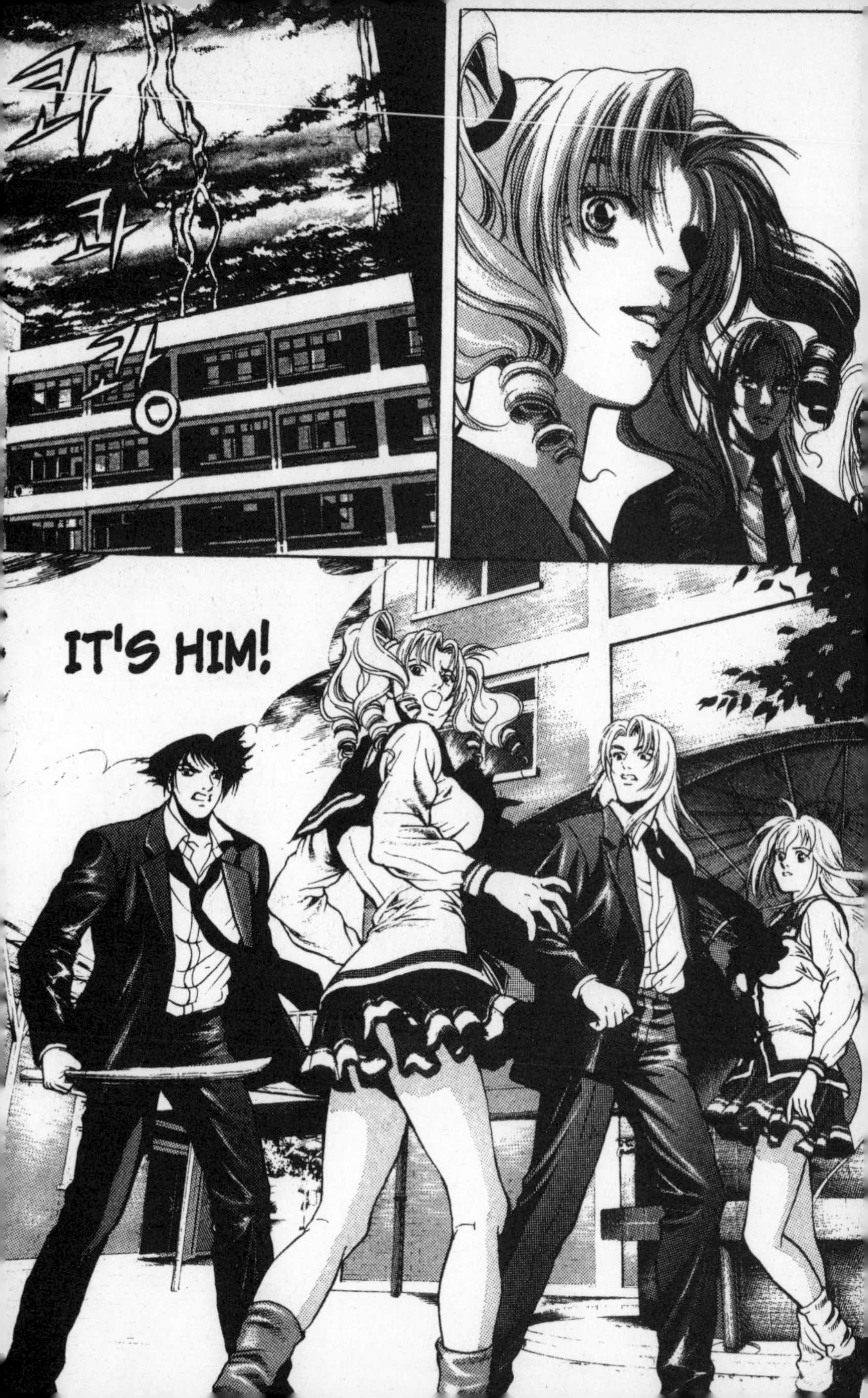
IT'S HIM!

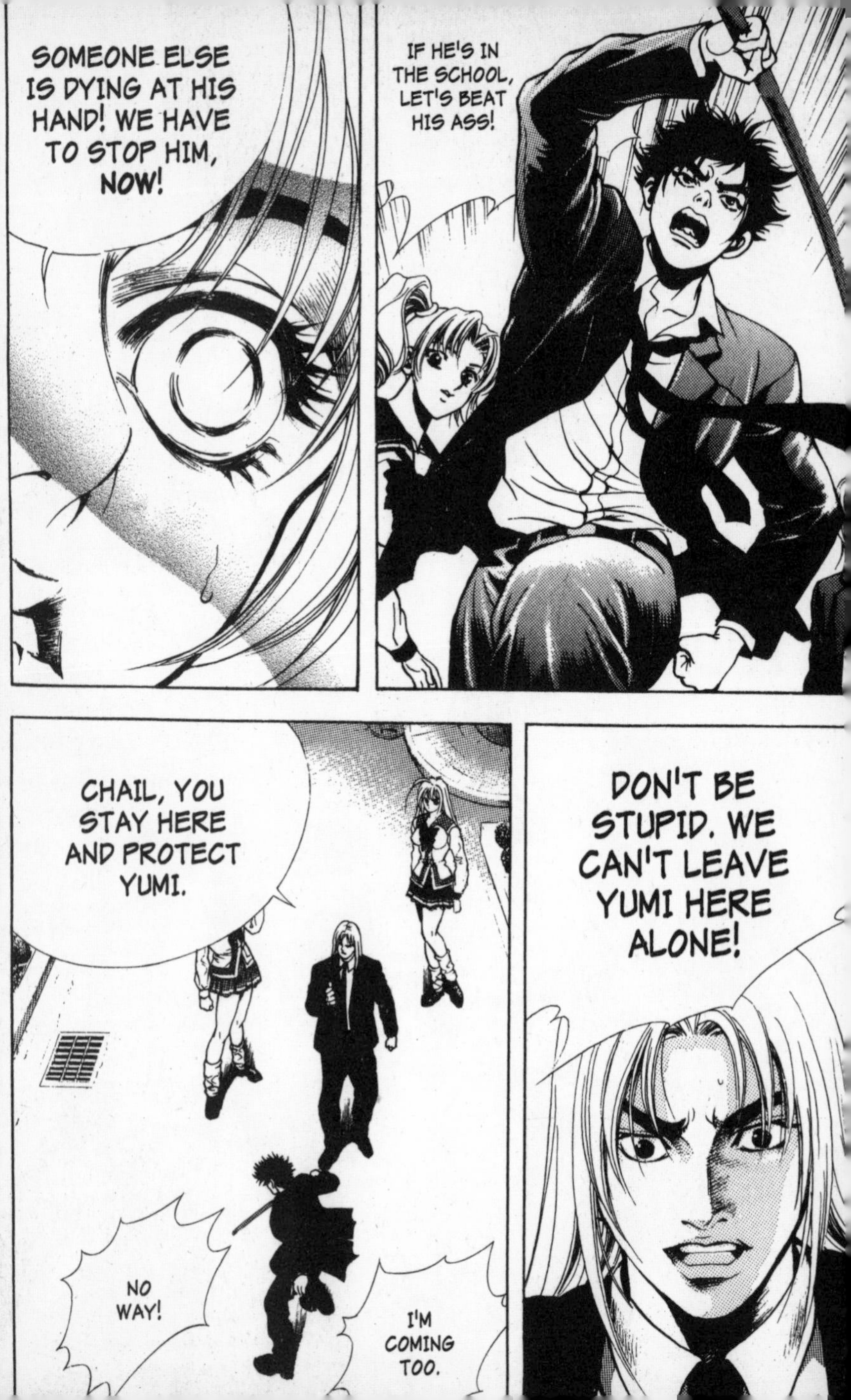
SOMEONE ELSE IS DYING AT HIS HAND! WE HAVE TO STOP HIM, NOW!
IF HE'S IN THE SCHOOL, LET'S BEAT HIS ASS!
CHAIL, YOU STAY HERE AND PROTECT YUMI.
NO WAY!
I'M COMING TOO.
DON'T BE STUPID. WE CAN'T LEAVE YUMI HERE ALONE!

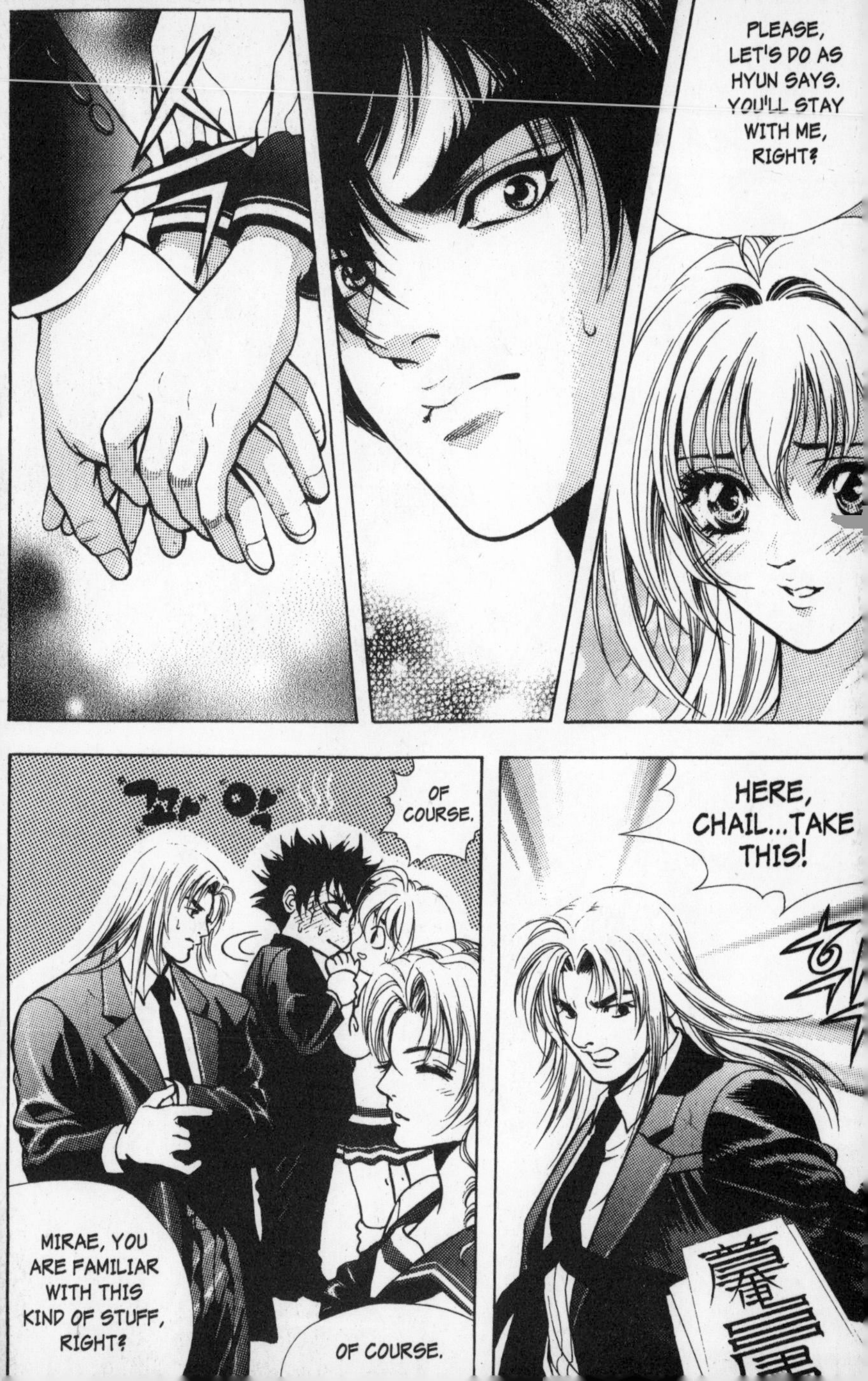
PLEASE, LET'S DO AS HYUN SAYS. YOU'LL STAY WITH ME, RIGHT?
OF COURSE.
MIRAE, YOU ARE FAMILIAR WITH THIS KIND OF STUFF, RIGHT?
OF COURSE.
HERE, CHAIL...TAKE THIS!

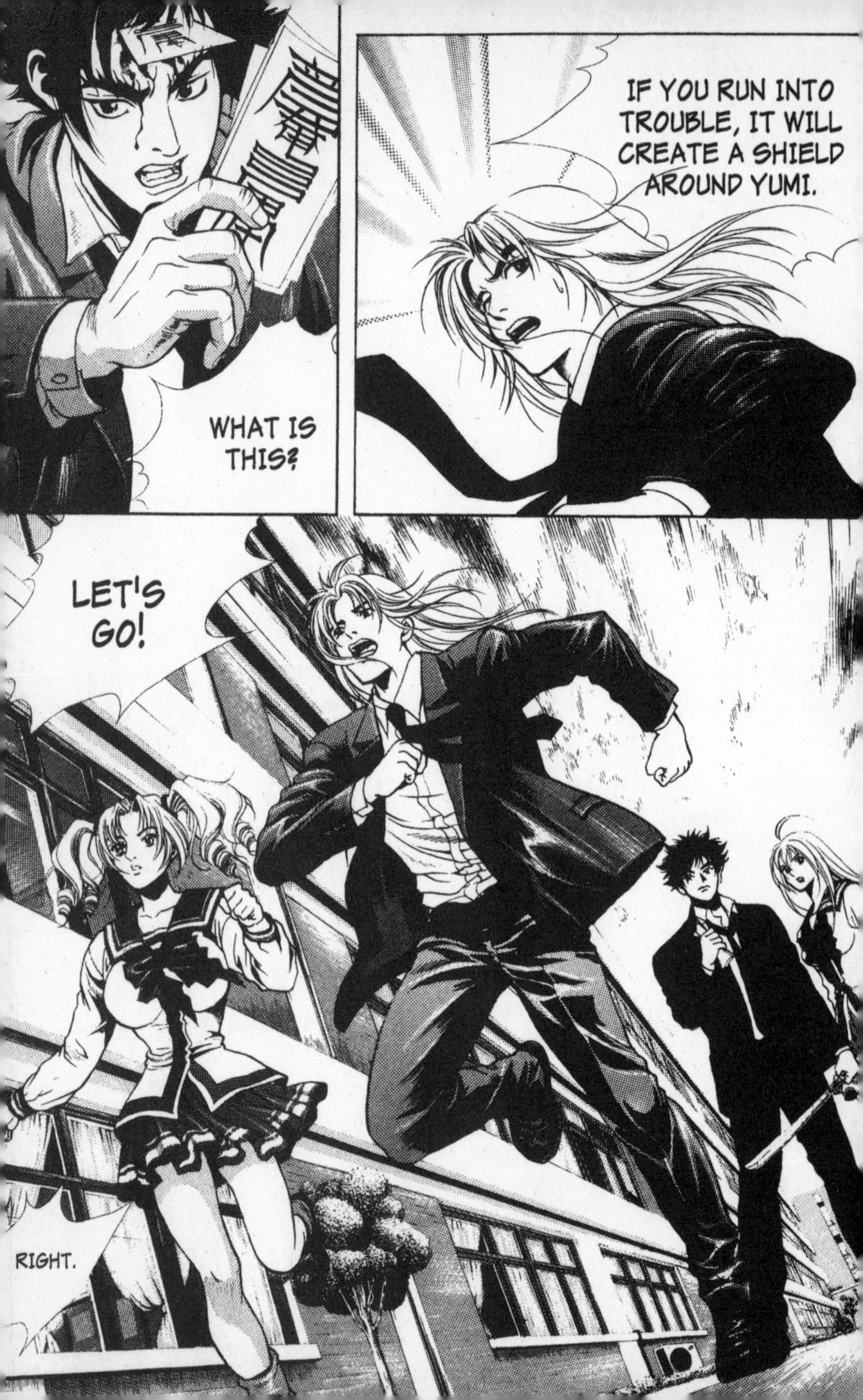
IF YOU RUN INTO TROUBLE, IT WILL CREATE A SHIELD AROUND YUMI.
WHAT IS THIS?
LET'S GO!
RIGHT.

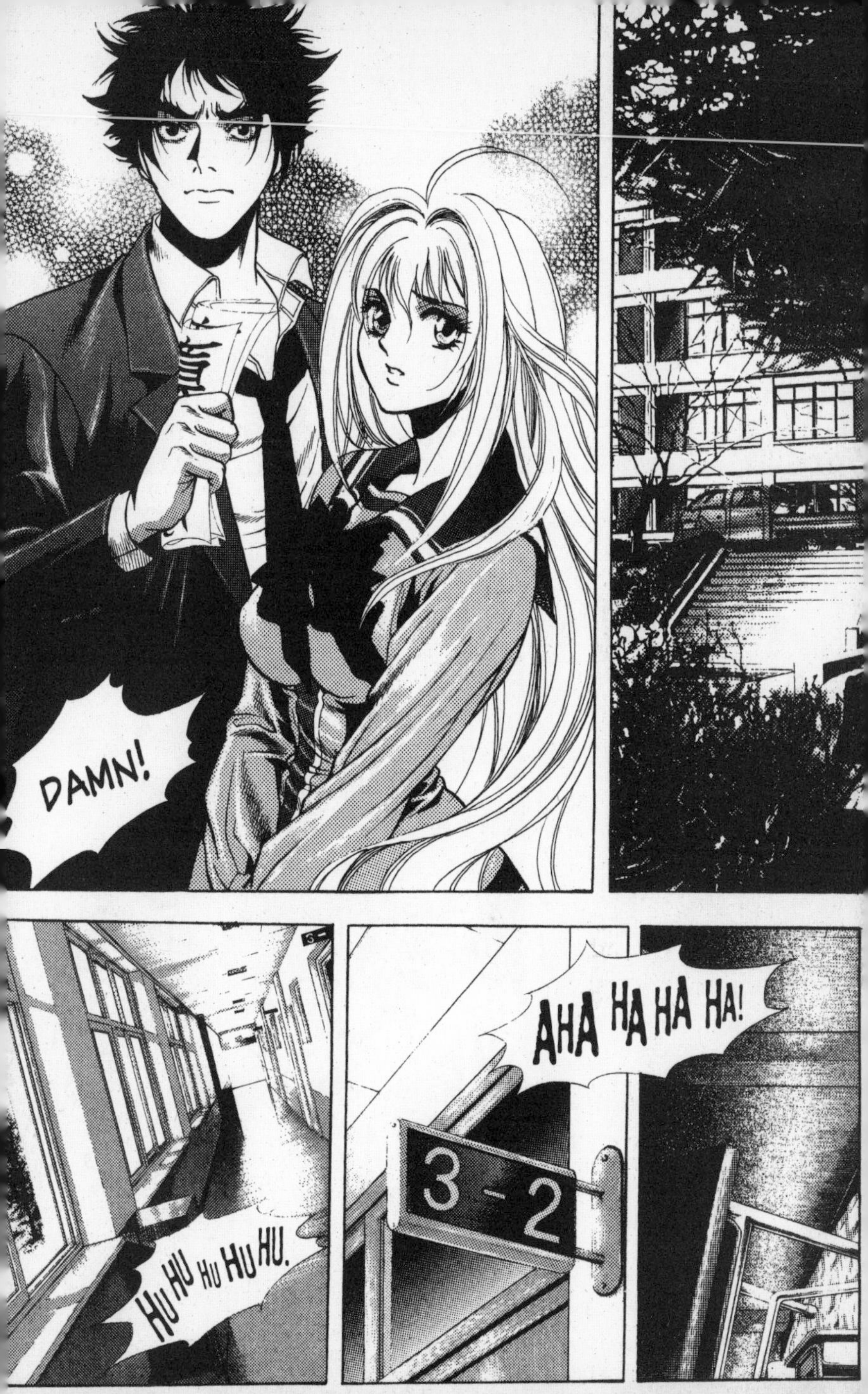

DAMN!
AHA HA HA HA!
HU HU HU HU HU.

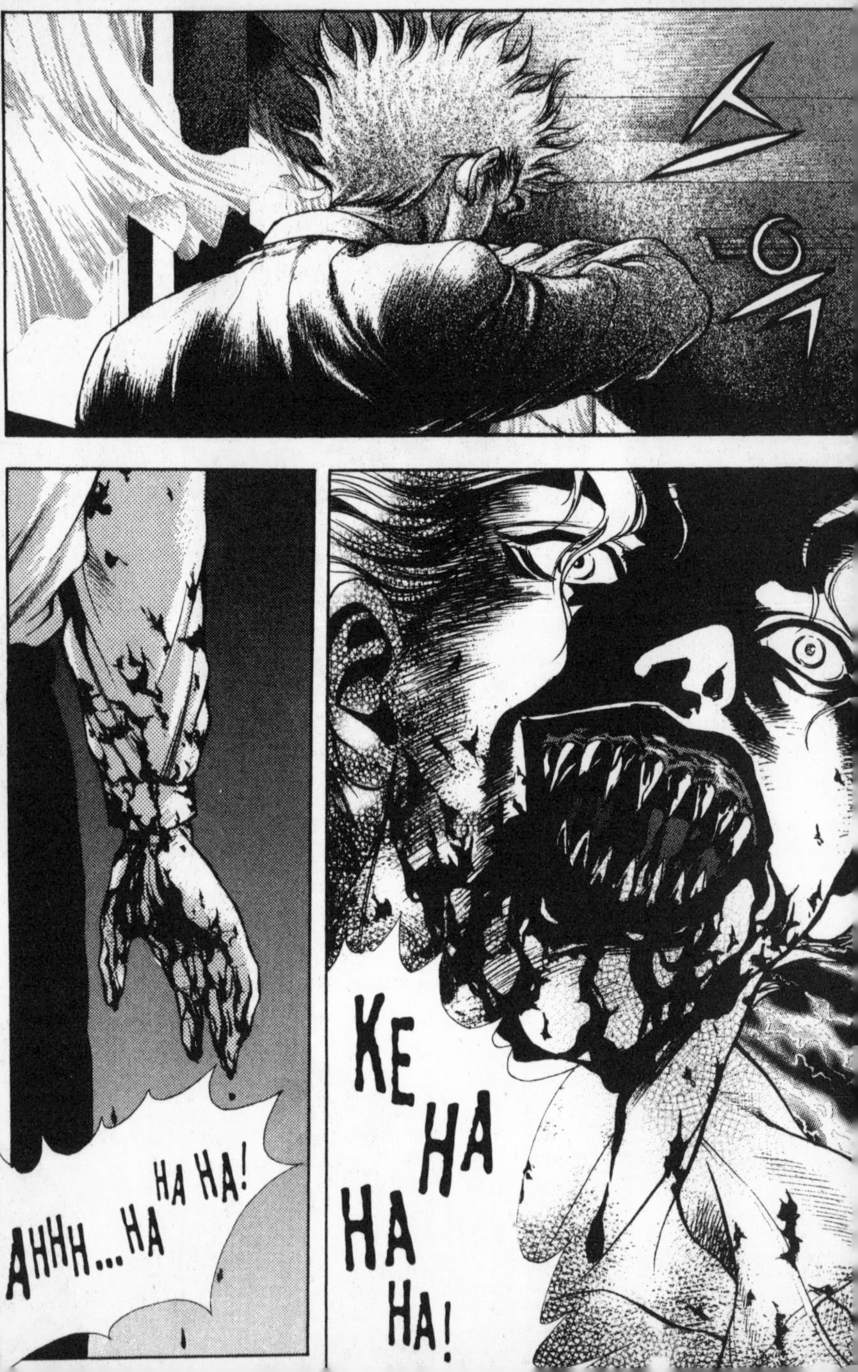
KE HA HA HA HA!
AHHH... HA HA HA!

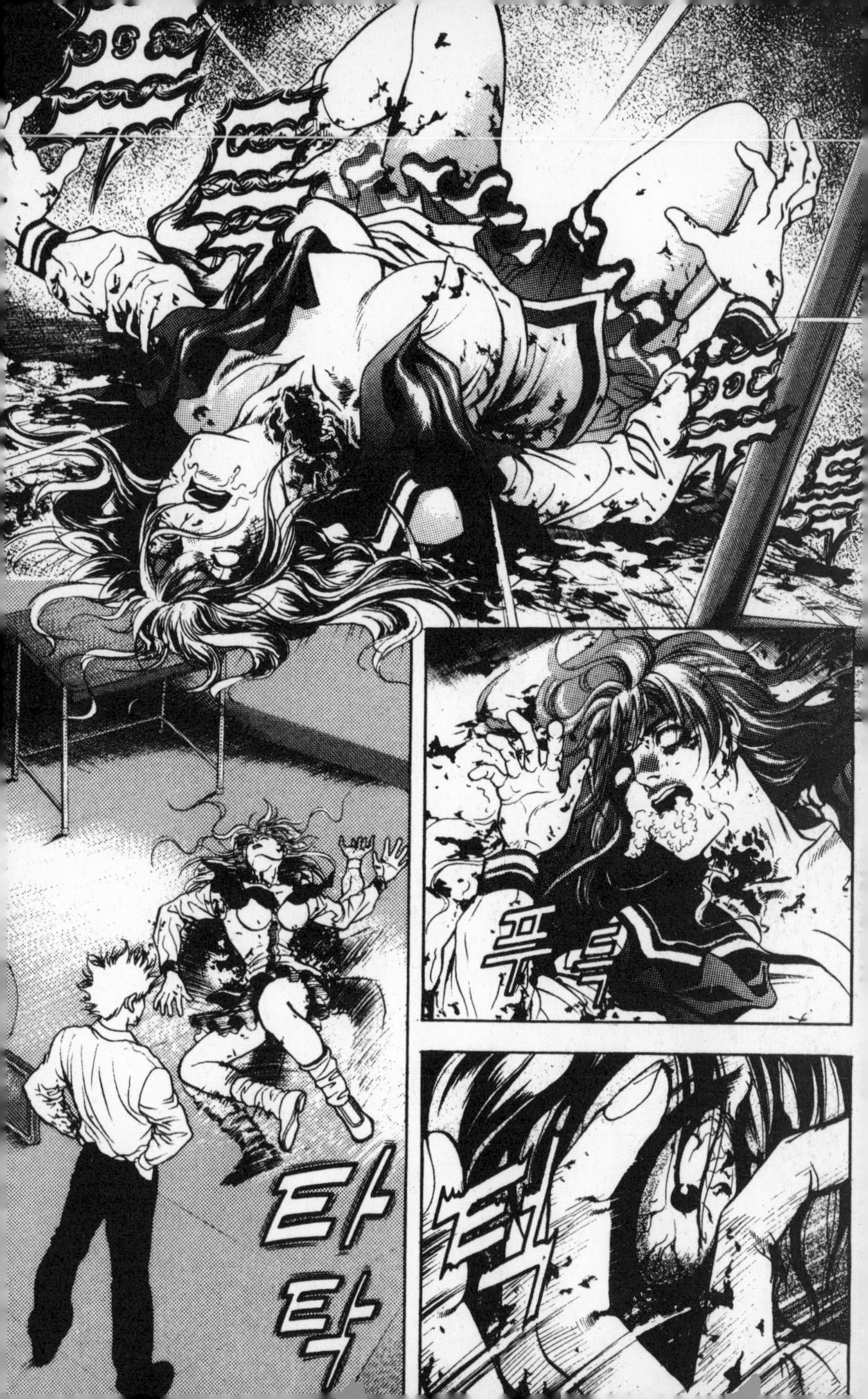
푸 득
타
탁
턱

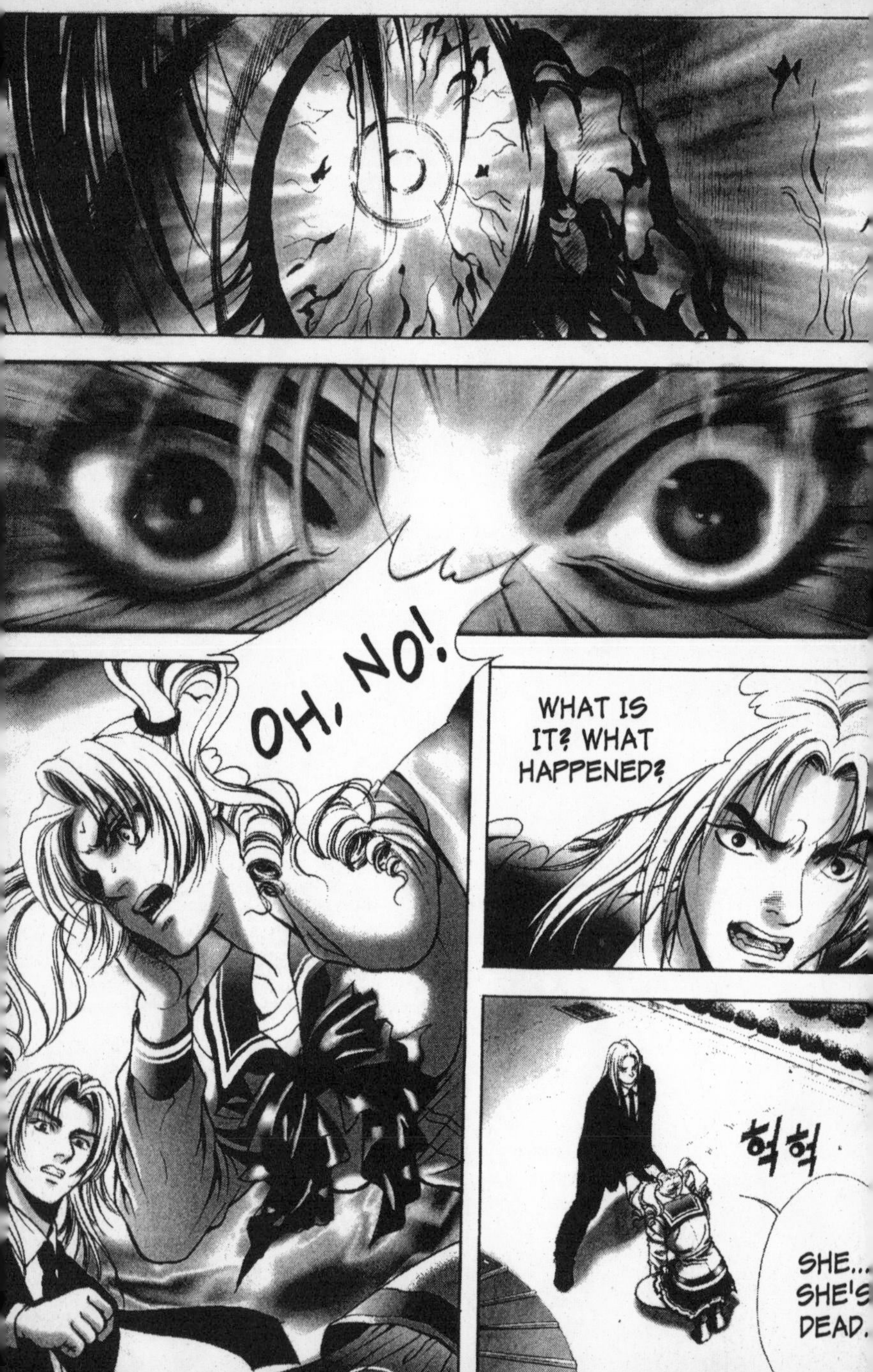
OH, NO!
WHAT IS IT? WHAT HAPPENED?
헉헉
SHE... SHE'S DEAD.

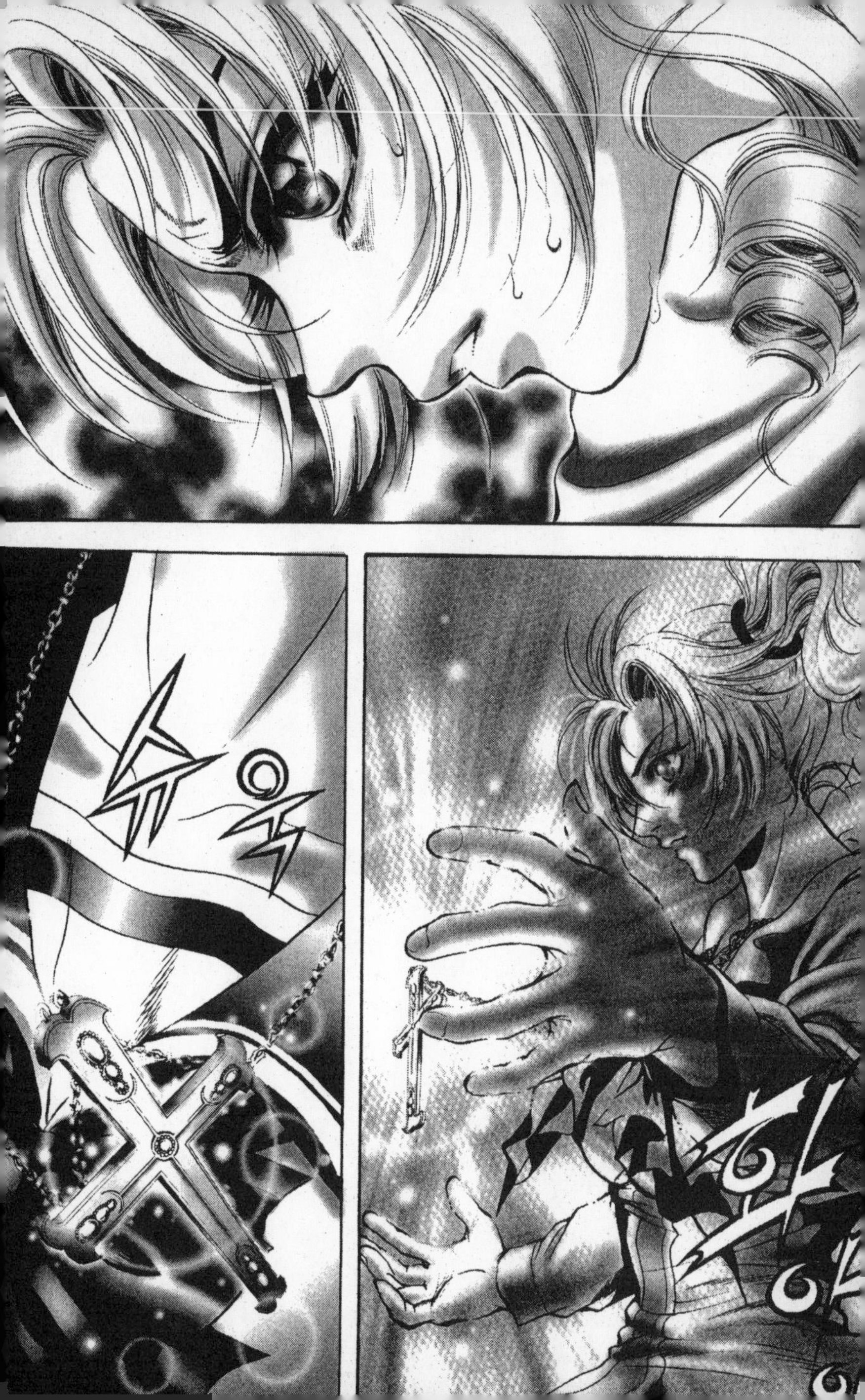

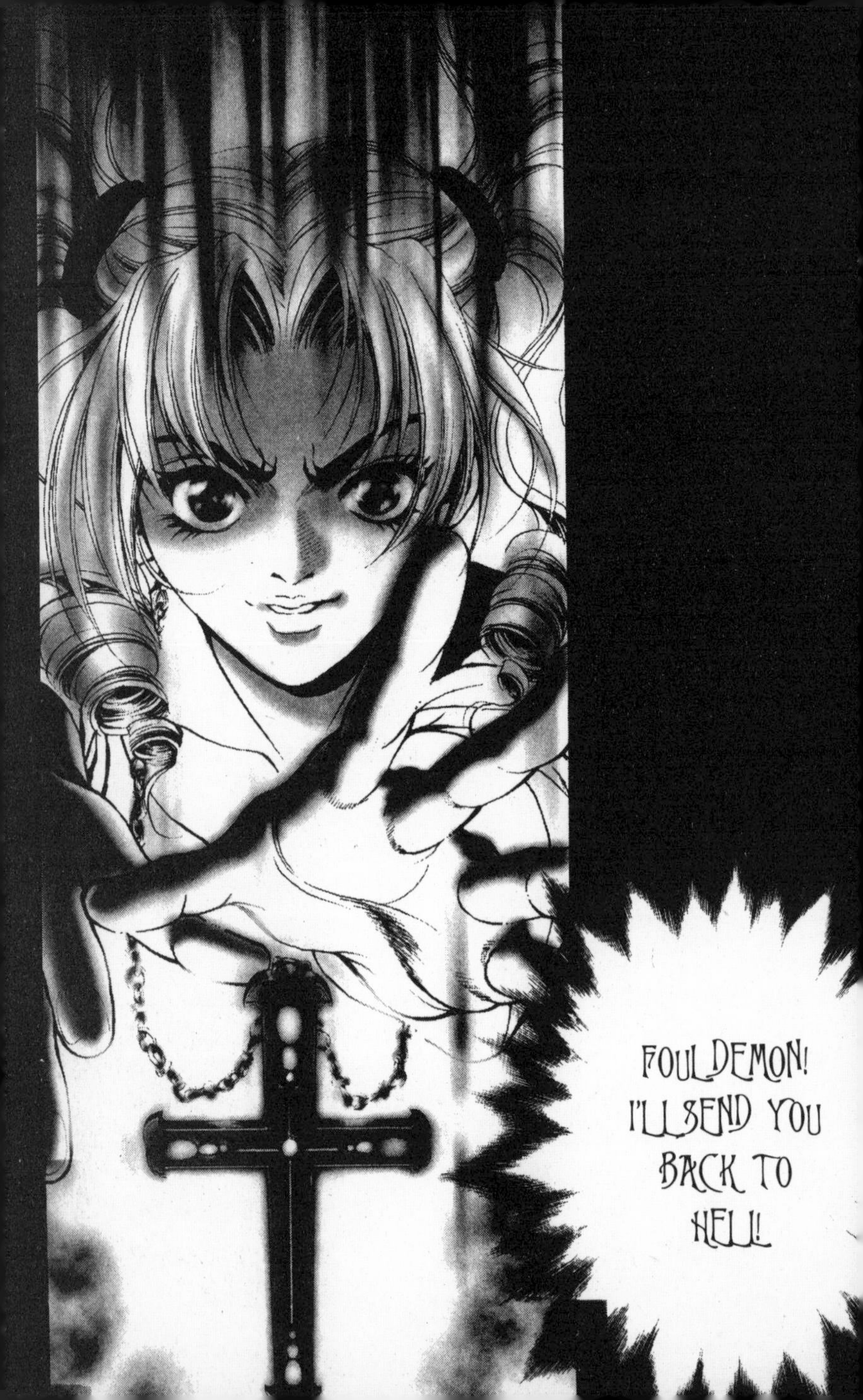
FOUL DEMON! I'LL SEND YOU BACK TO HELL!

天 천

地 지

人 인

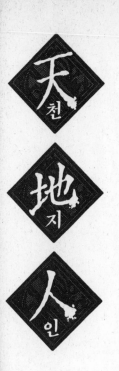

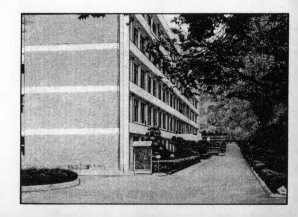

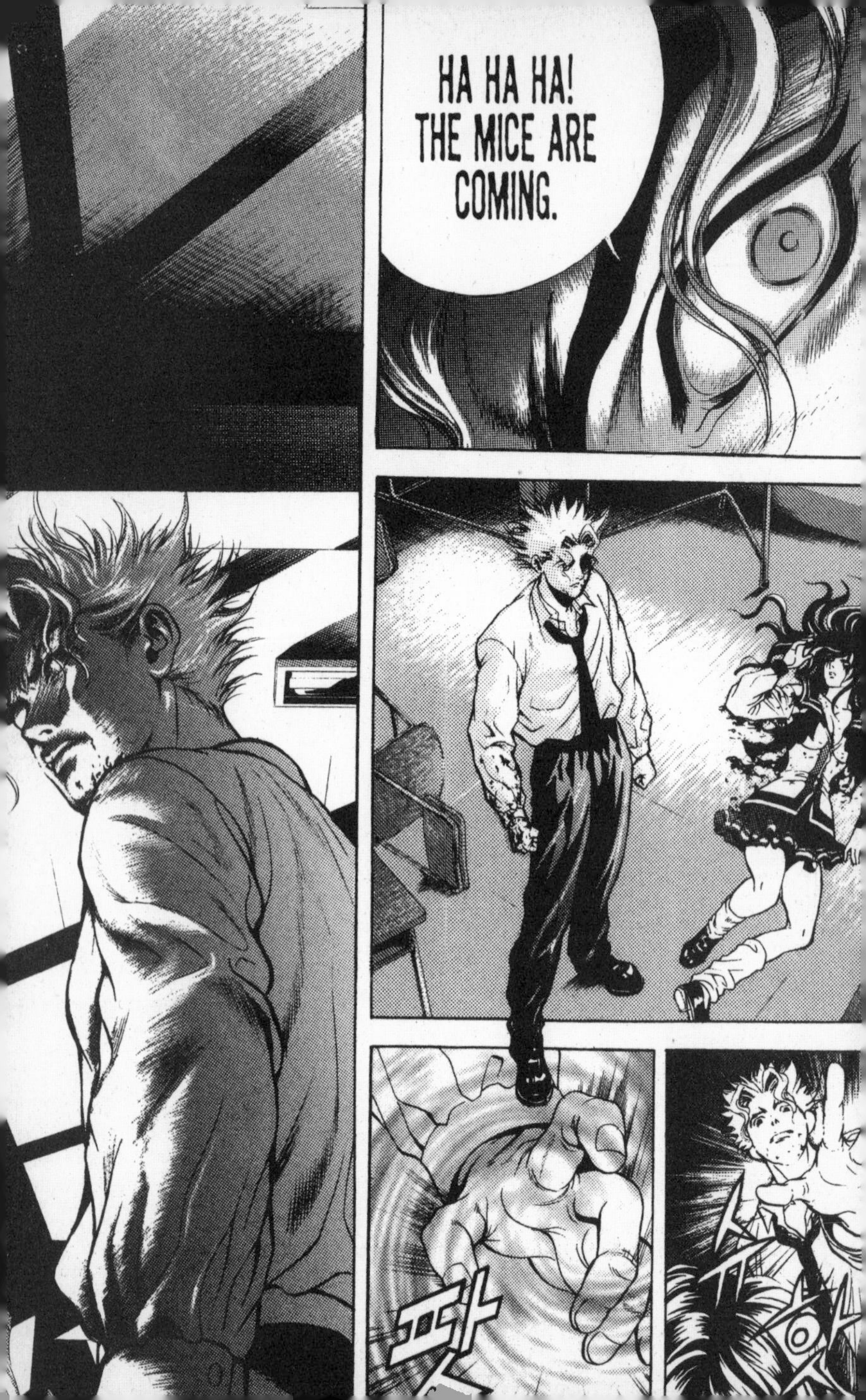
HA HA HA! THE MICE ARE COMING.

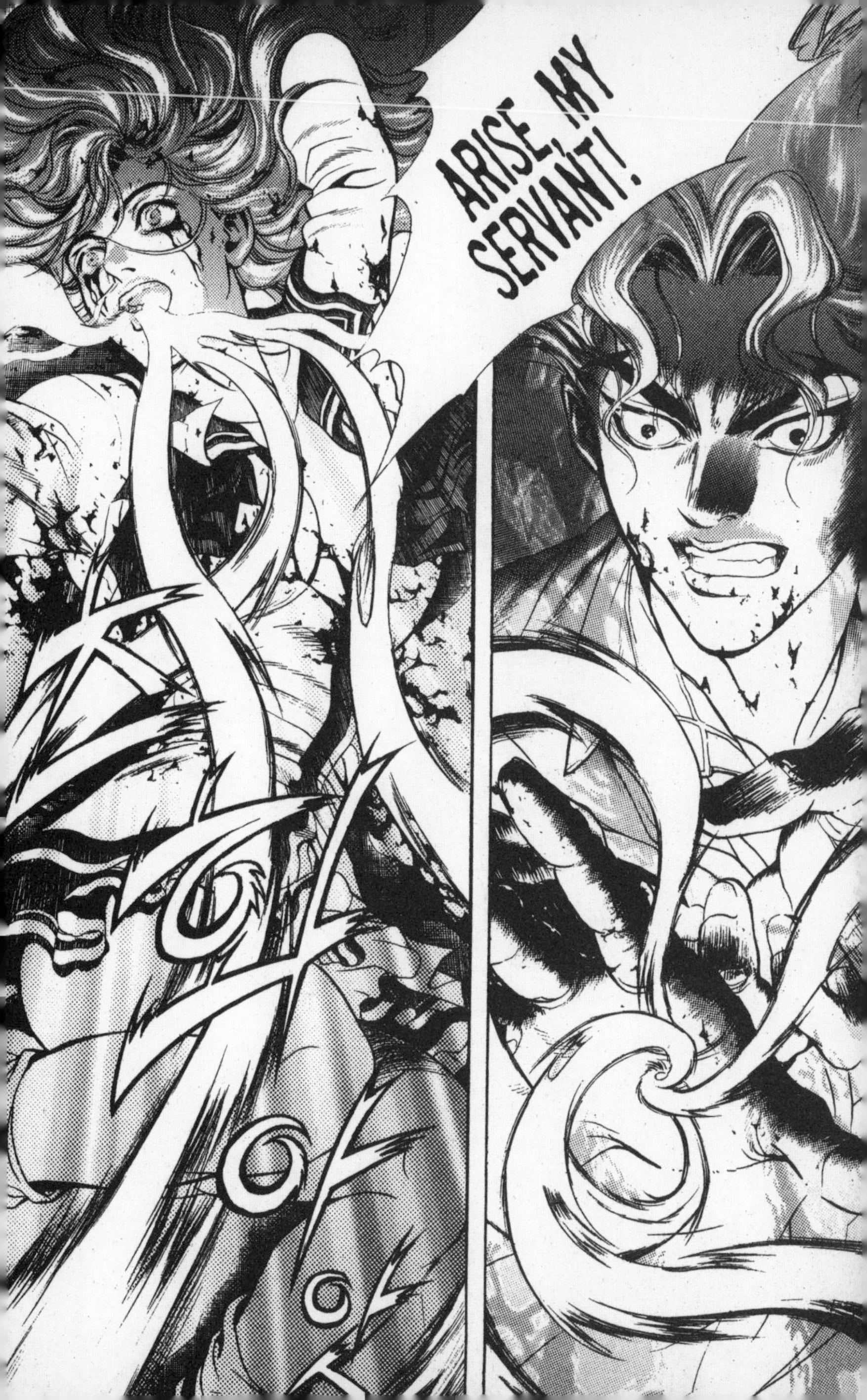
ARISE, MY SERVANT!

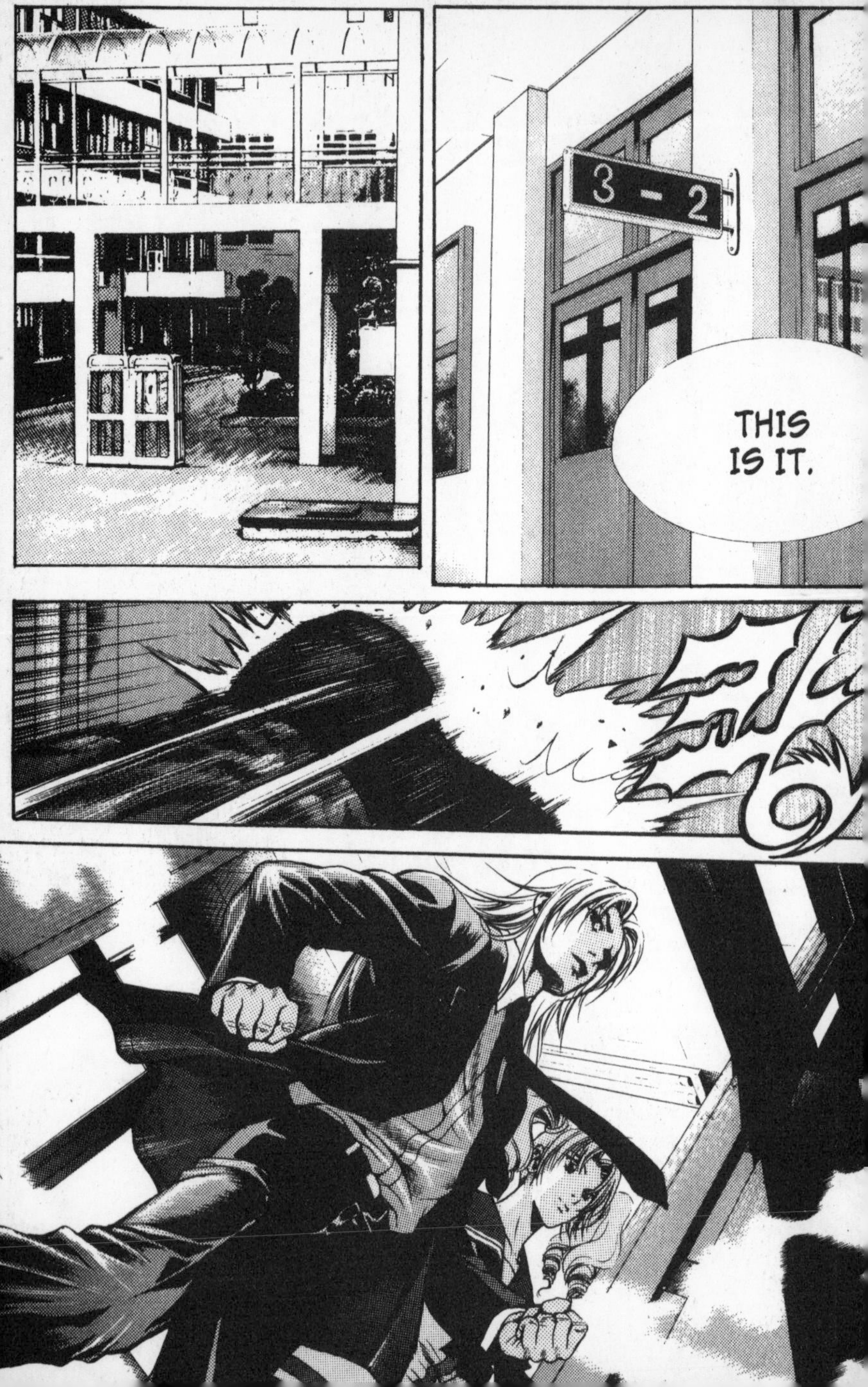
3-2
THIS IS IT.

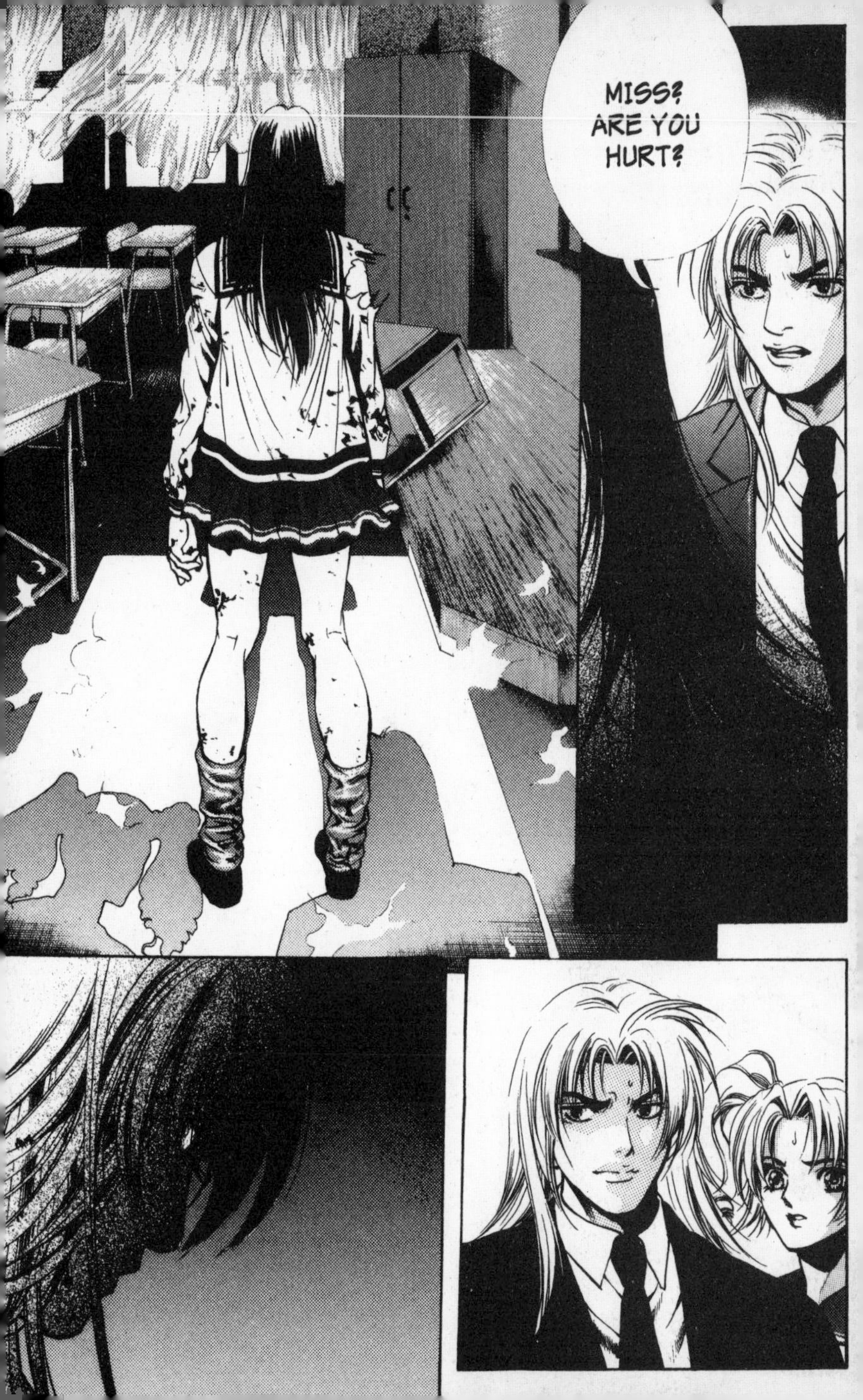
MISS? ARE YOU HURT?

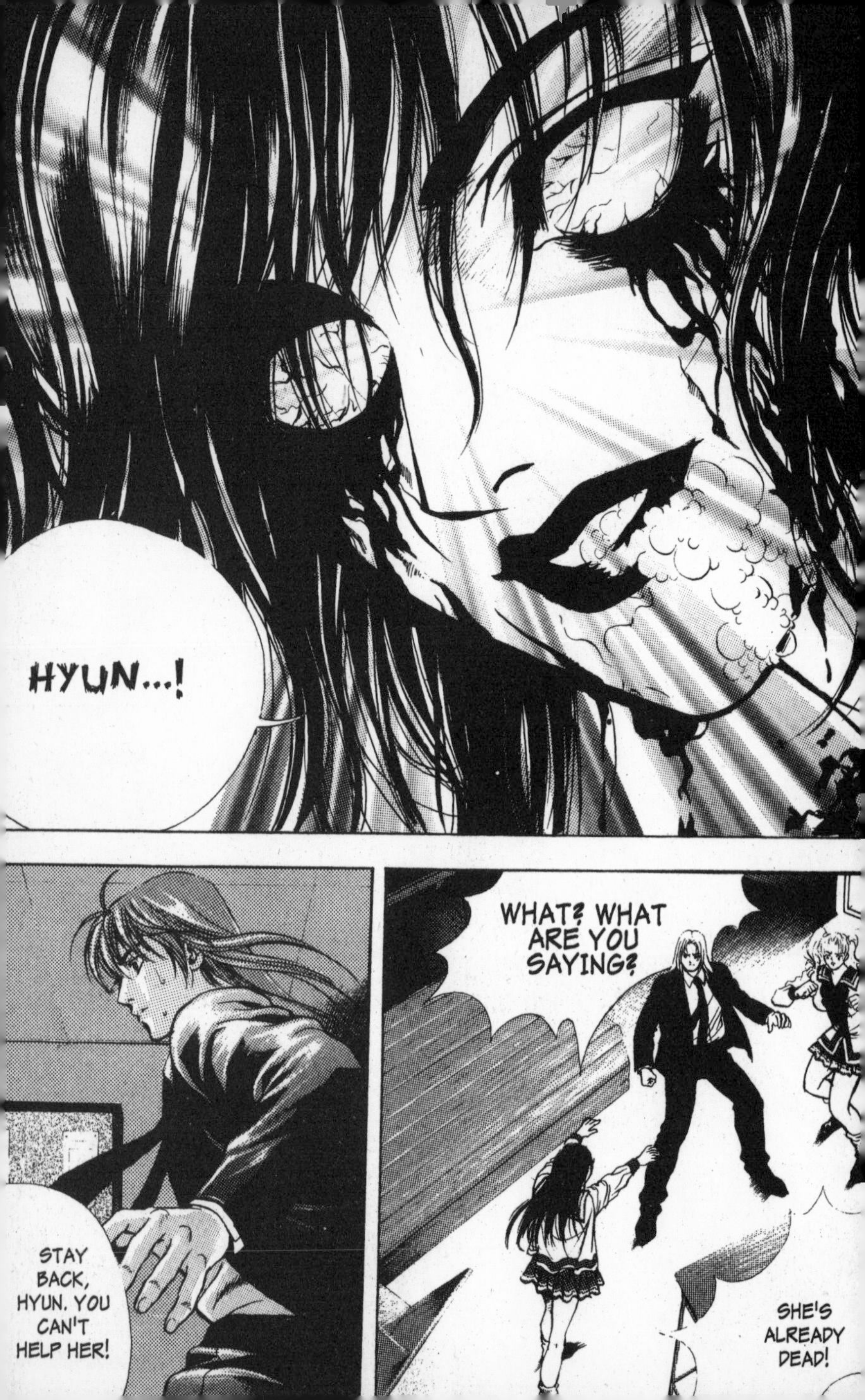
HYUN...!
STAY BACK, HYUN. YOU CAN'T HELP HER!
WHAT? WHAT ARE YOU SAYING?
SHE'S ALREADY DEAD!

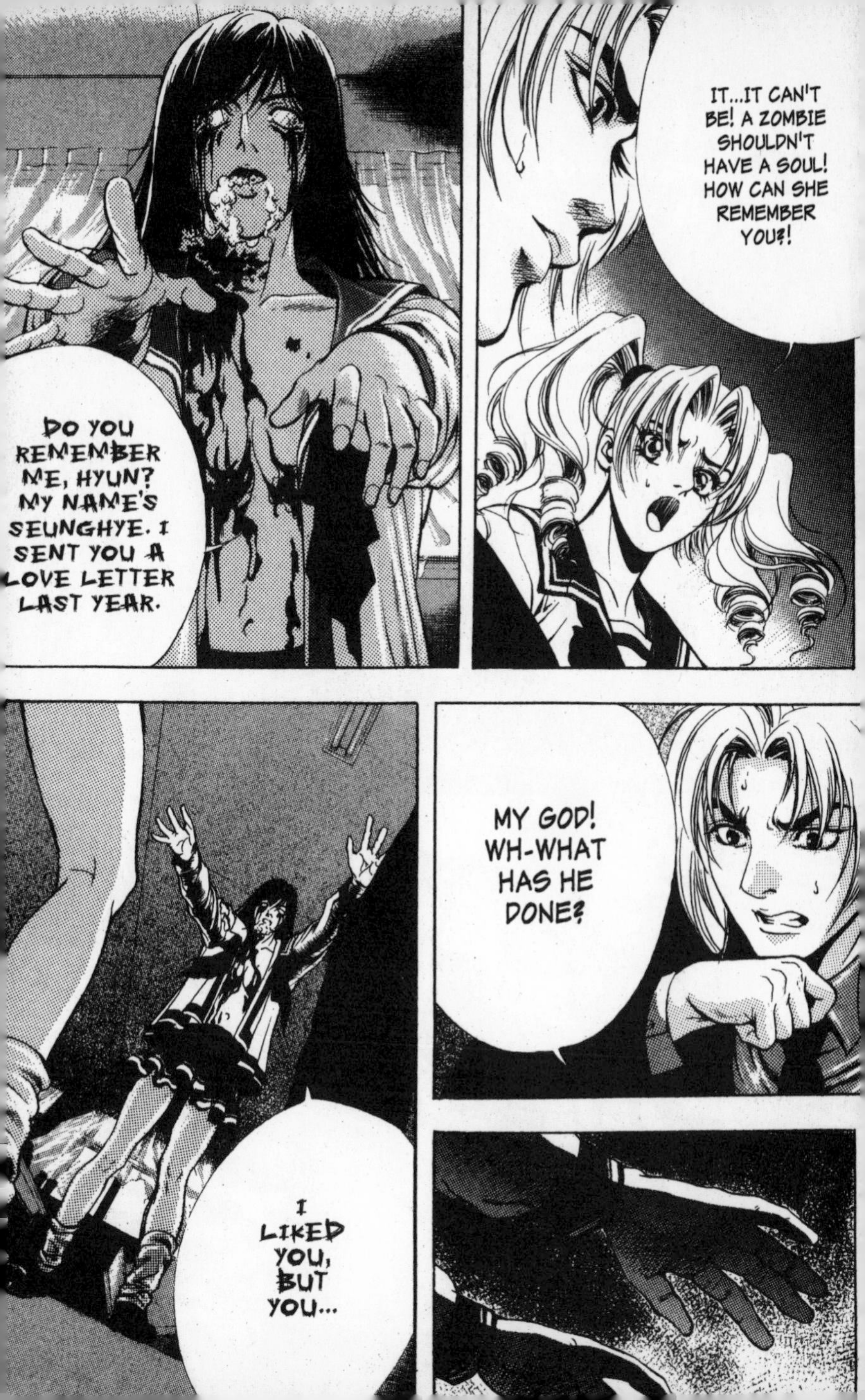
DO YOU REMEMBER ME, HYUN? MY NAME'S SEUNGHYE. I SENT YOU A LOVE LETTER LAST YEAR.
IT...IT CAN'T BE! A ZOMBIE SHOULDN'T HAVE A SOUL! HOW CAN SHE REMEMBER YOU?!
I LIKED YOU, BUT YOU...
MY GOD! WH-WHAT HAS HE DONE?

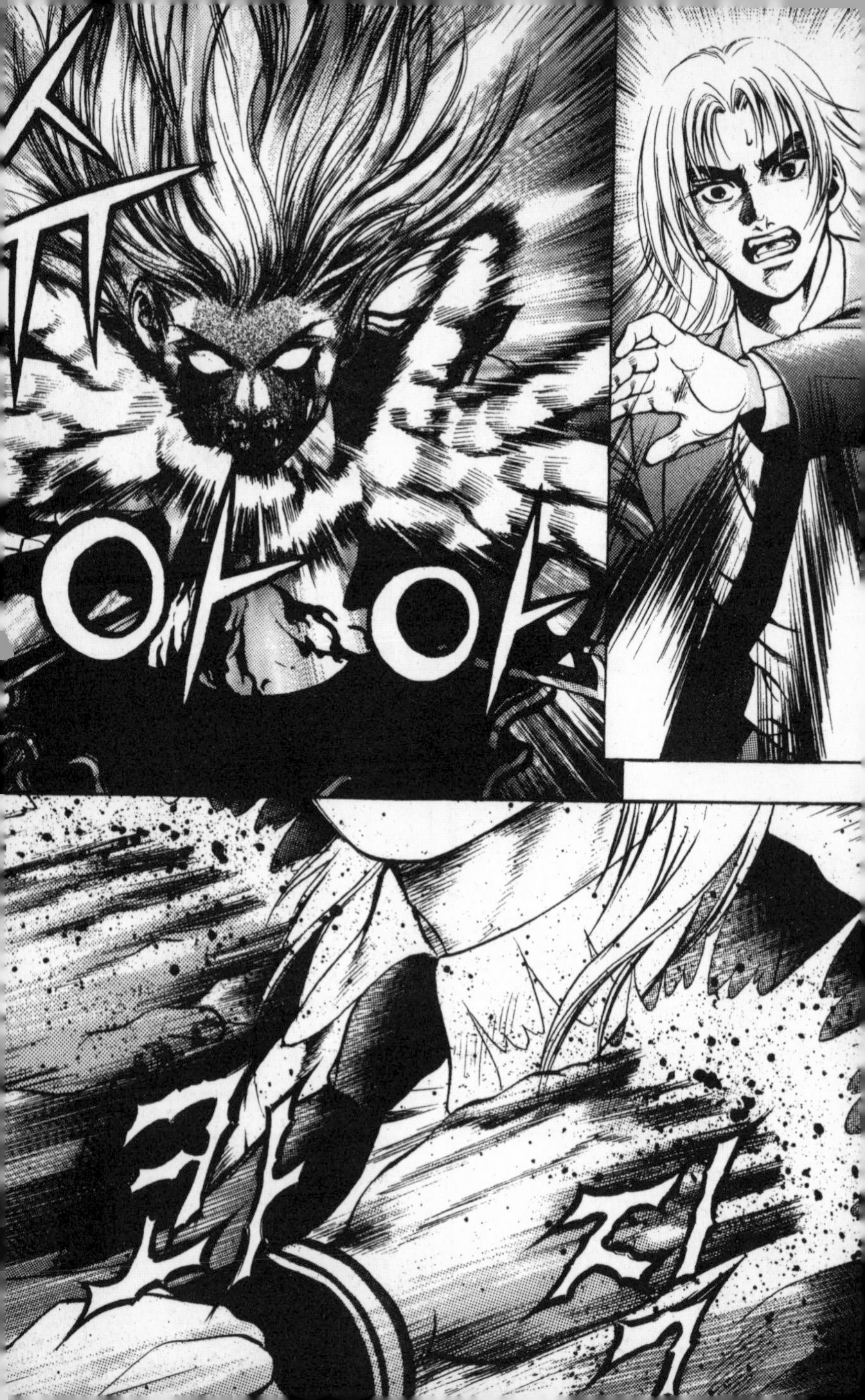

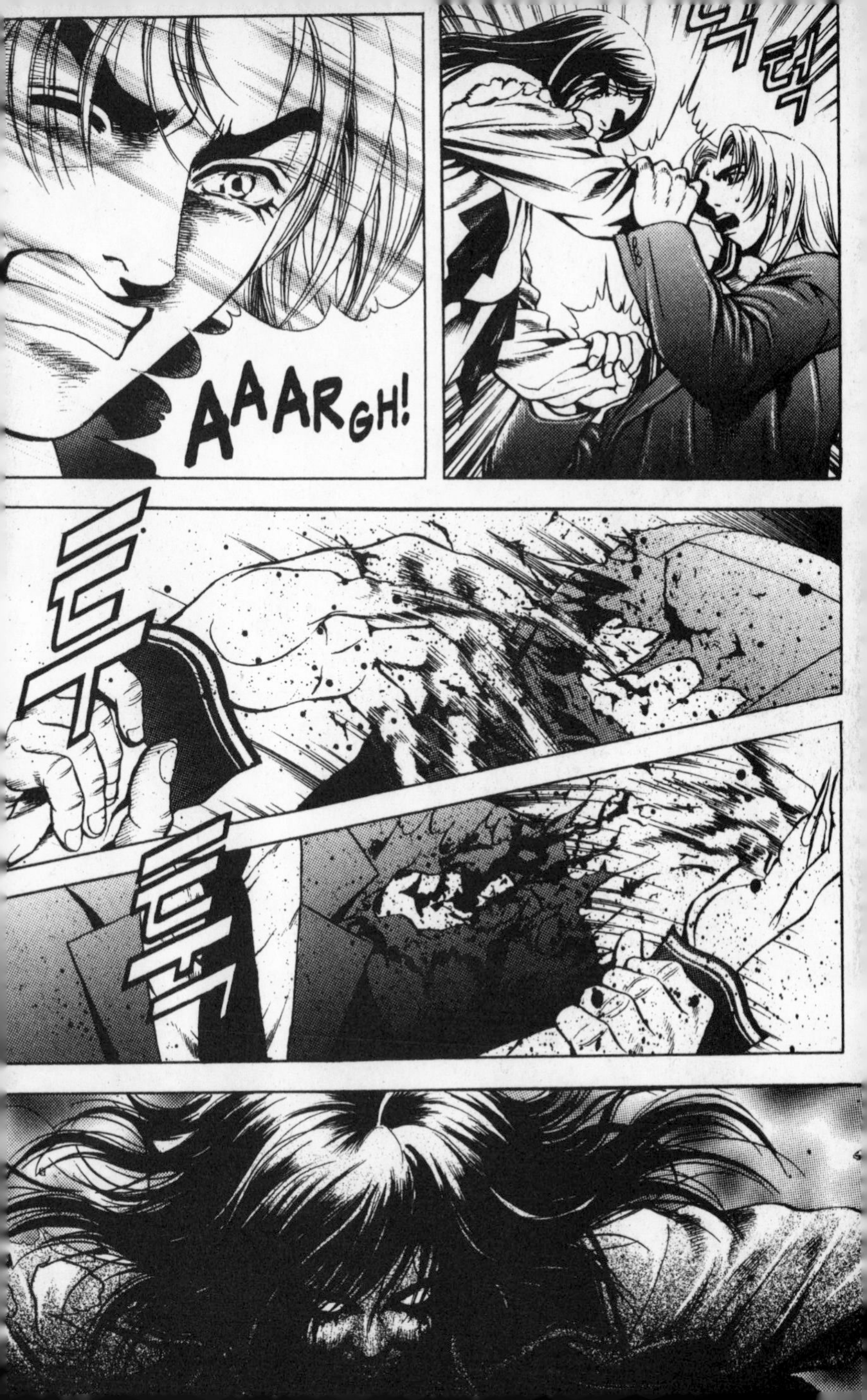
AAARGH!

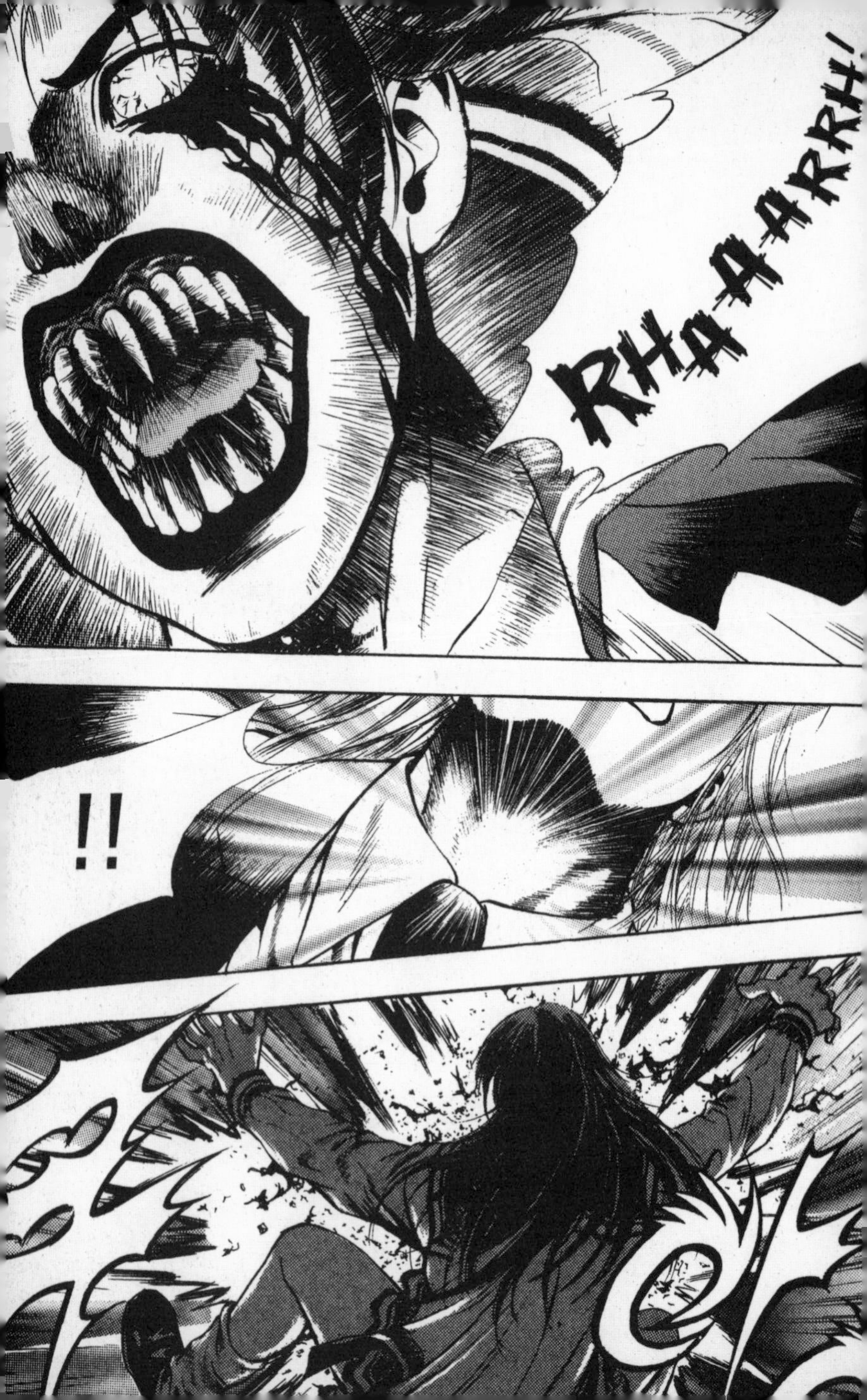
RHA-A-ARRH!
!!

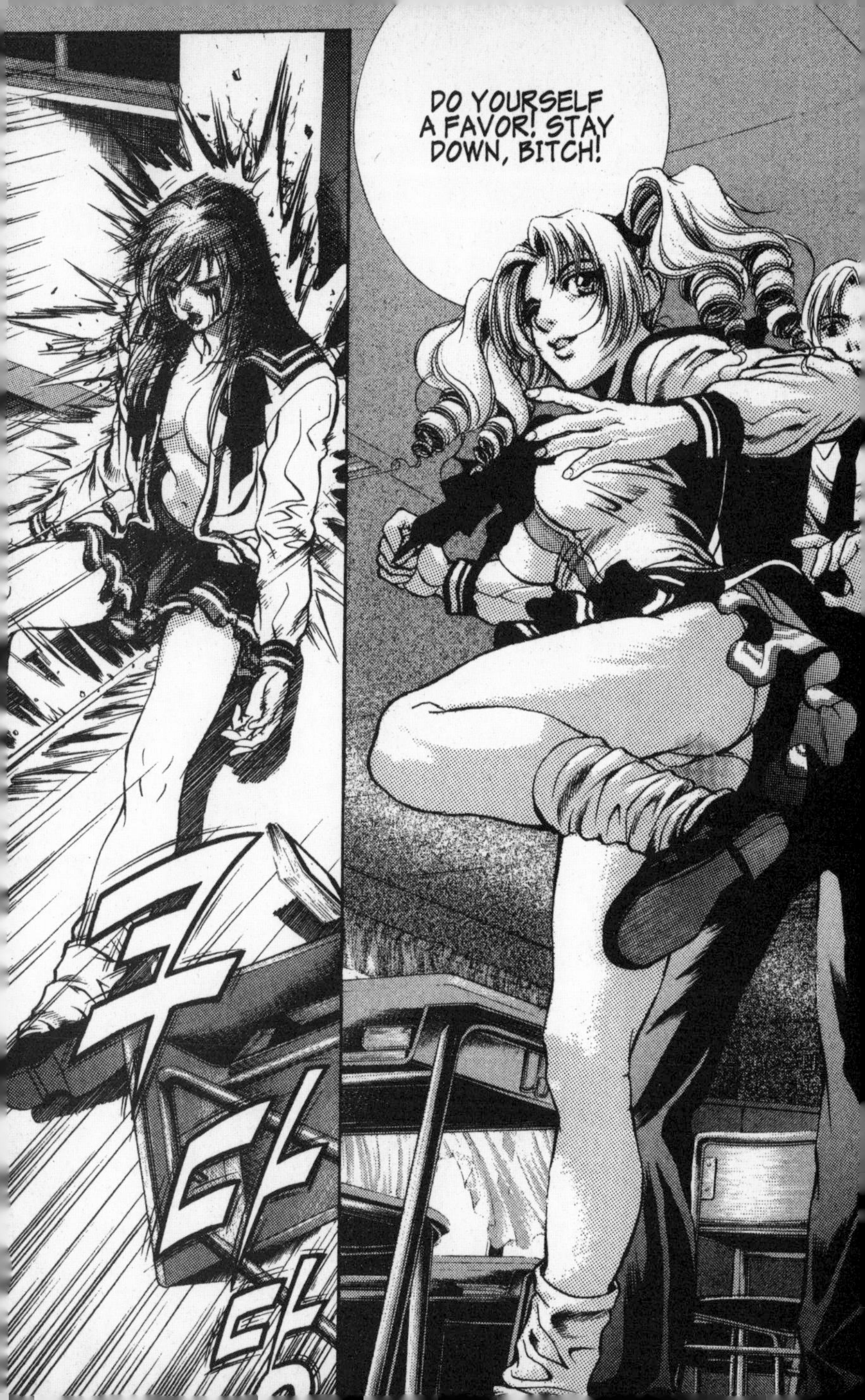
DO YOURSELF A FAVOR! STAY DOWN, BITCH!

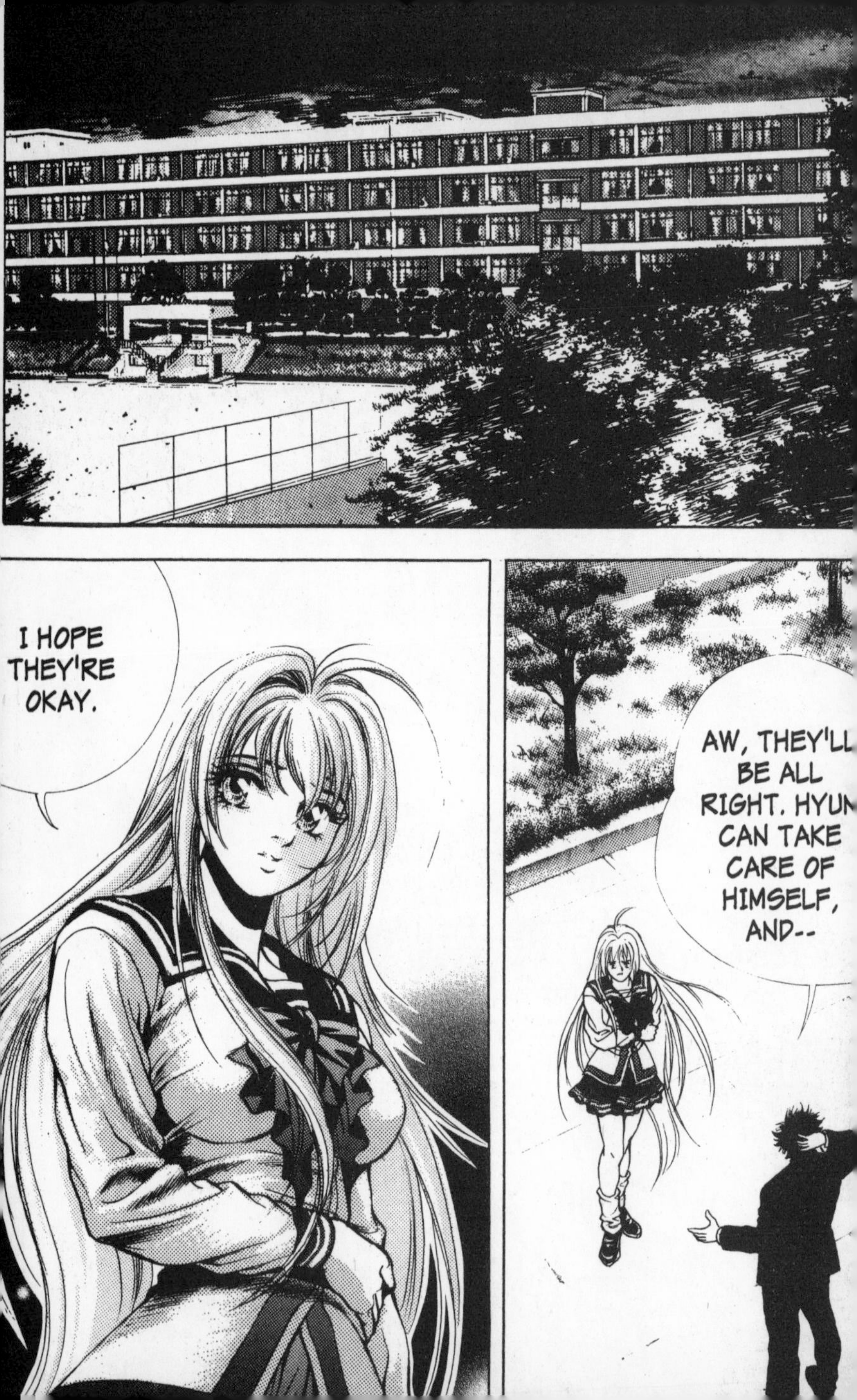
I HOPE THEY'RE OKAY.
AW, THEY'LL BE ALL RIGHT. HYUN CAN TAKE CARE OF HIMSELF, AND--

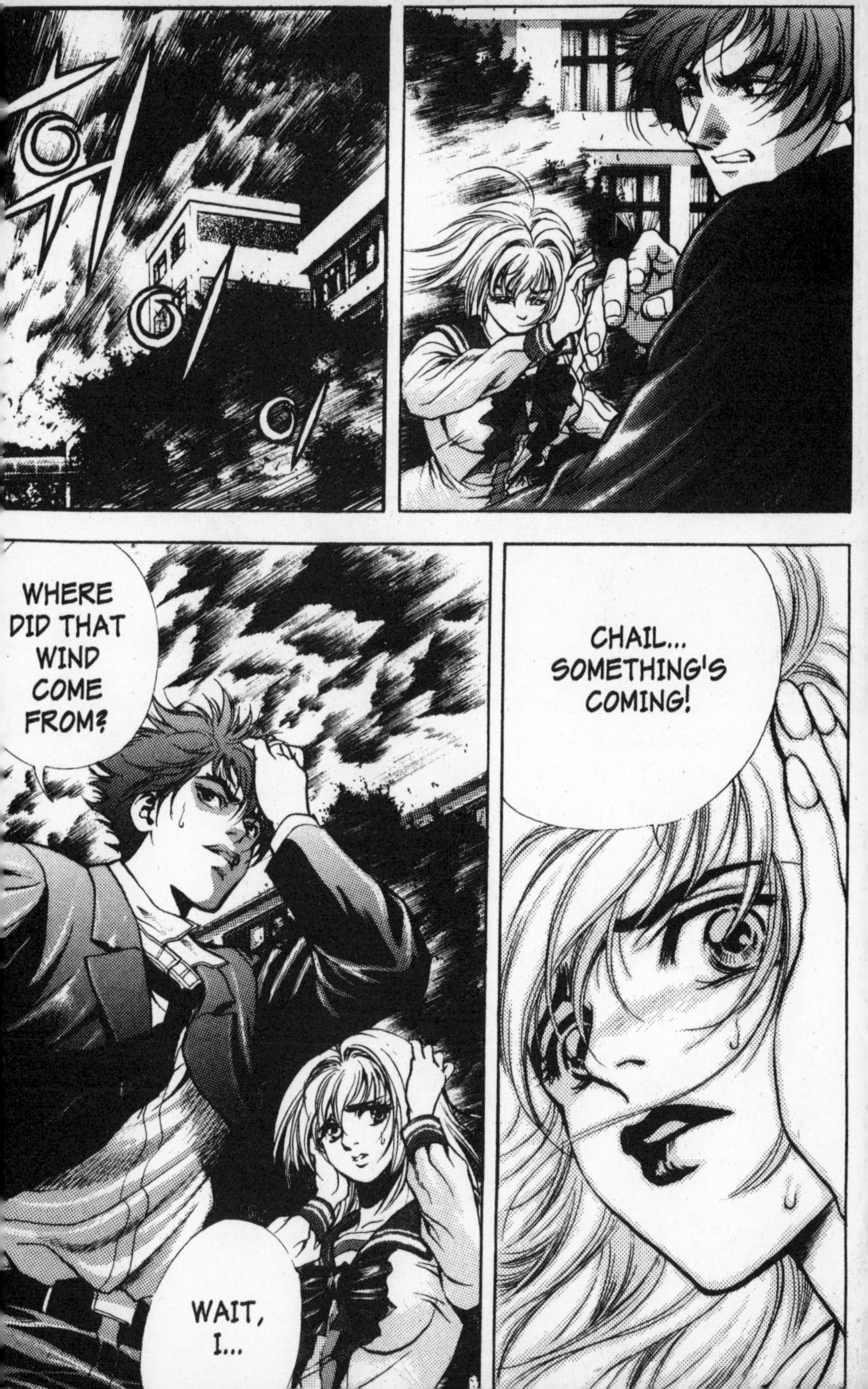
CHAIL... SOMETHING'S COMING!
WHERE DID THAT WIND COME FROM?
WAIT, I...

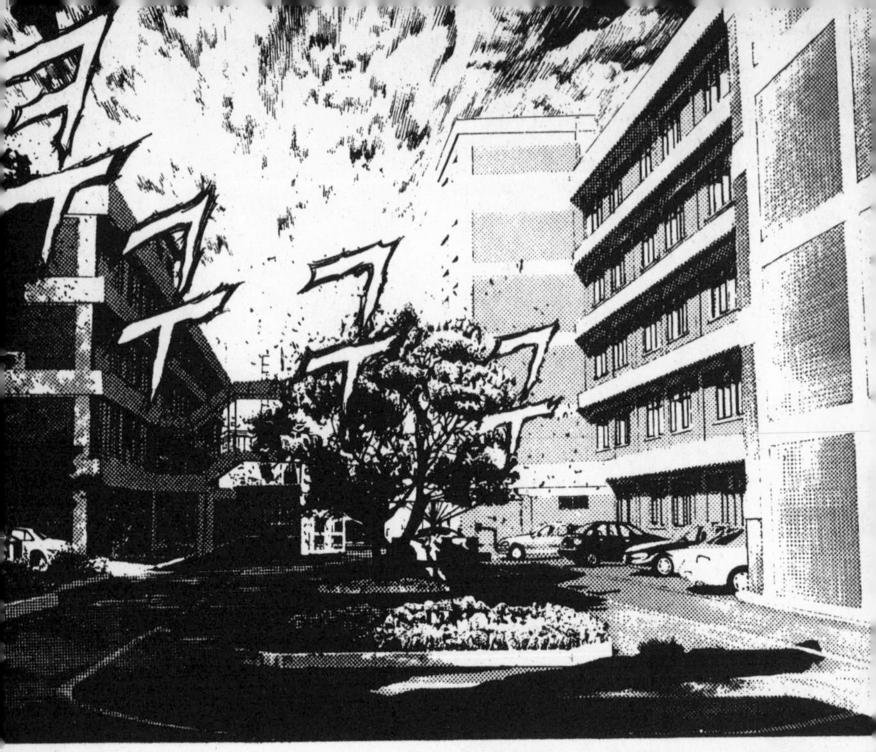

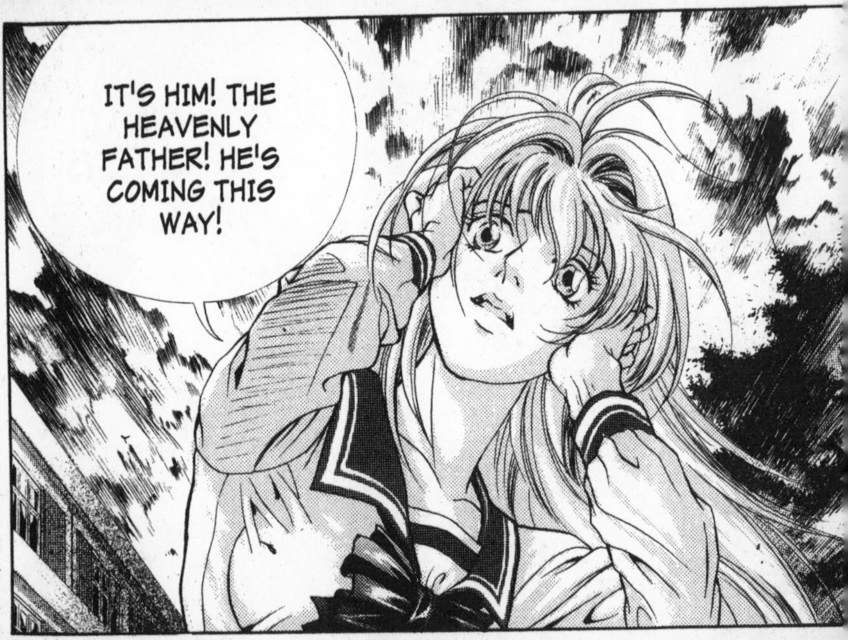
IT'S HIM! THE HEAVENLY FATHER! HE'S COMING THIS WAY!

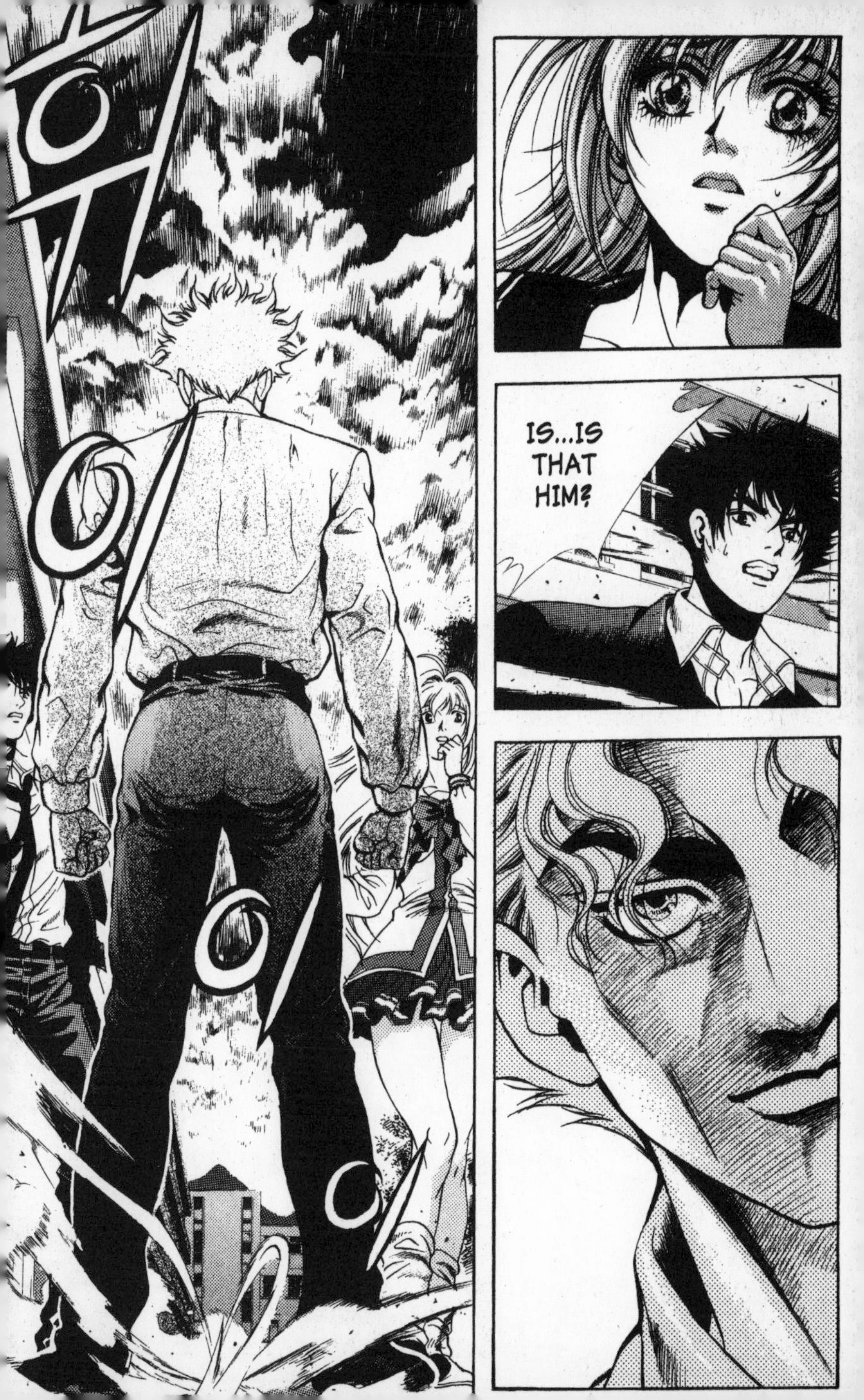
IS...IS
THAT
HIM?

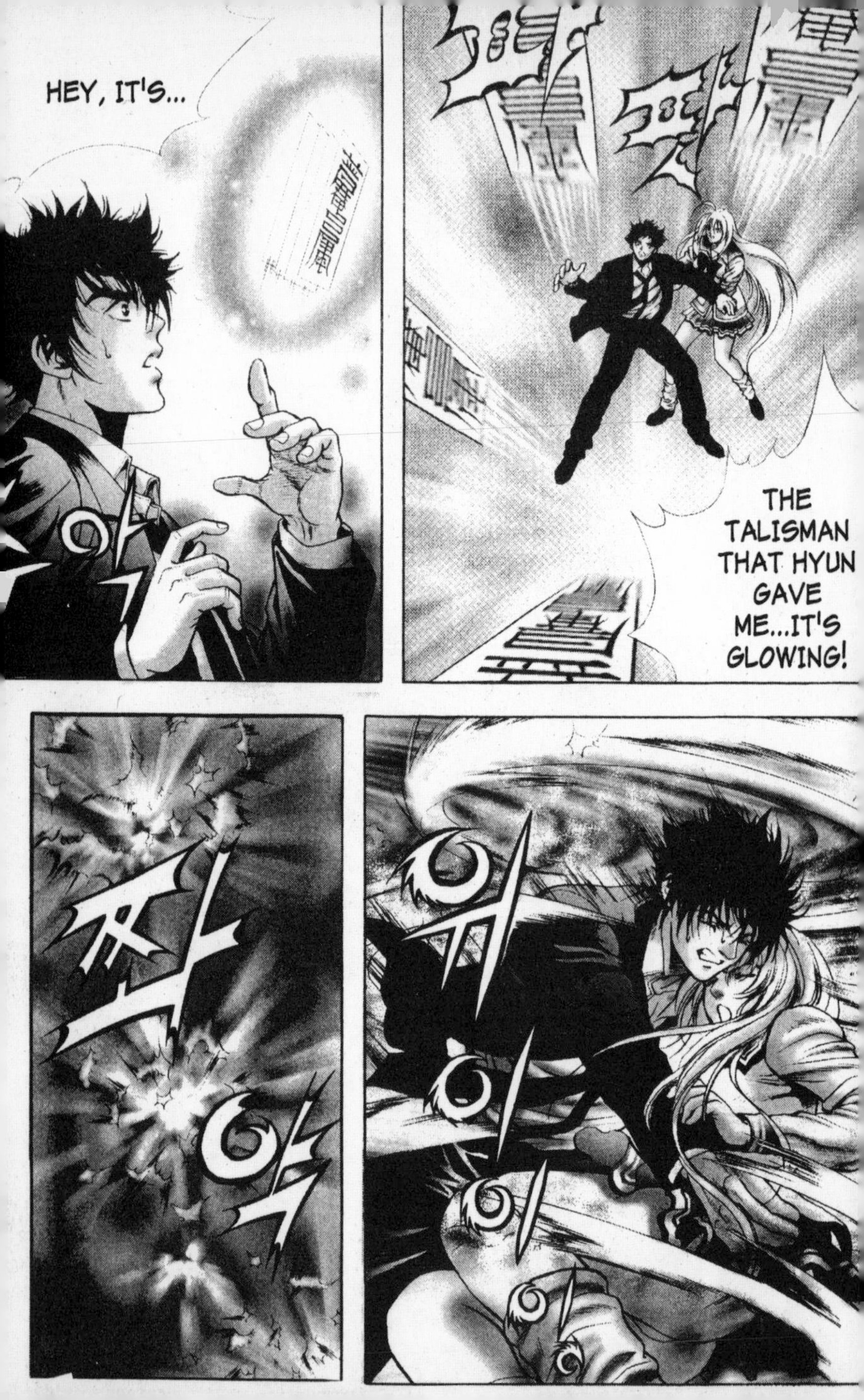
HEY, IT'S...
THE TALISMAN THAT HYUN GAVE ME...IT'S GLOWING!

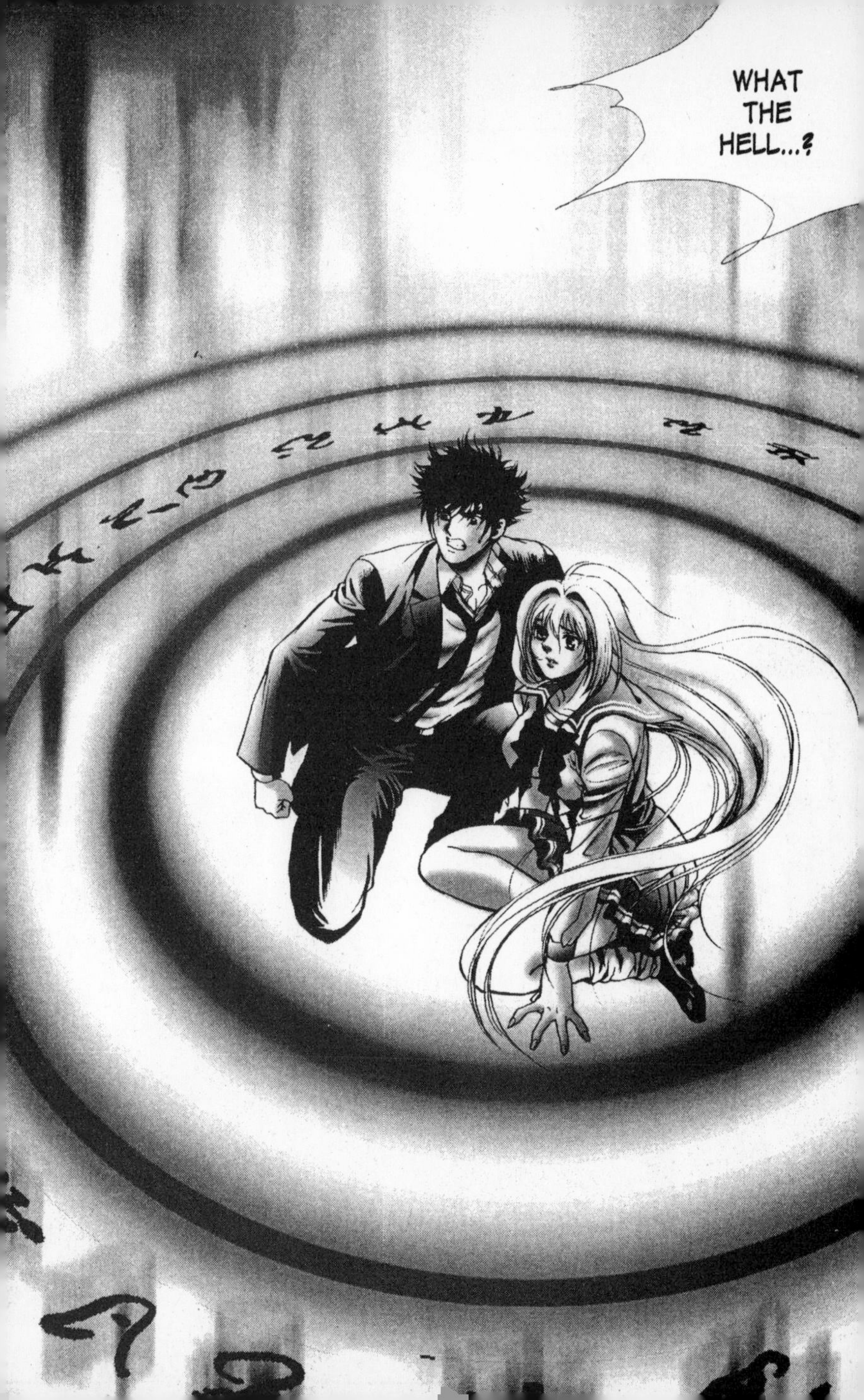
WHAT THE HELL...?

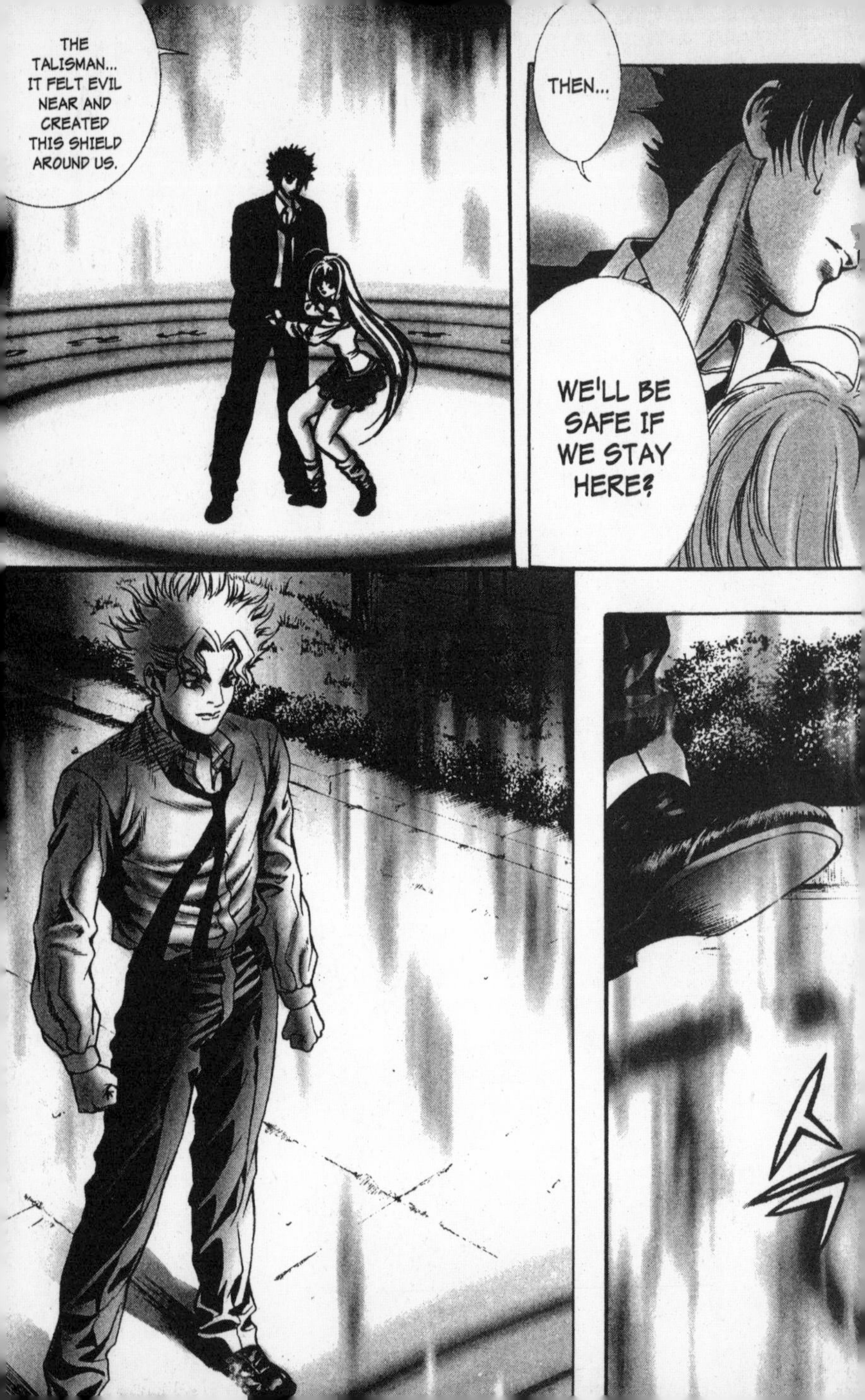
THEN...
WE'LL BE SAFE IF WE STAY HERE?
THE TALISMAN... IT FELT EVIL NEAR AND CREATED THIS SHIELD AROUND US.

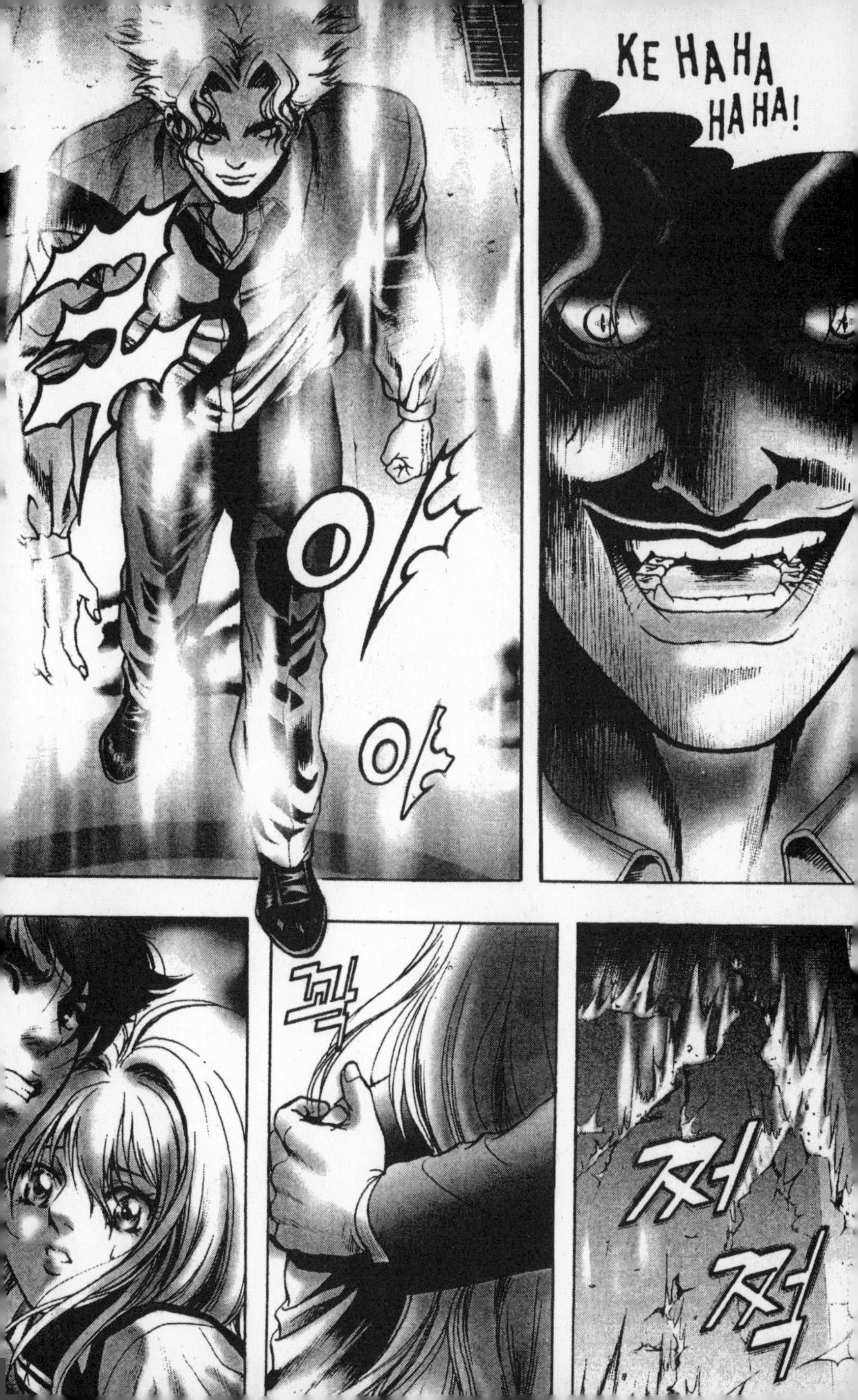
아
아
KE HAHA HAHA!
꽉
저
적

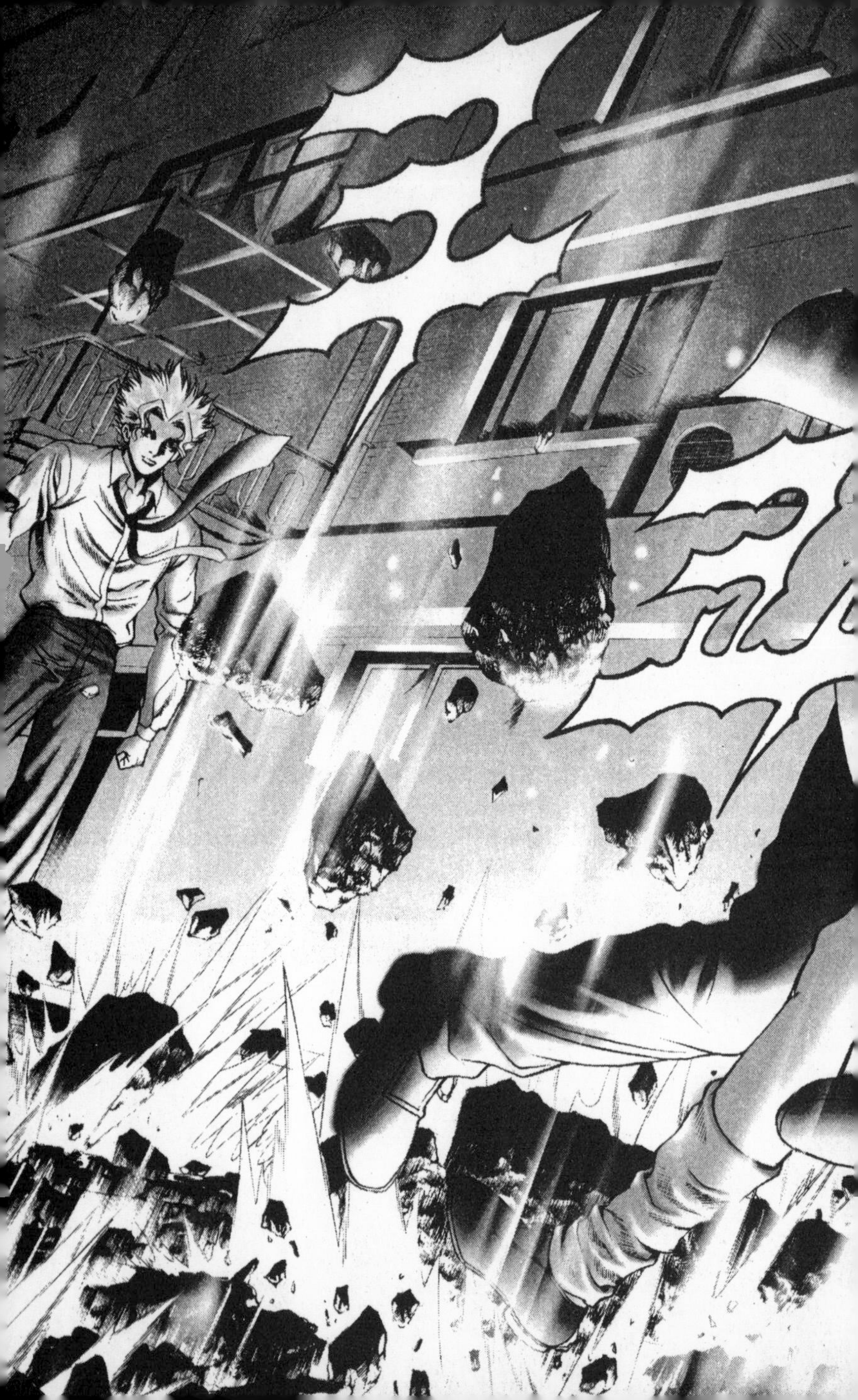

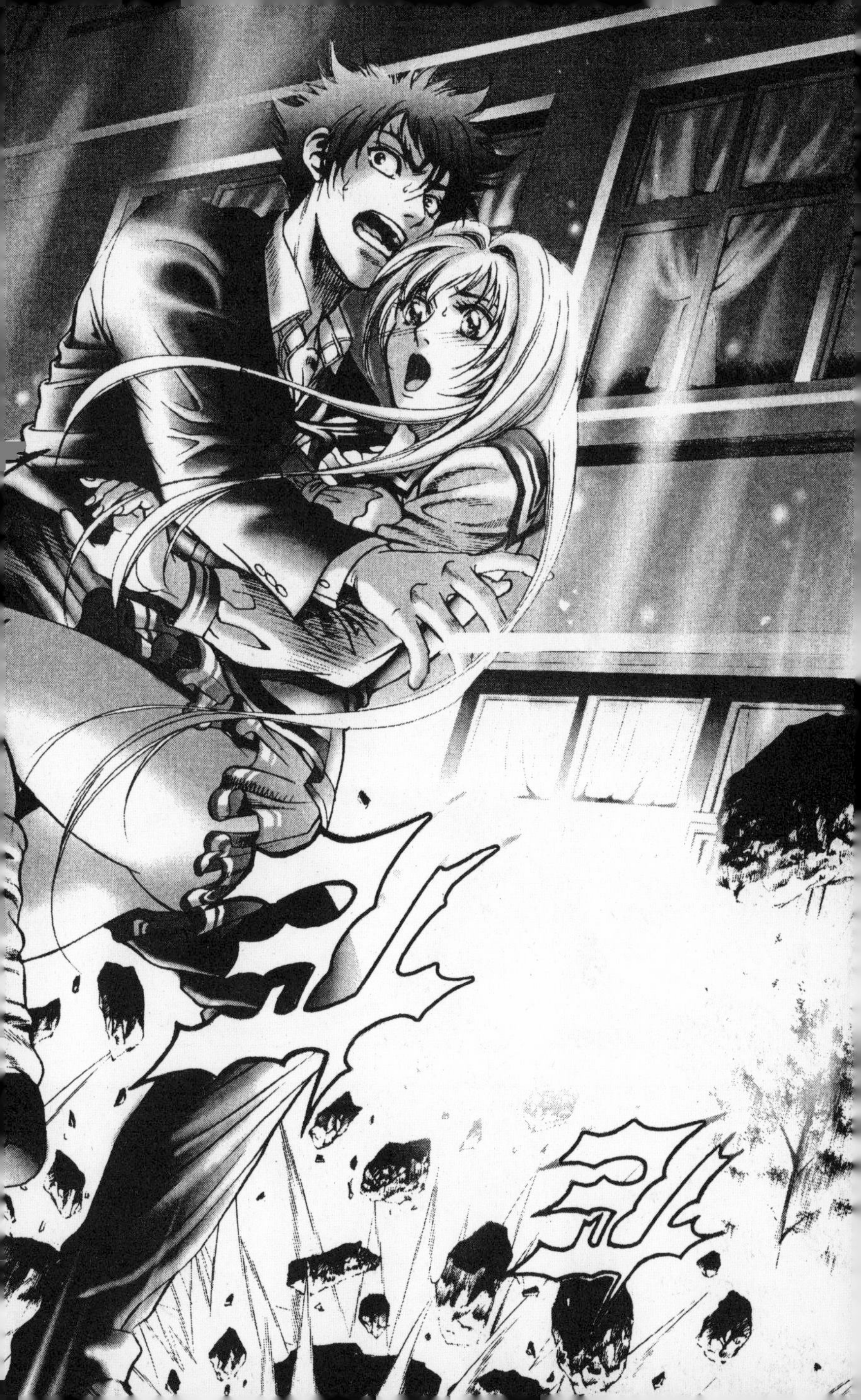

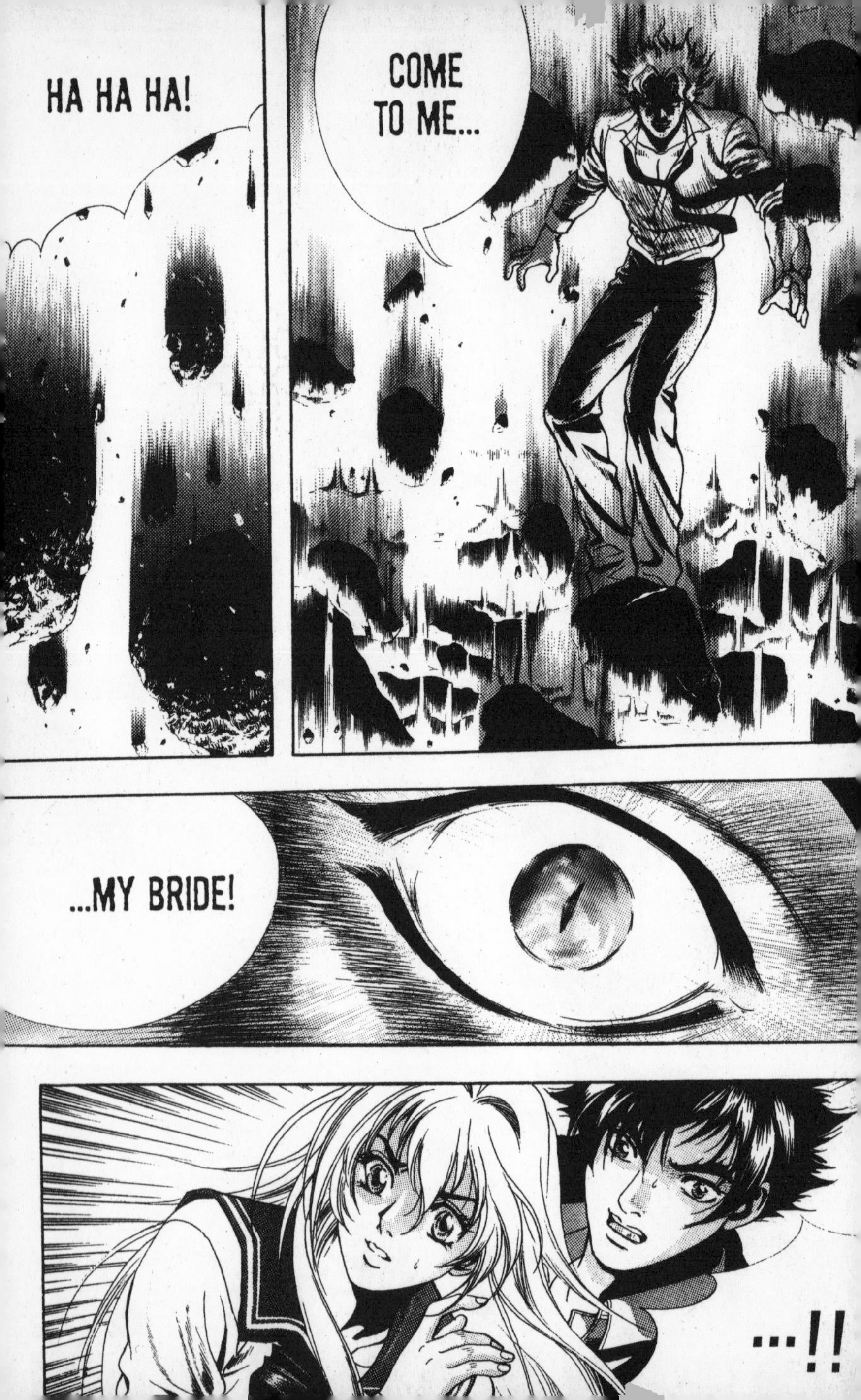
COME TO ME...
HA HA HA!
...MY BRIDE!
...!!

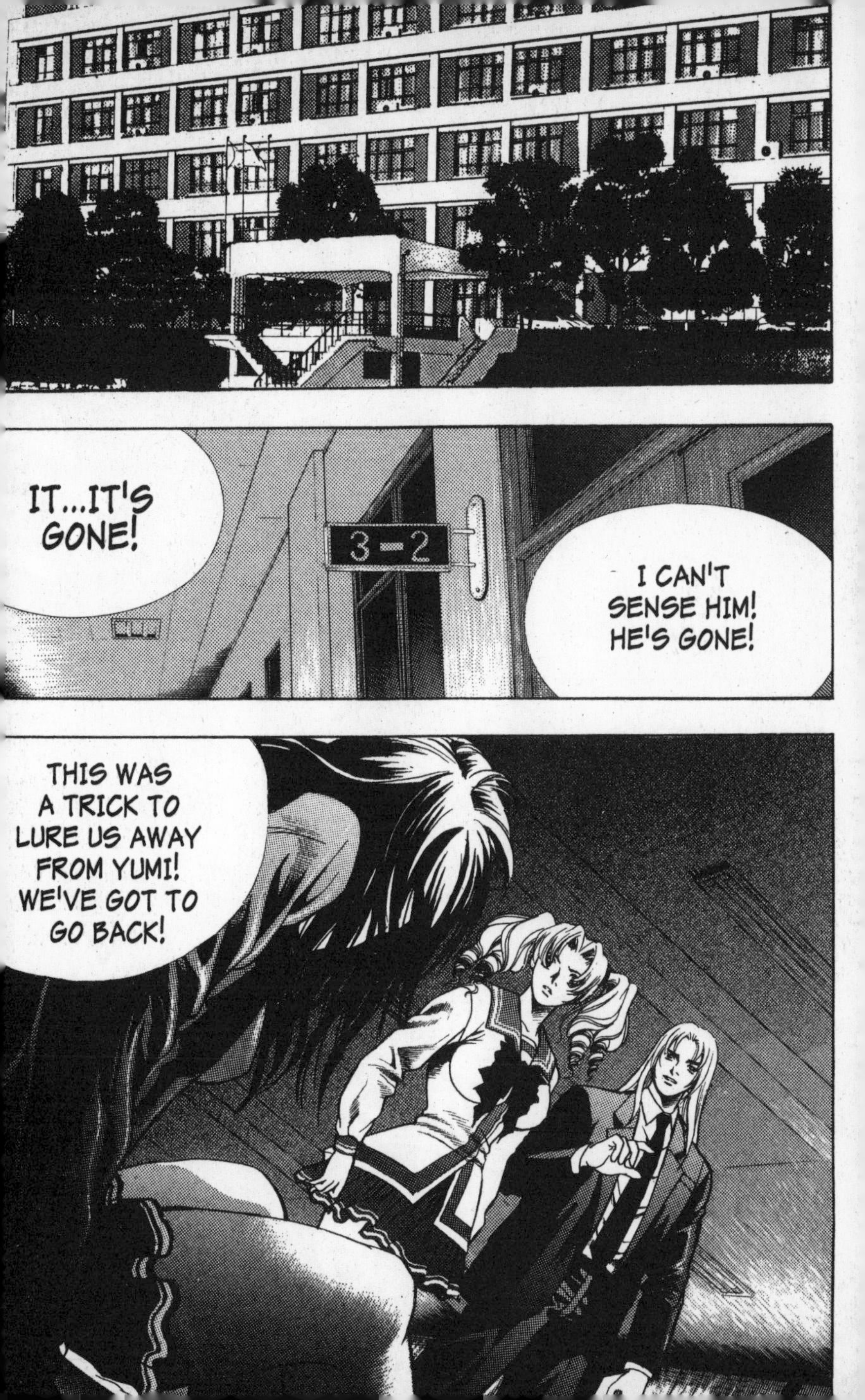

I CAN'T SENSE HIM! HE'S GONE!
IT...IT'S GONE!
THIS WAS A TRICK TO LURE US AWAY FROM YUMI! WE'VE GOT TO GO BACK!

음질

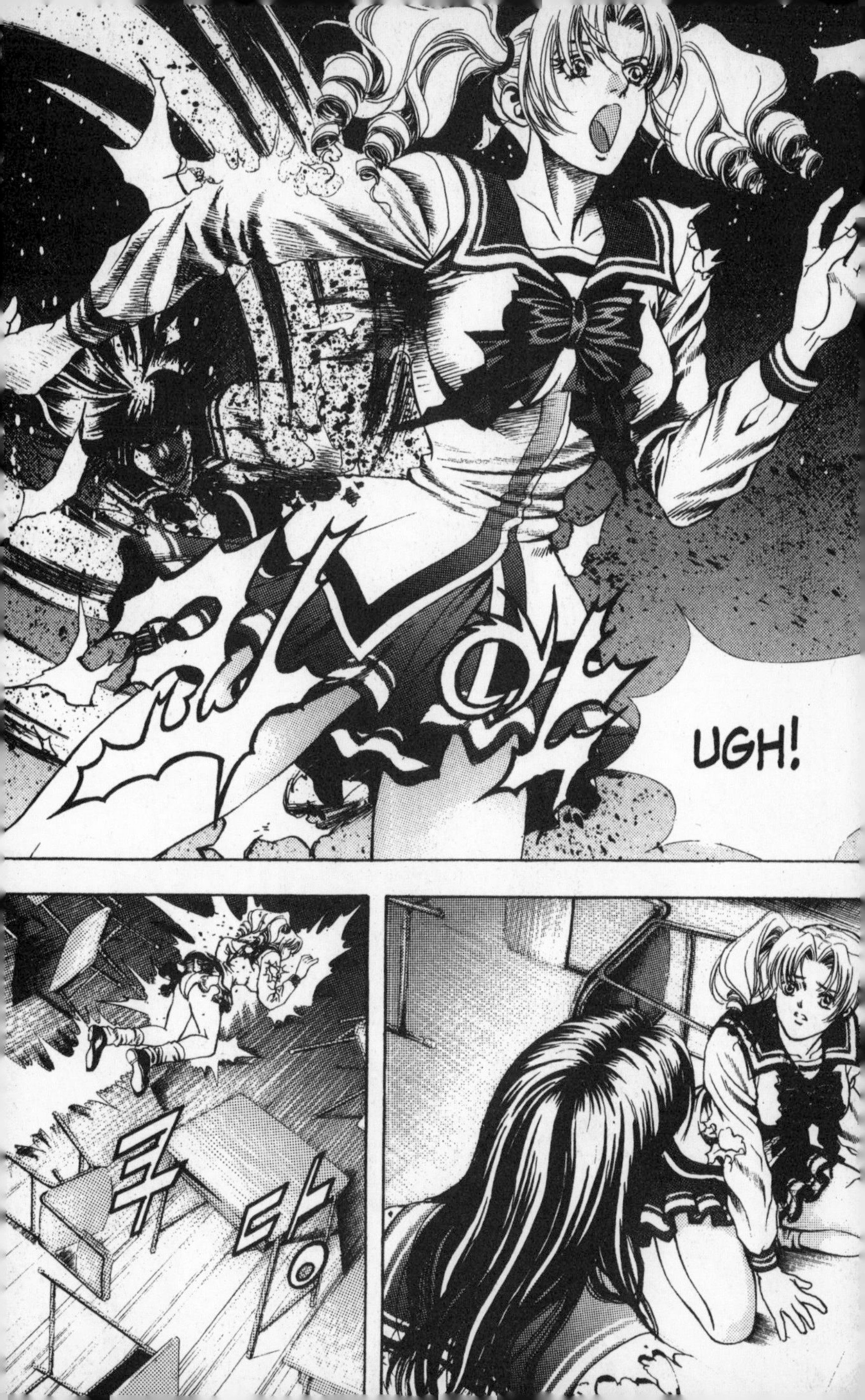
UGH!

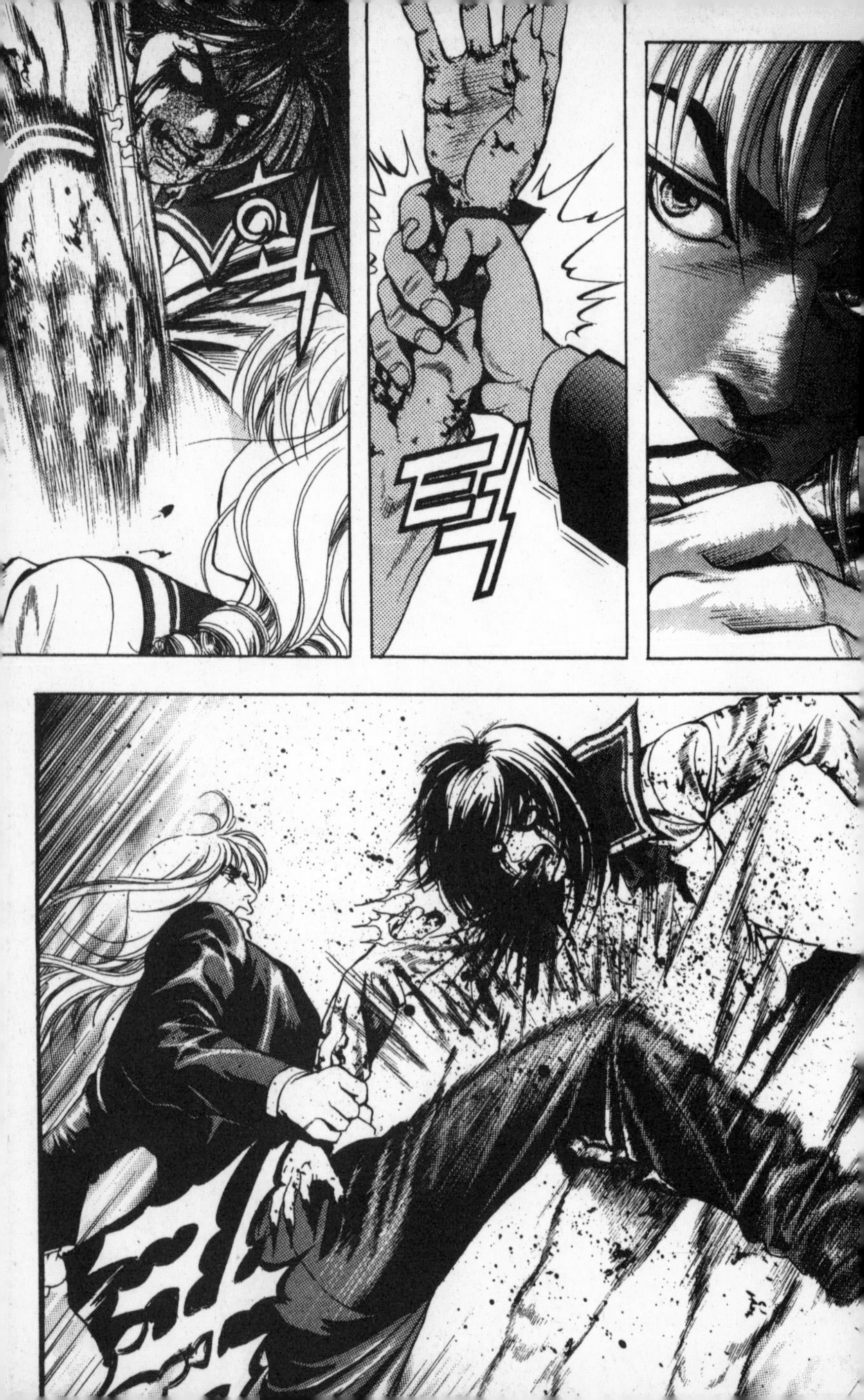
턱

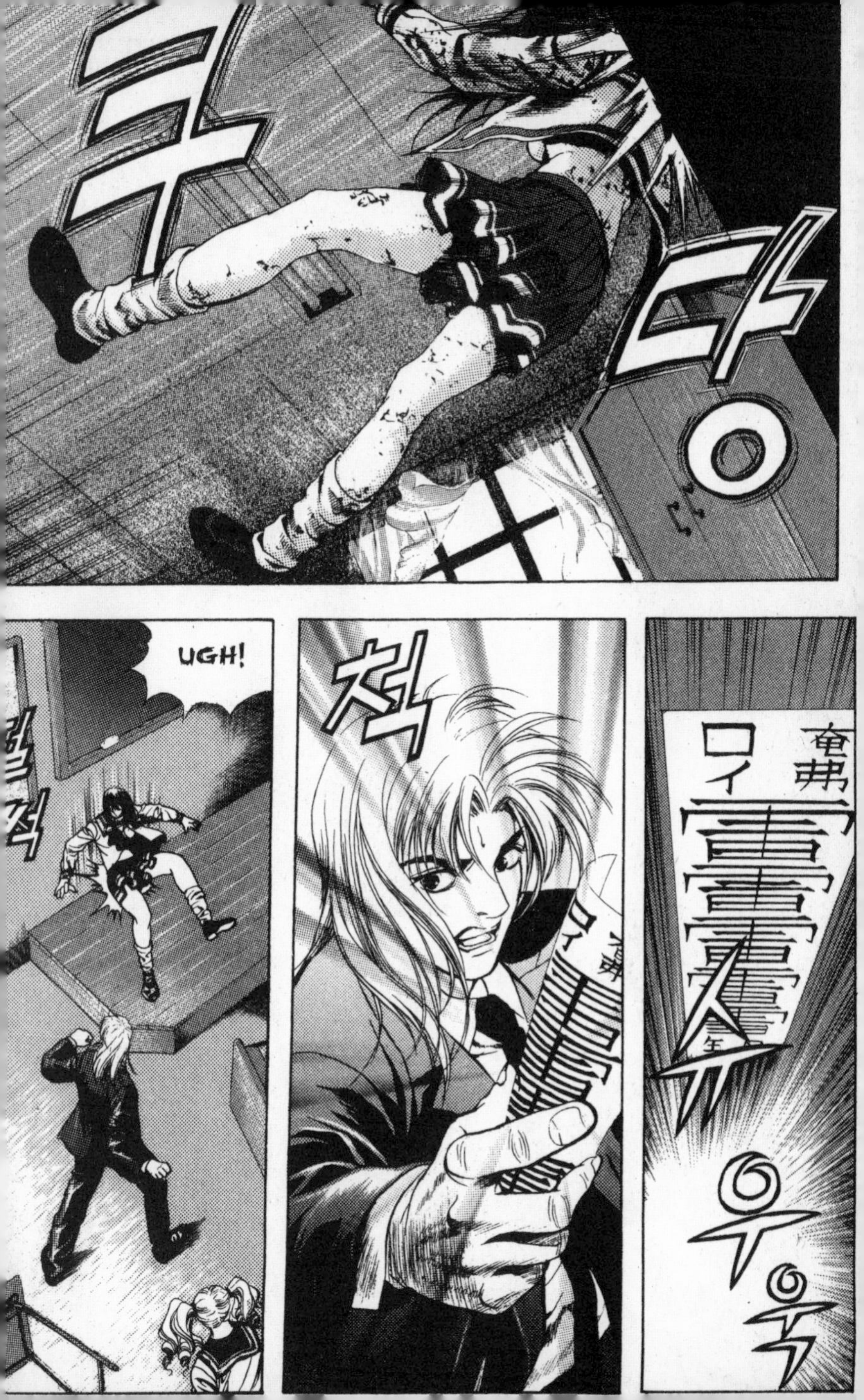
UGH!

GHUUH!

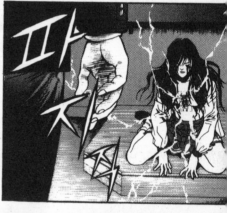

H...
HYUN!

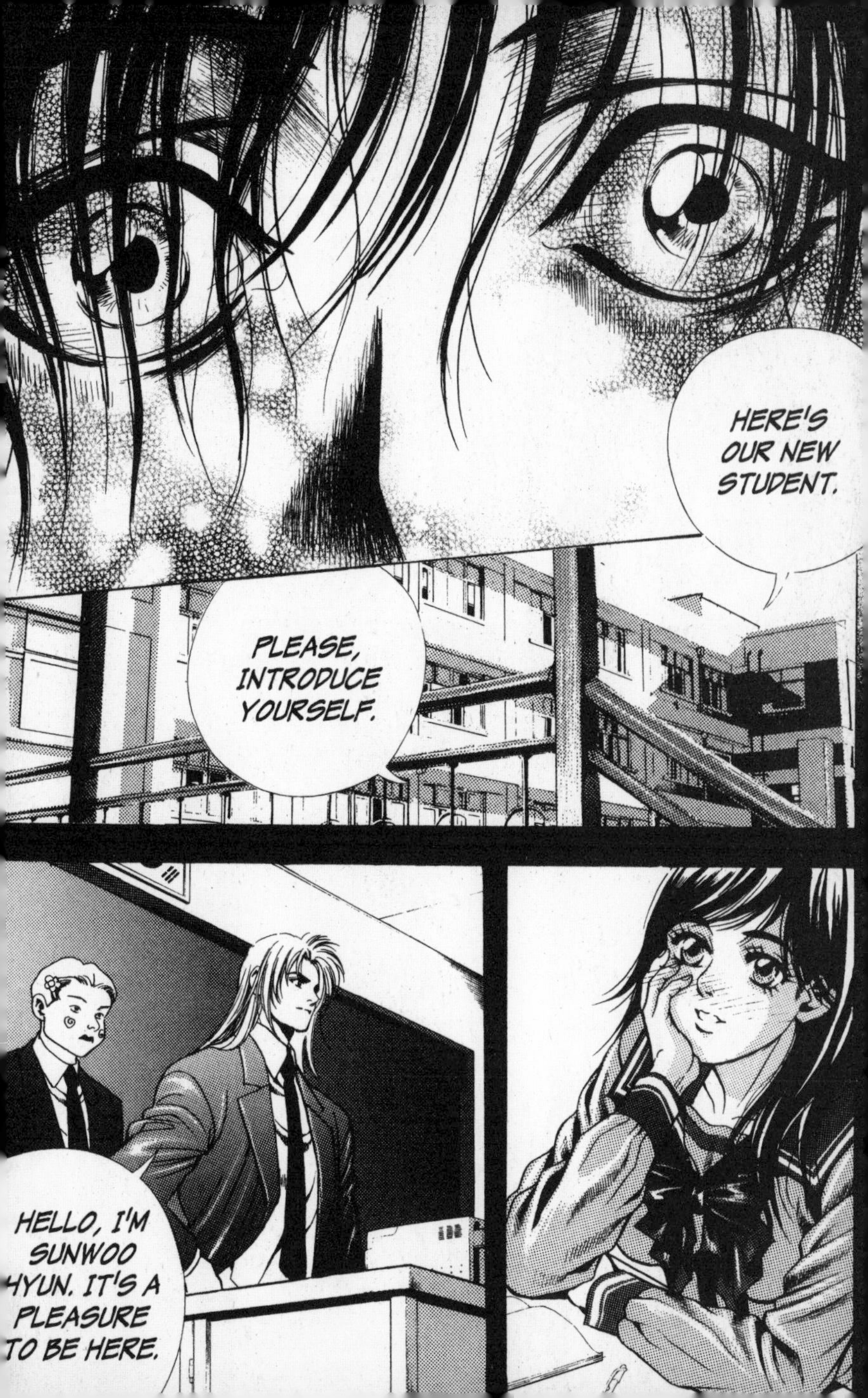
HERE'S OUR NEW STUDENT.
PLEASE, INTRODUCE YOURSELF.
HELLO, I'M SUNWOO HYUN. IT'S A PLEASURE TO BE HERE.

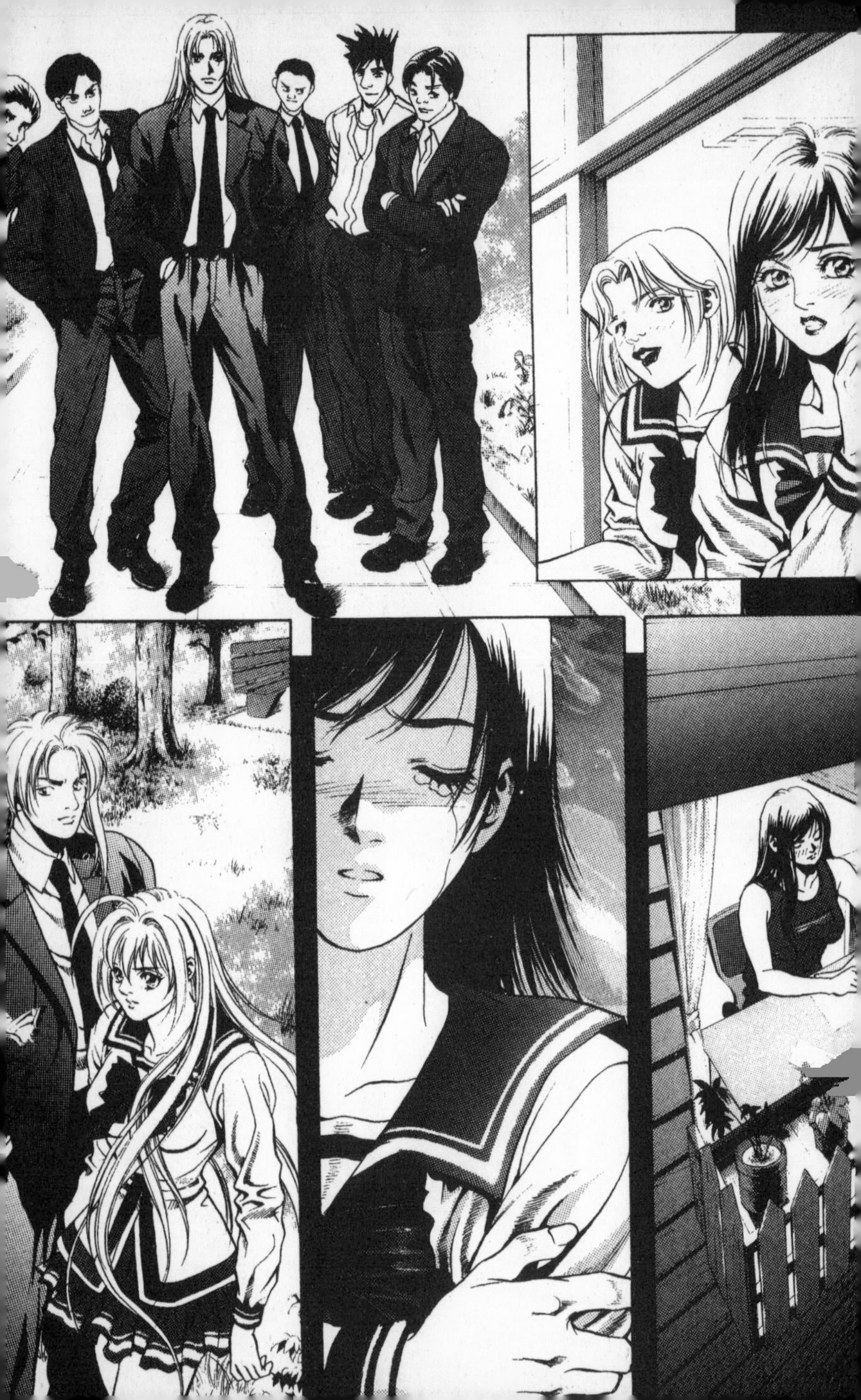

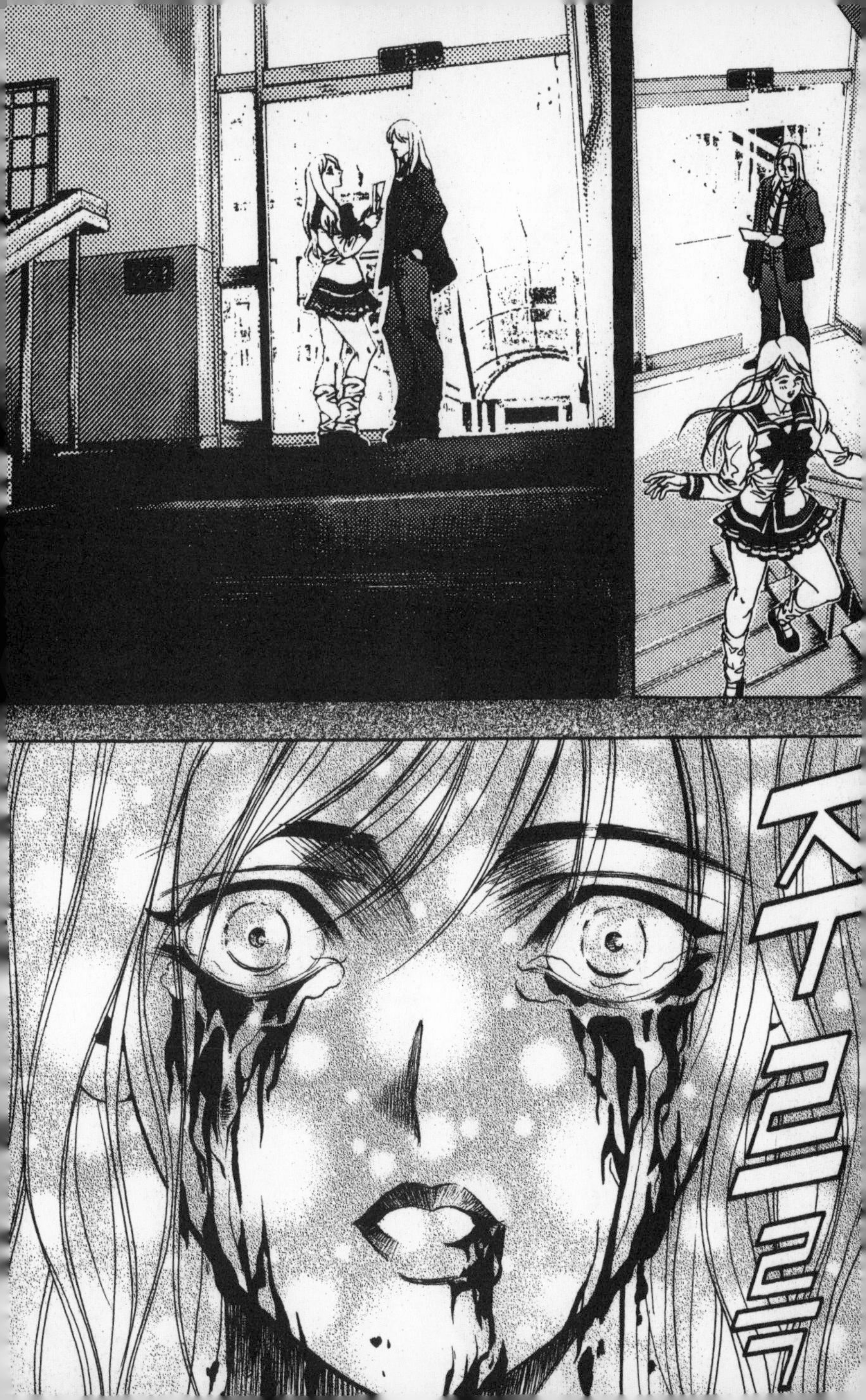

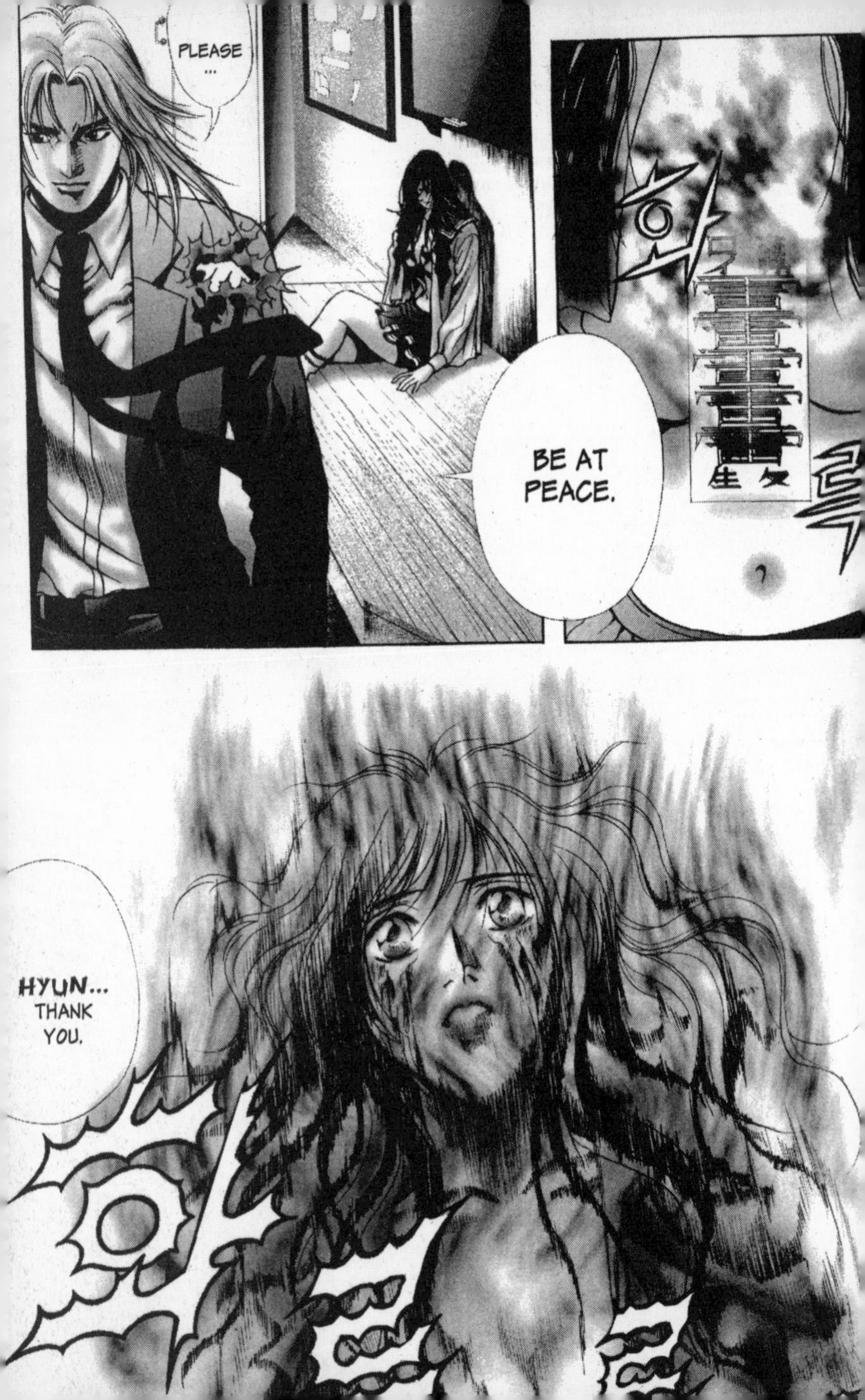
PLEASE ...
BE AT PEACE.
HYUN... THANK YOU.

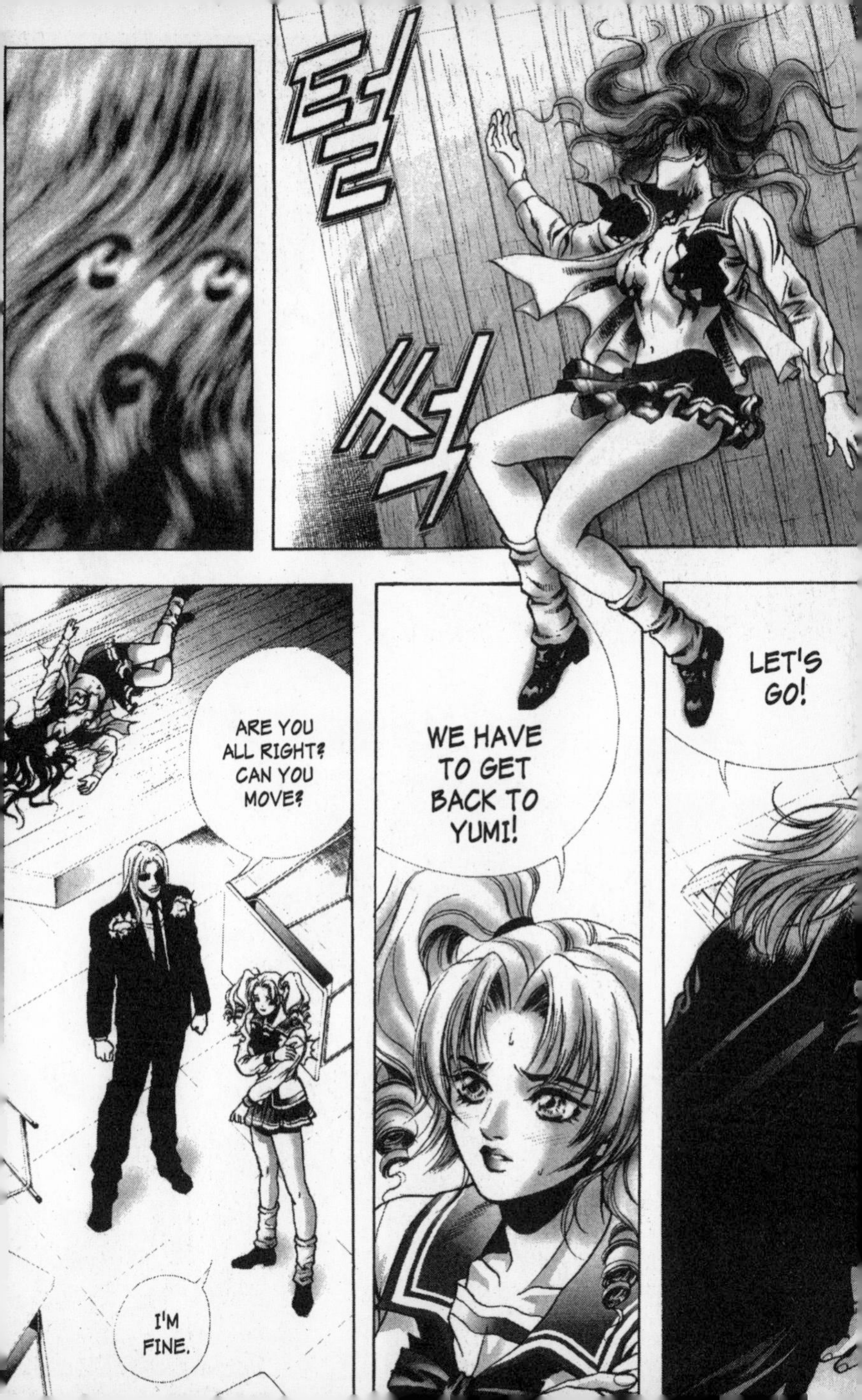

털
썩
LET'S GO!
WE HAVE TO GET BACK TO YUMI!
ARE YOU ALL RIGHT? CAN YOU MOVE?
I'M FINE.

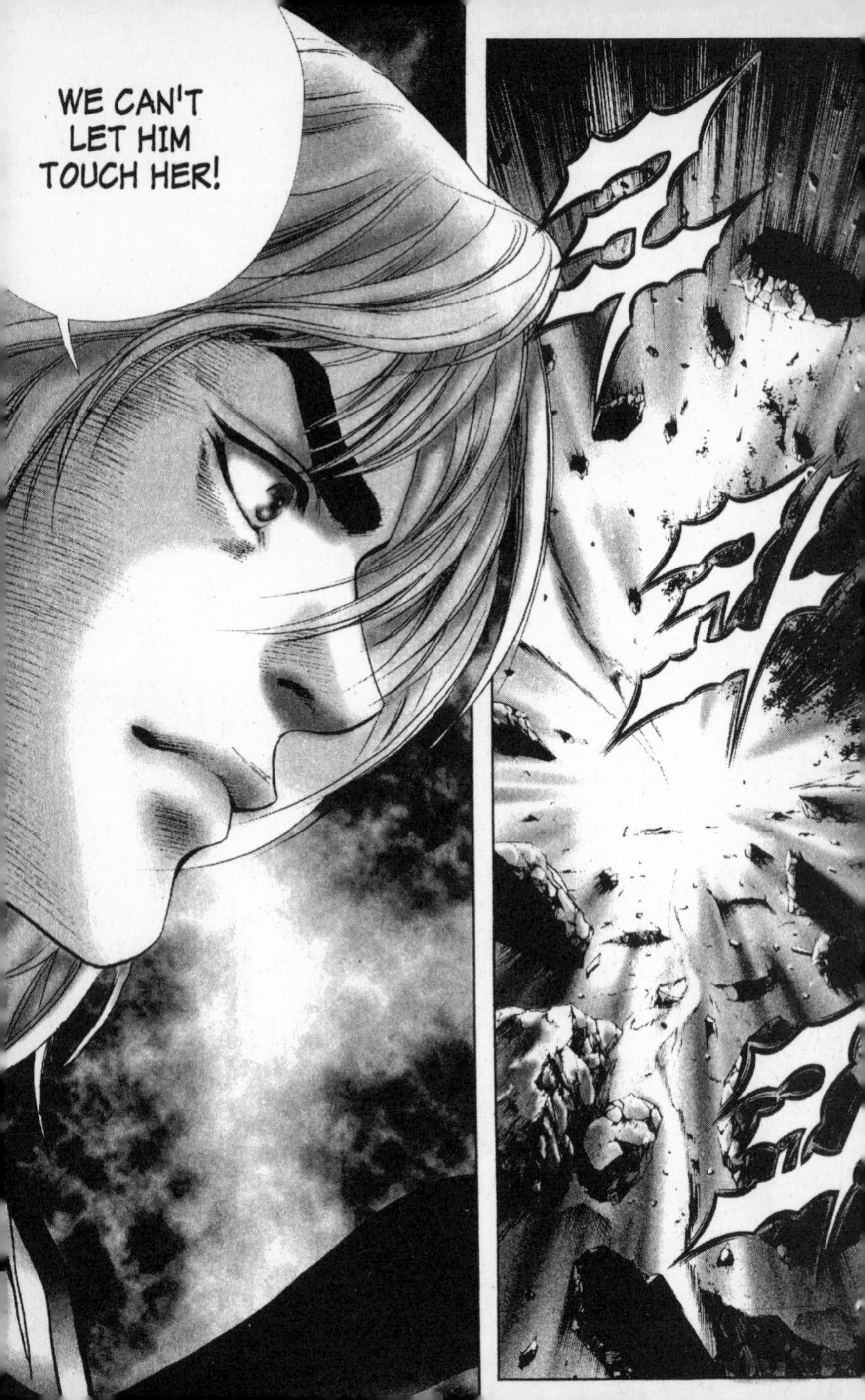
WE CAN'T LET HIM TOUCH HER!

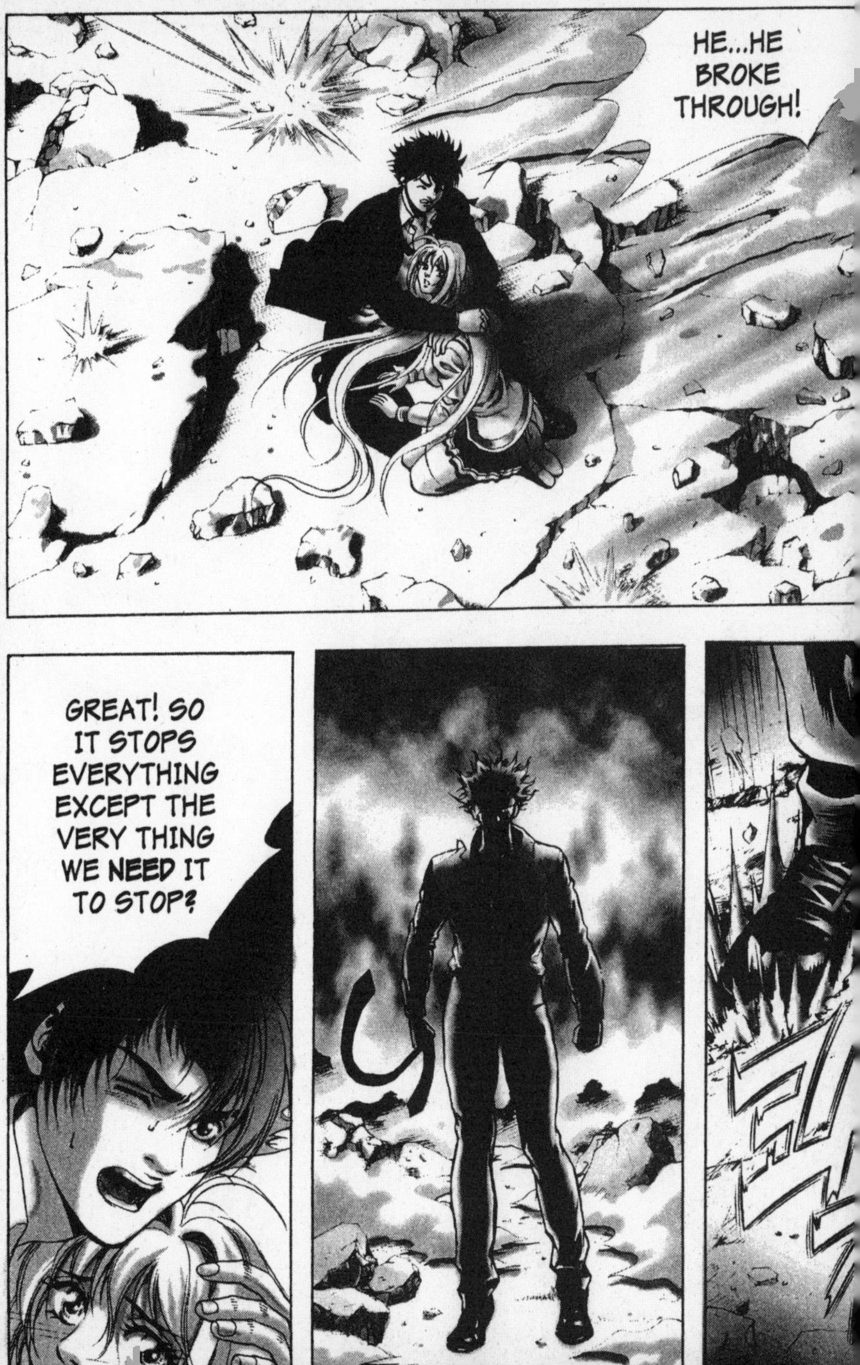
HE...HE BROKE THROUGH!
GREAT! SO IT STOPS EVERYTHING EXCEPT THE VERY THING WE NEED IT TO STOP?

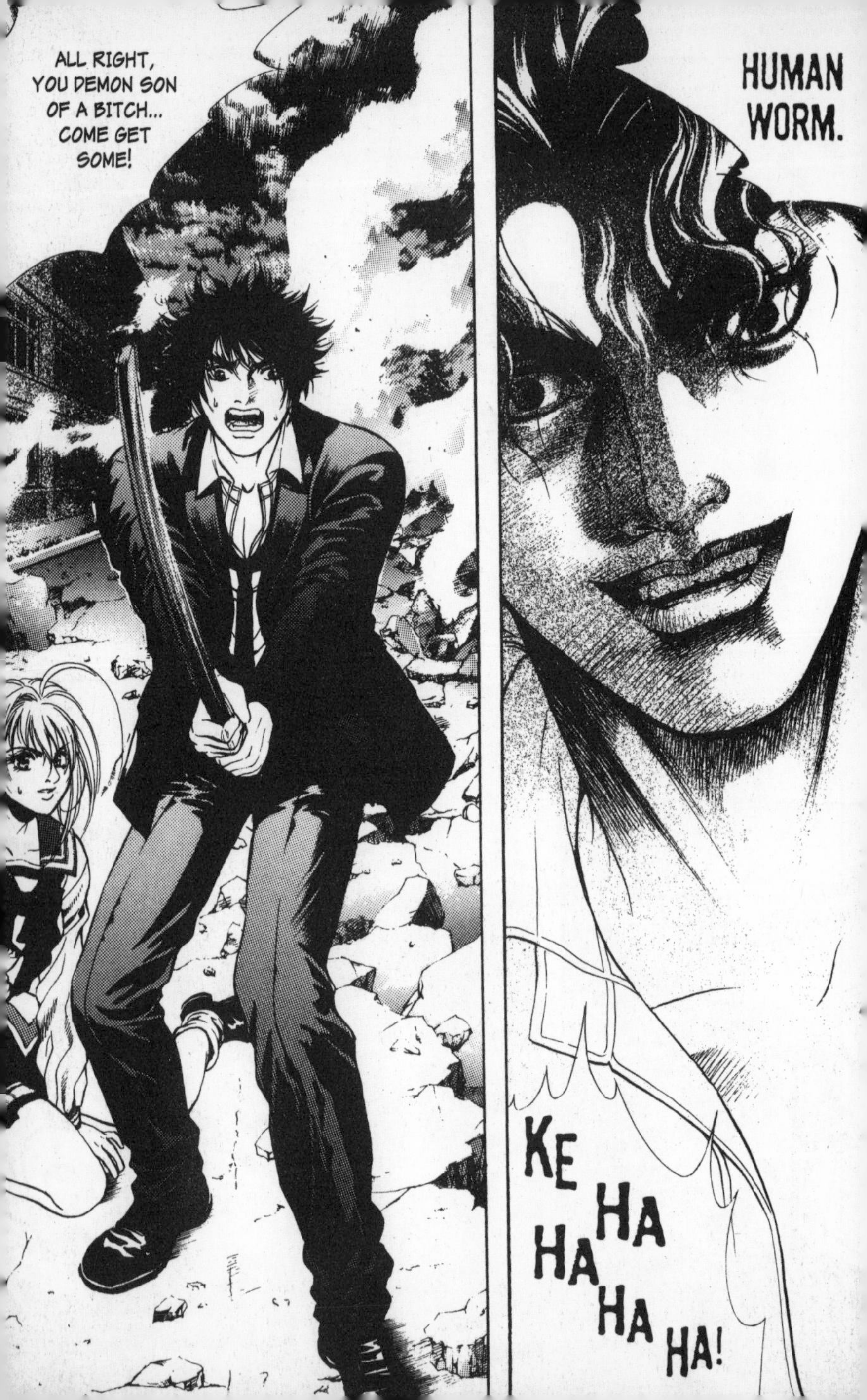
HUMAN WORM.
KE HA HA HA HA HA!
ALL RIGHT, YOU DEMON SON OF A BITCH... COME GET SOME!

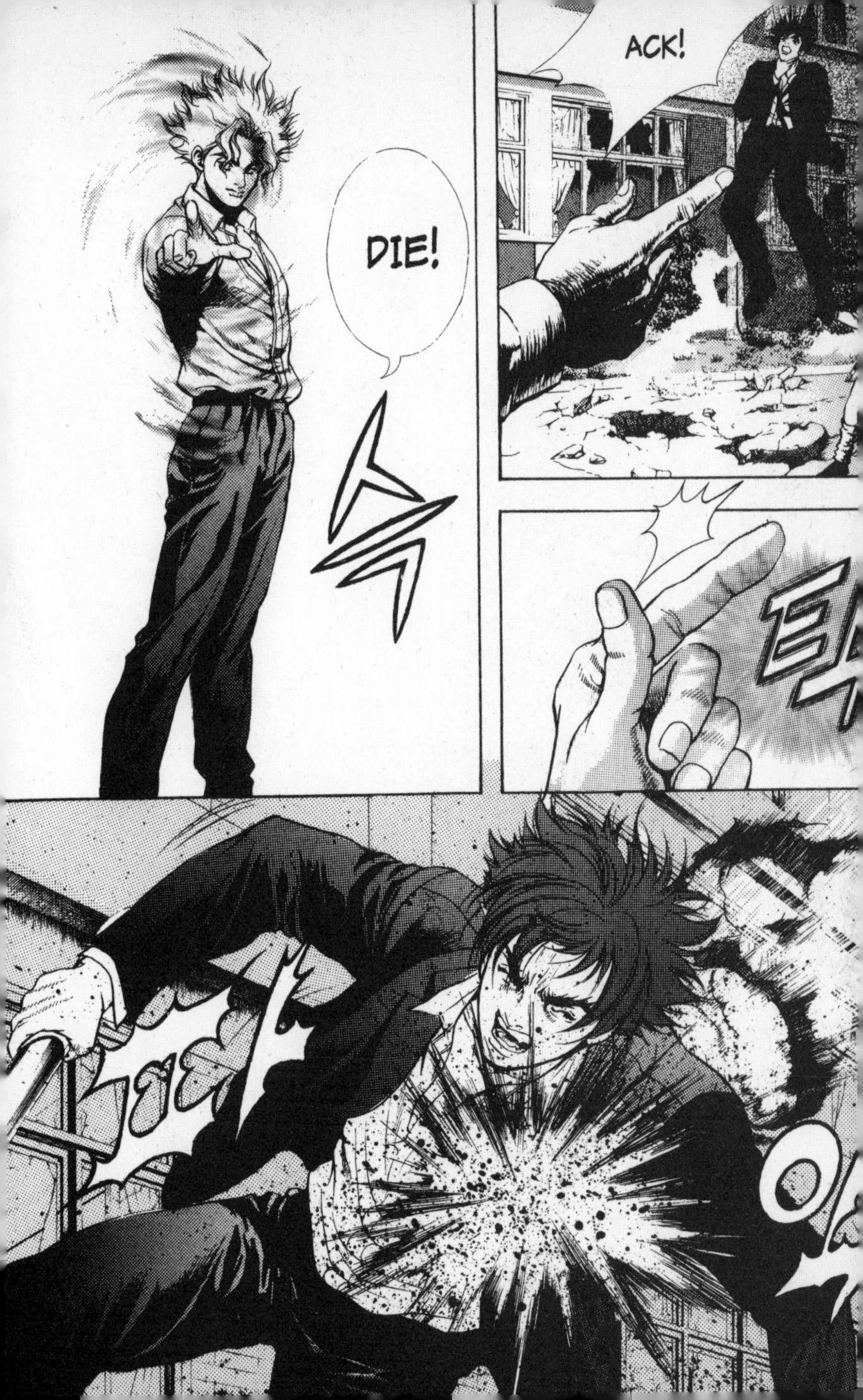
ACK!
DIE!

CHAIL!

NOOO!!

AHH!

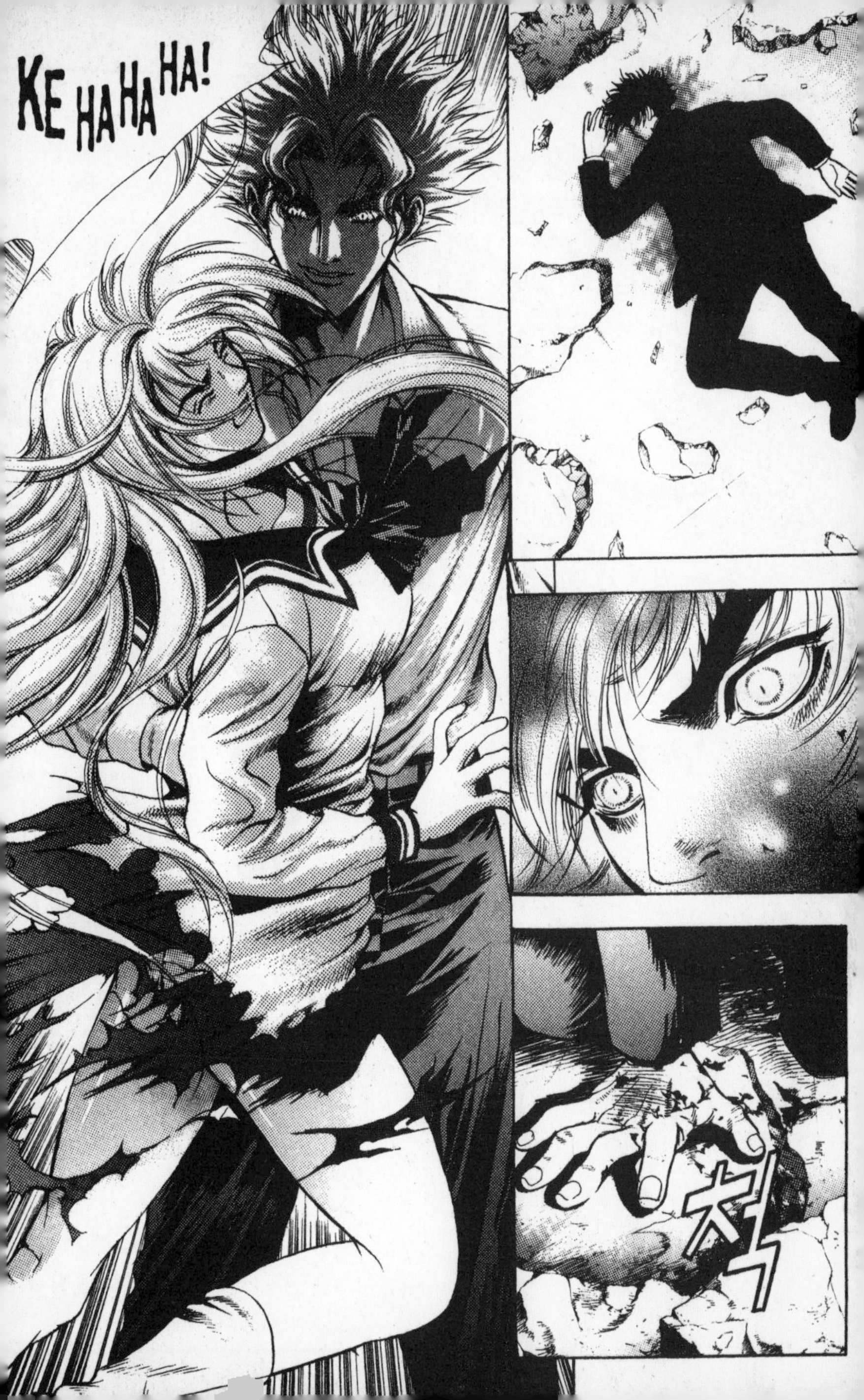
KE HA HA HA!

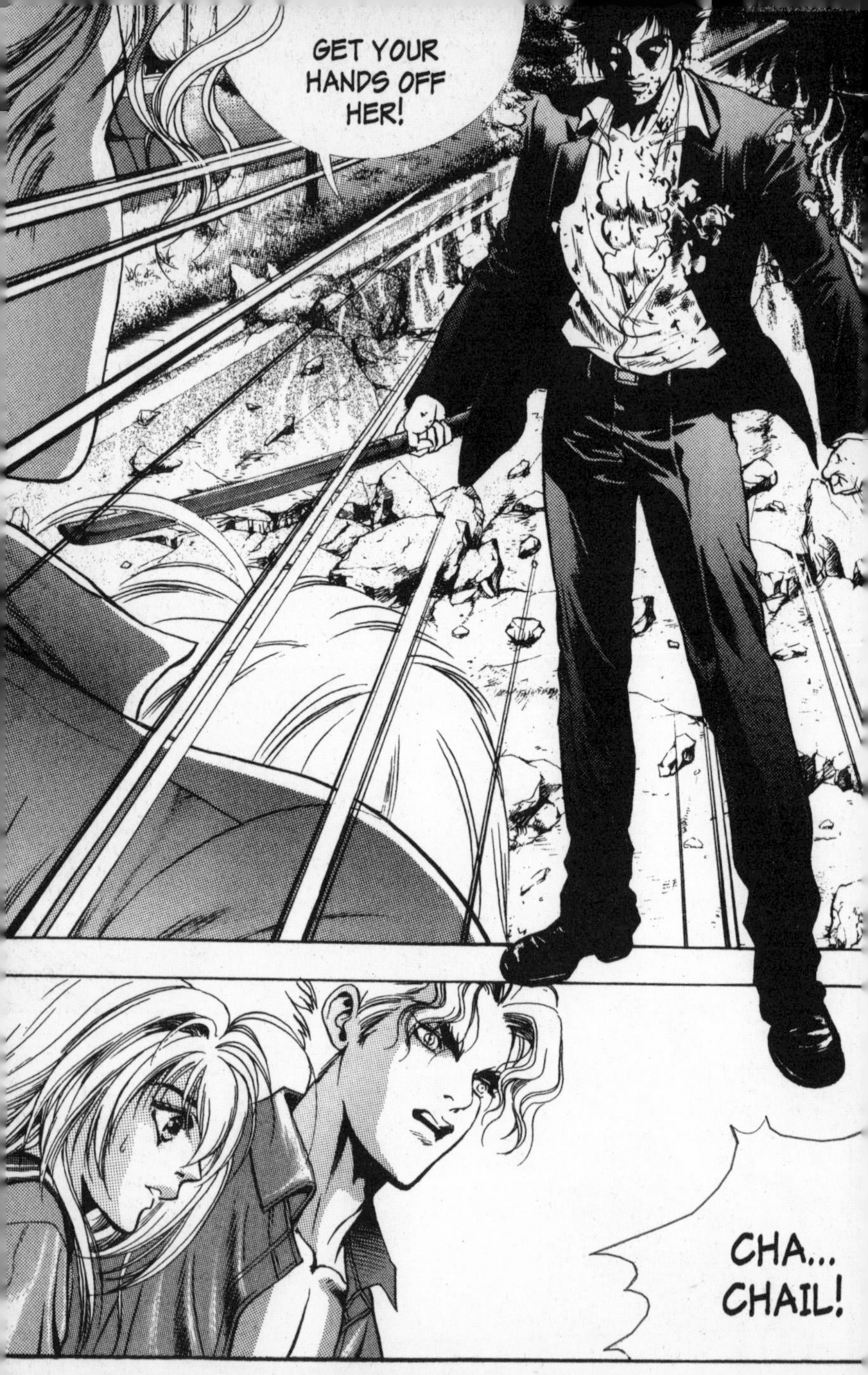
GET YOUR HANDS OFF HER!
CHA... CHAIL!

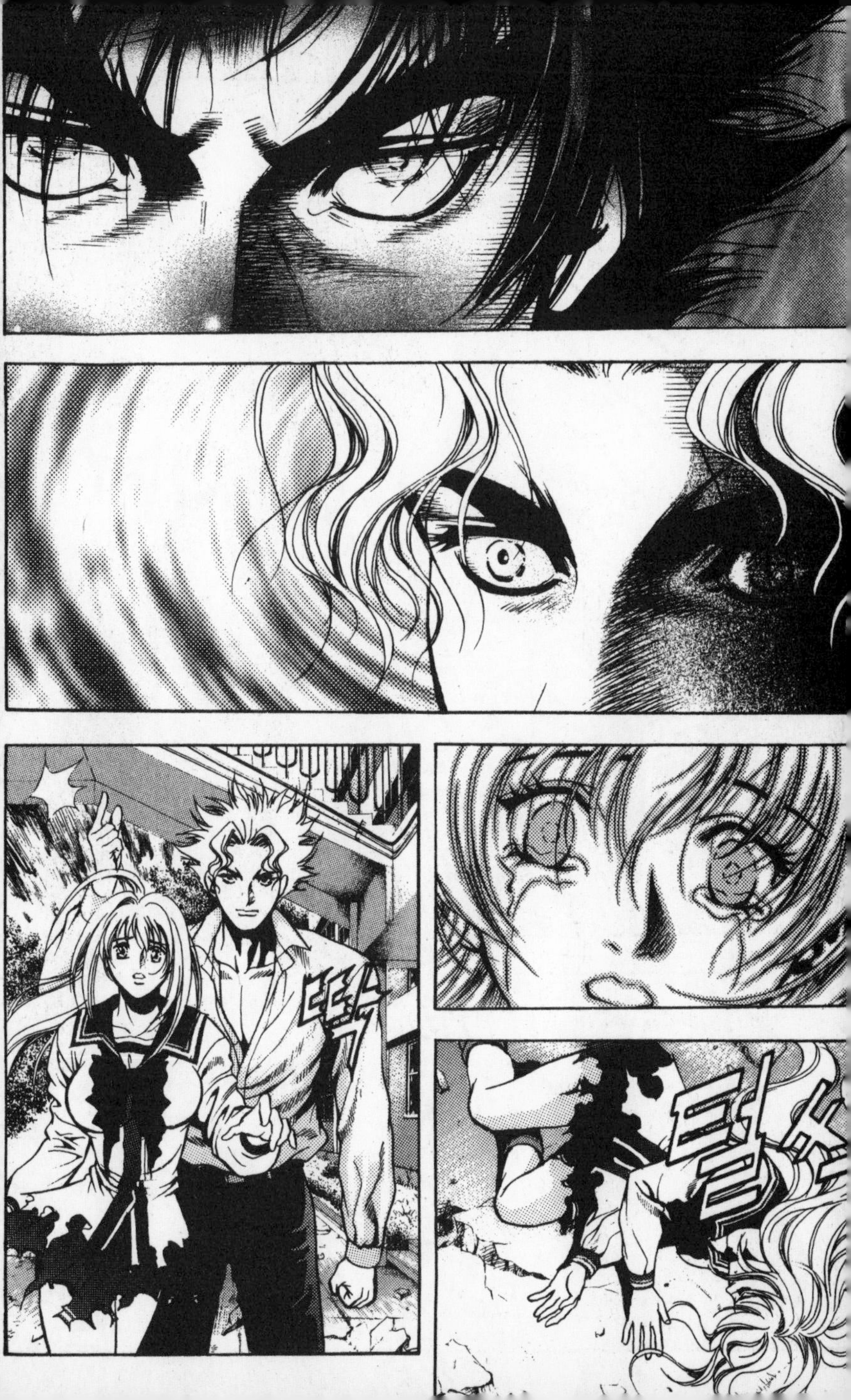

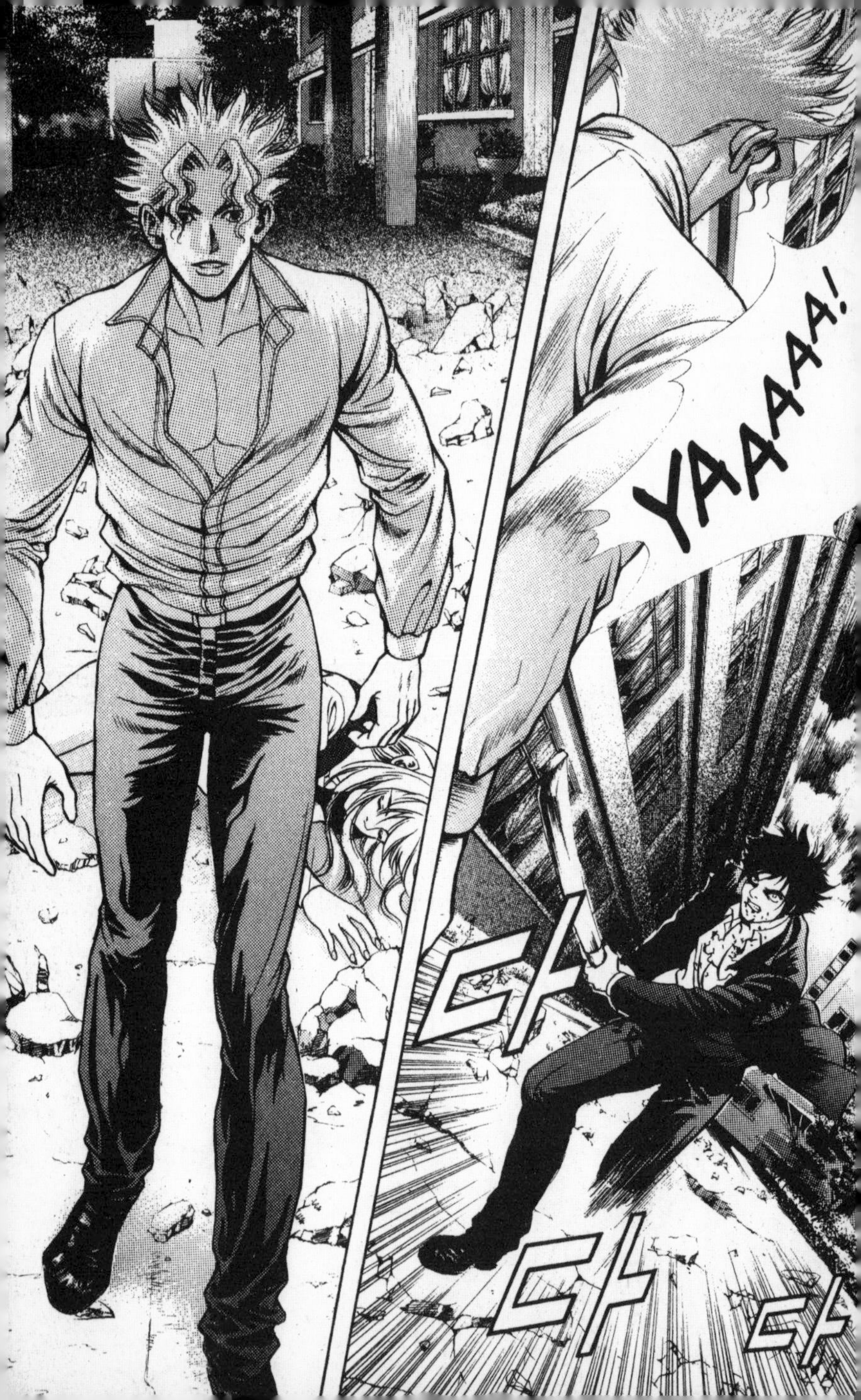
YAAAA!
다
다
다

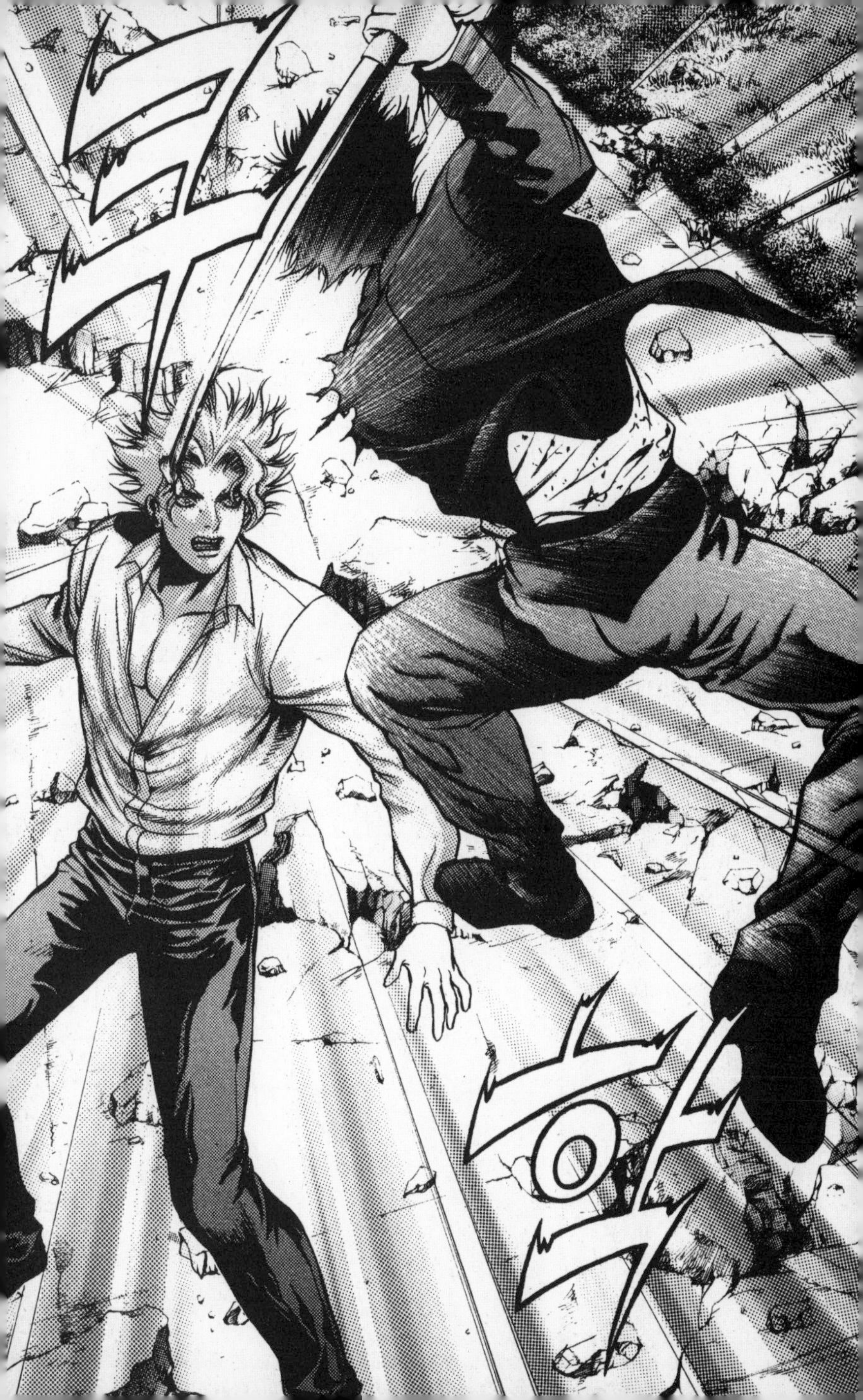

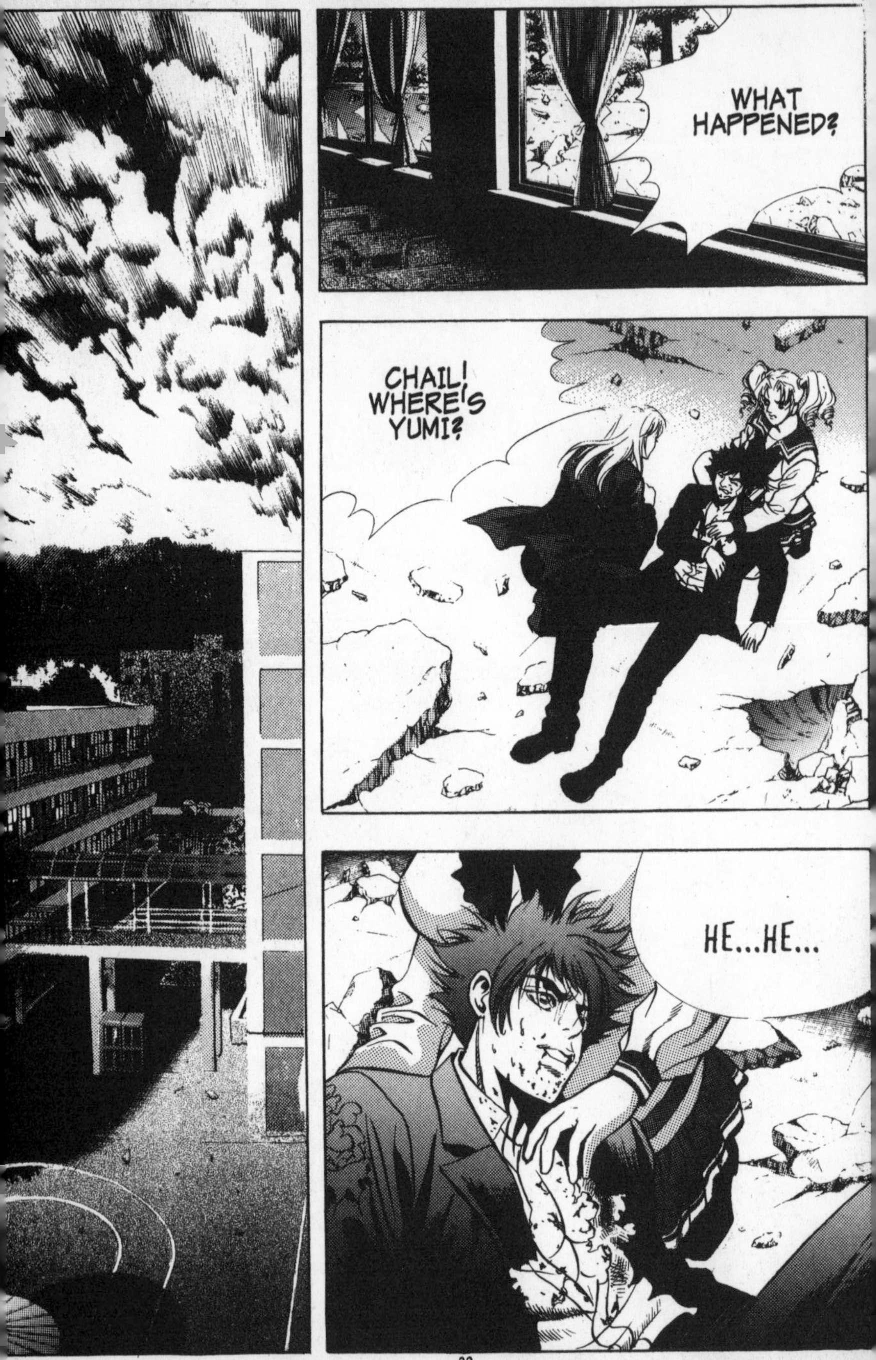
WHAT HAPPENED?
CHAIL! WHERE'S YUMI?
HE...HE...

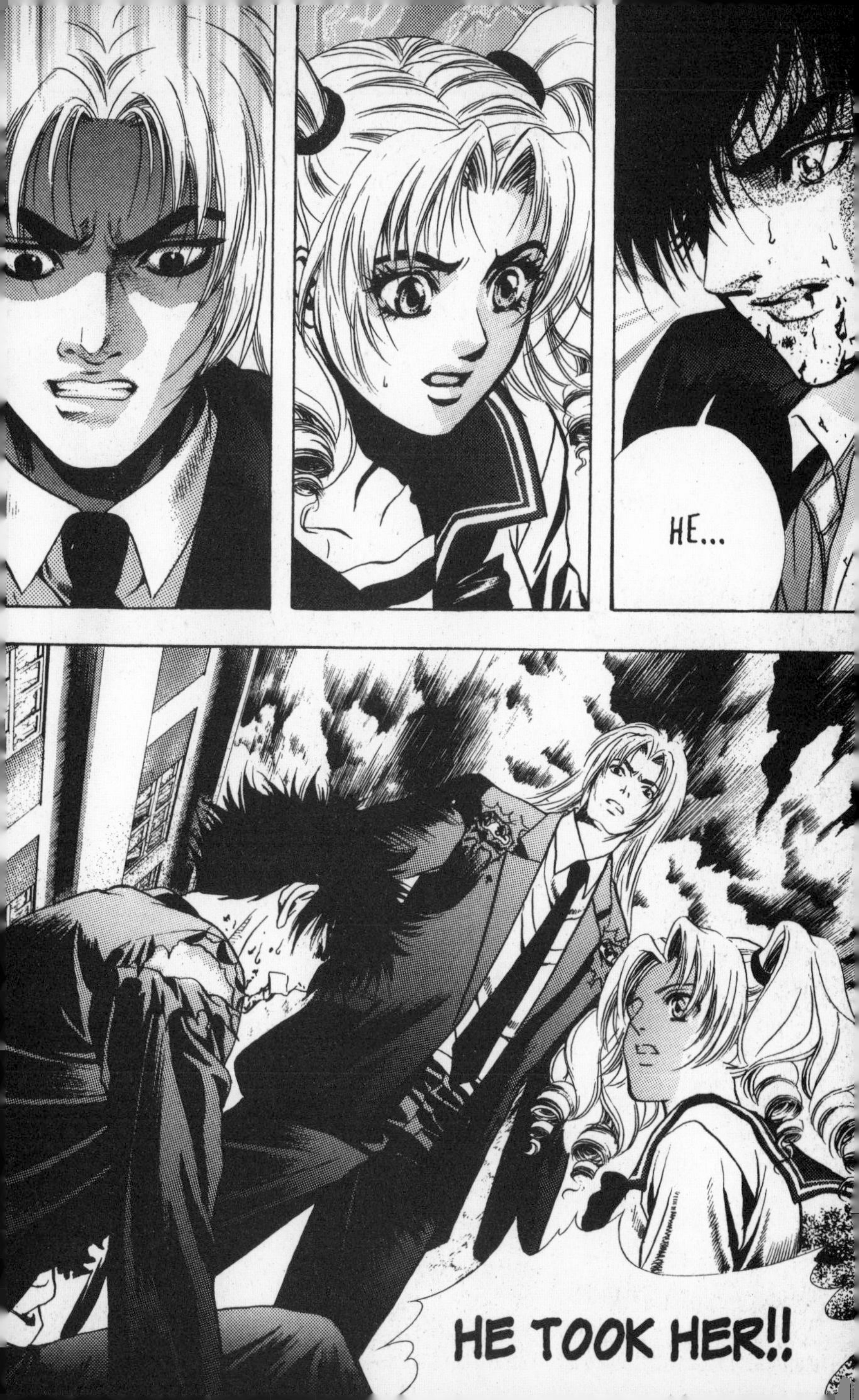
HE...
HE TOOK HER!!

天 천

地 지

人 인

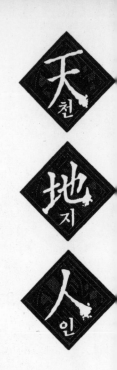

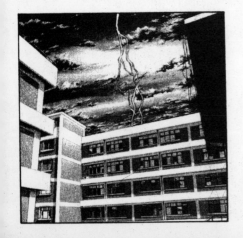

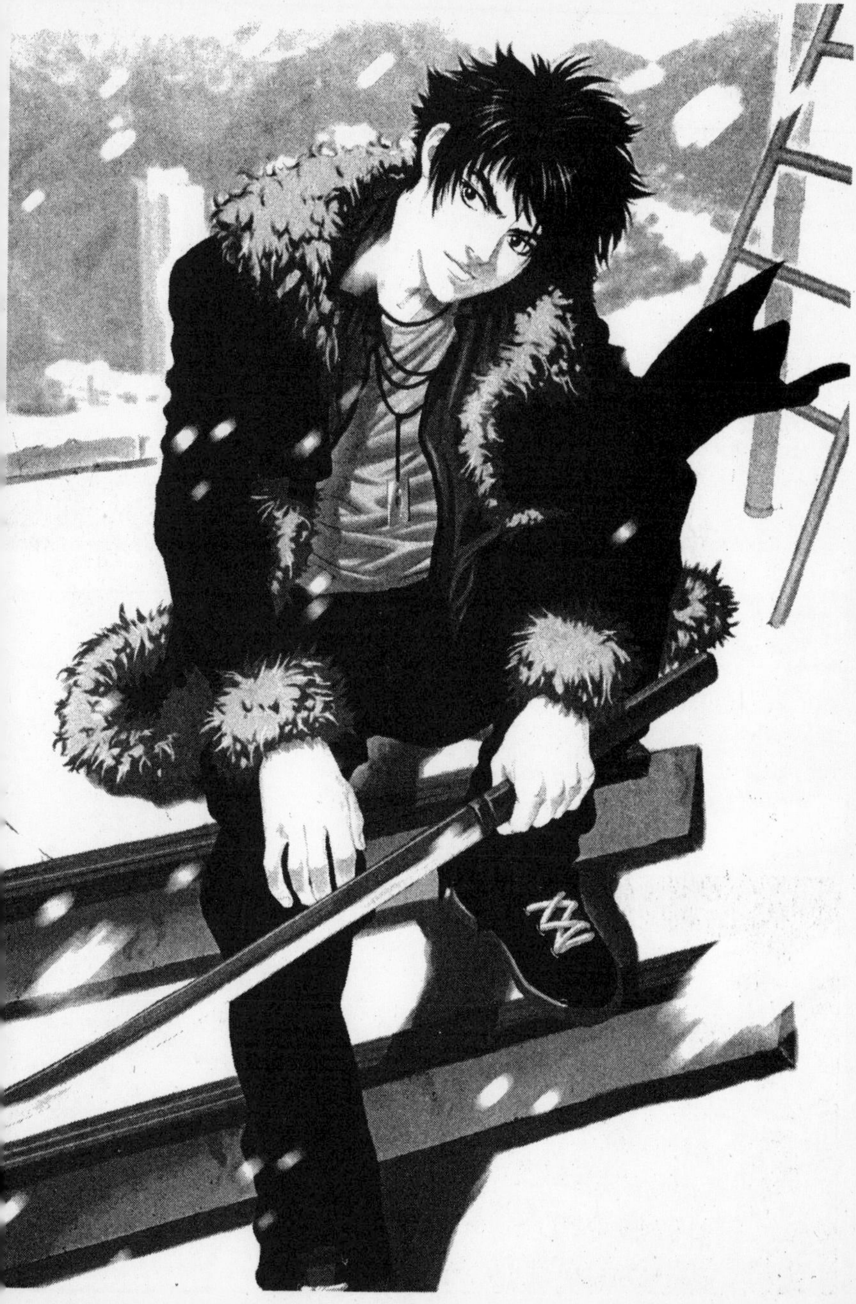

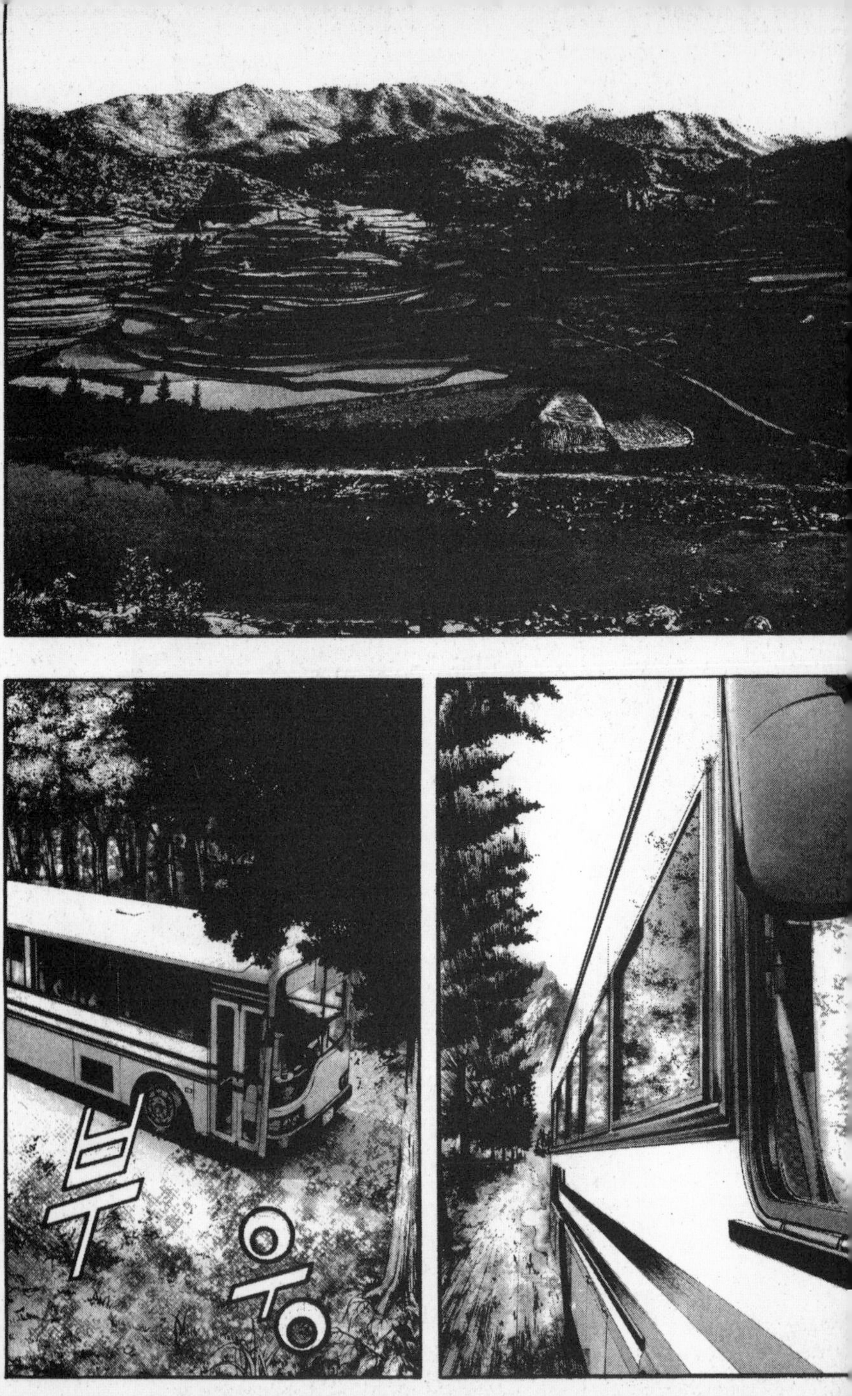
부웅

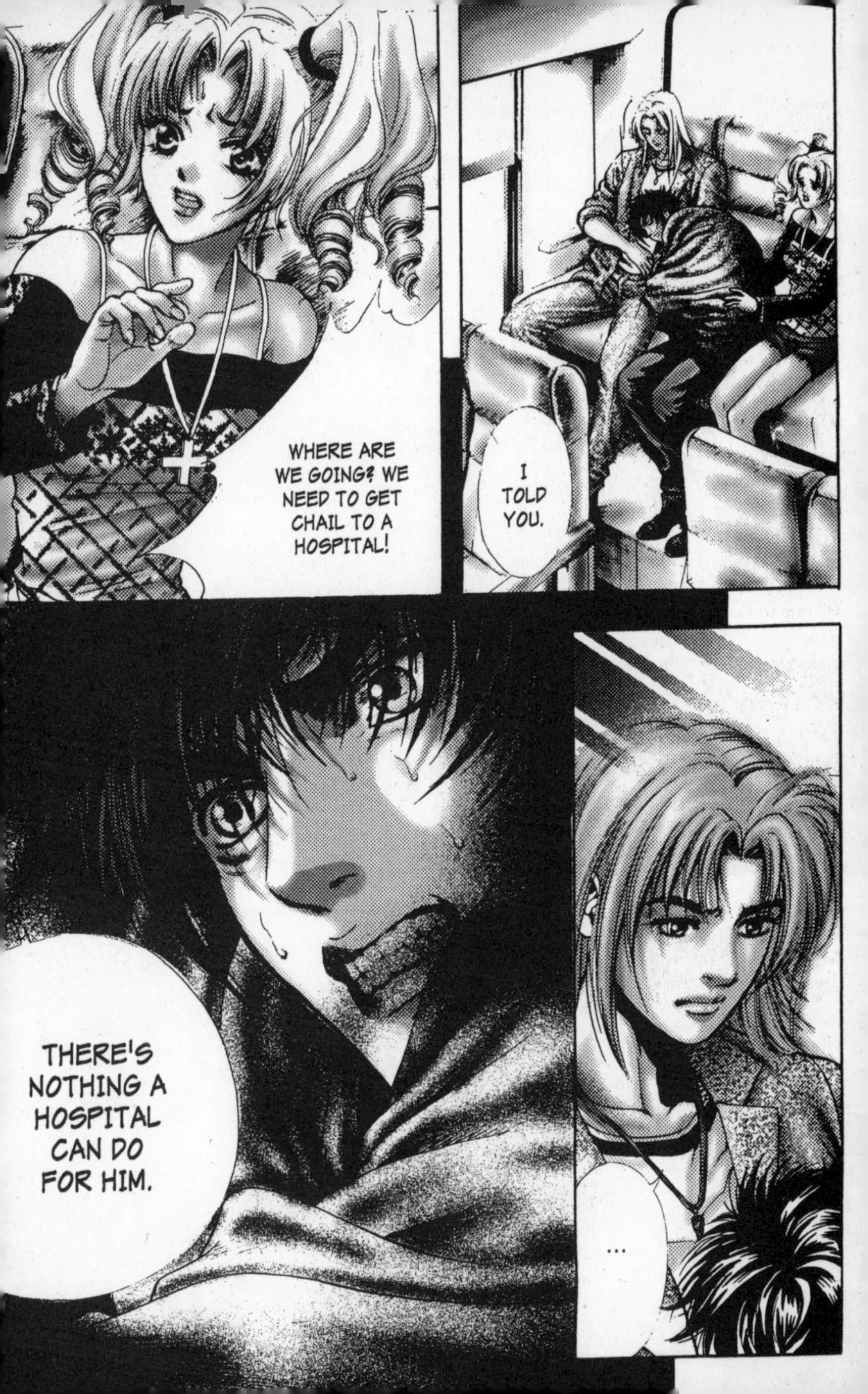
WHERE ARE WE GOING? WE NEED TO GET CHAIL TO A HOSPITAL!
I TOLD YOU.
THERE'S NOTHING A HOSPITAL CAN DO FOR HIM.
...

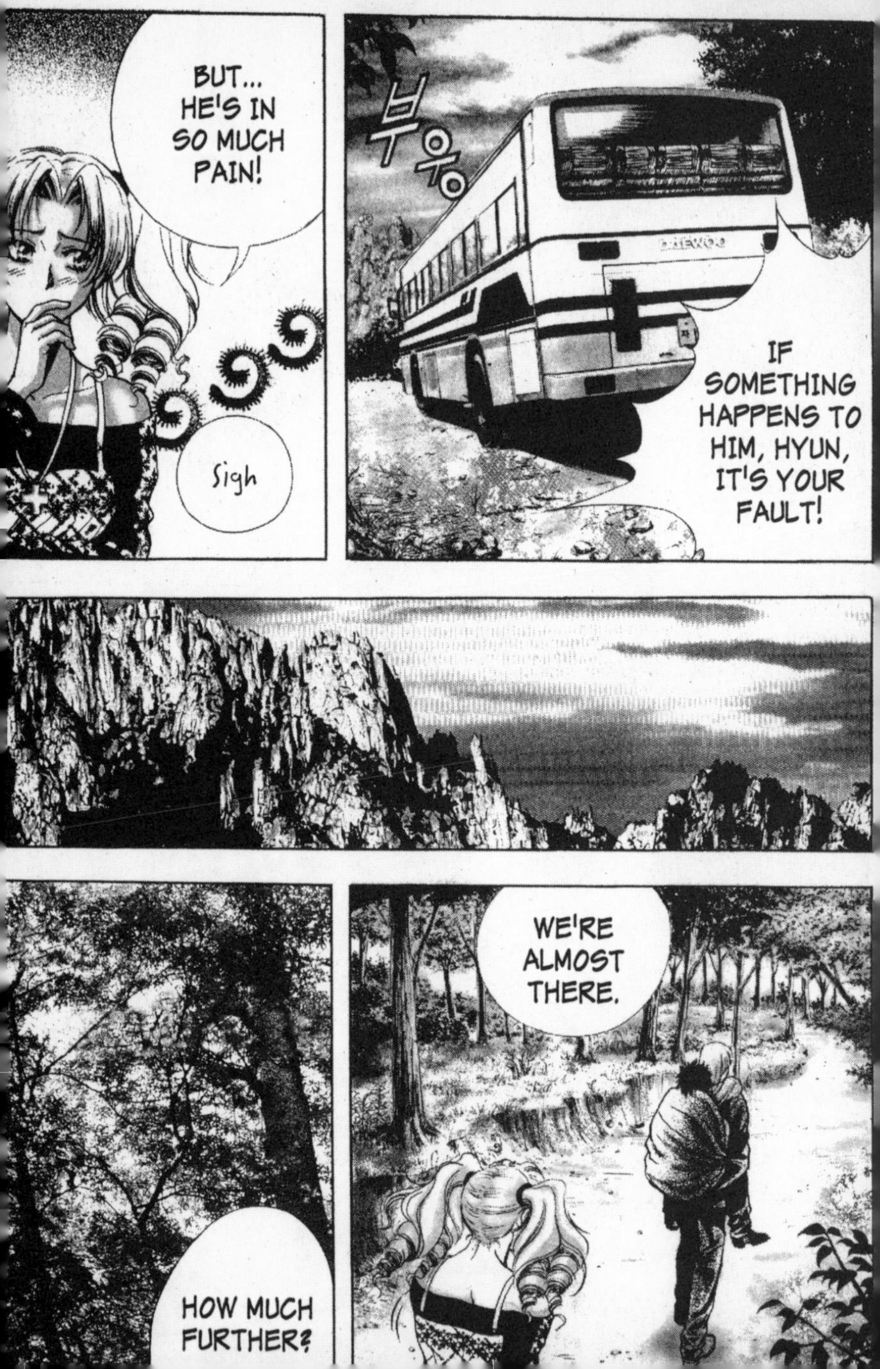
BUT... HE'S IN SO MUCH PAIN!
Sigh
부웅
IF SOMETHING HAPPENS TO HIM, HYUN, IT'S YOUR FAULT!
HOW MUCH FURTHER?
WE'RE ALMOST THERE.

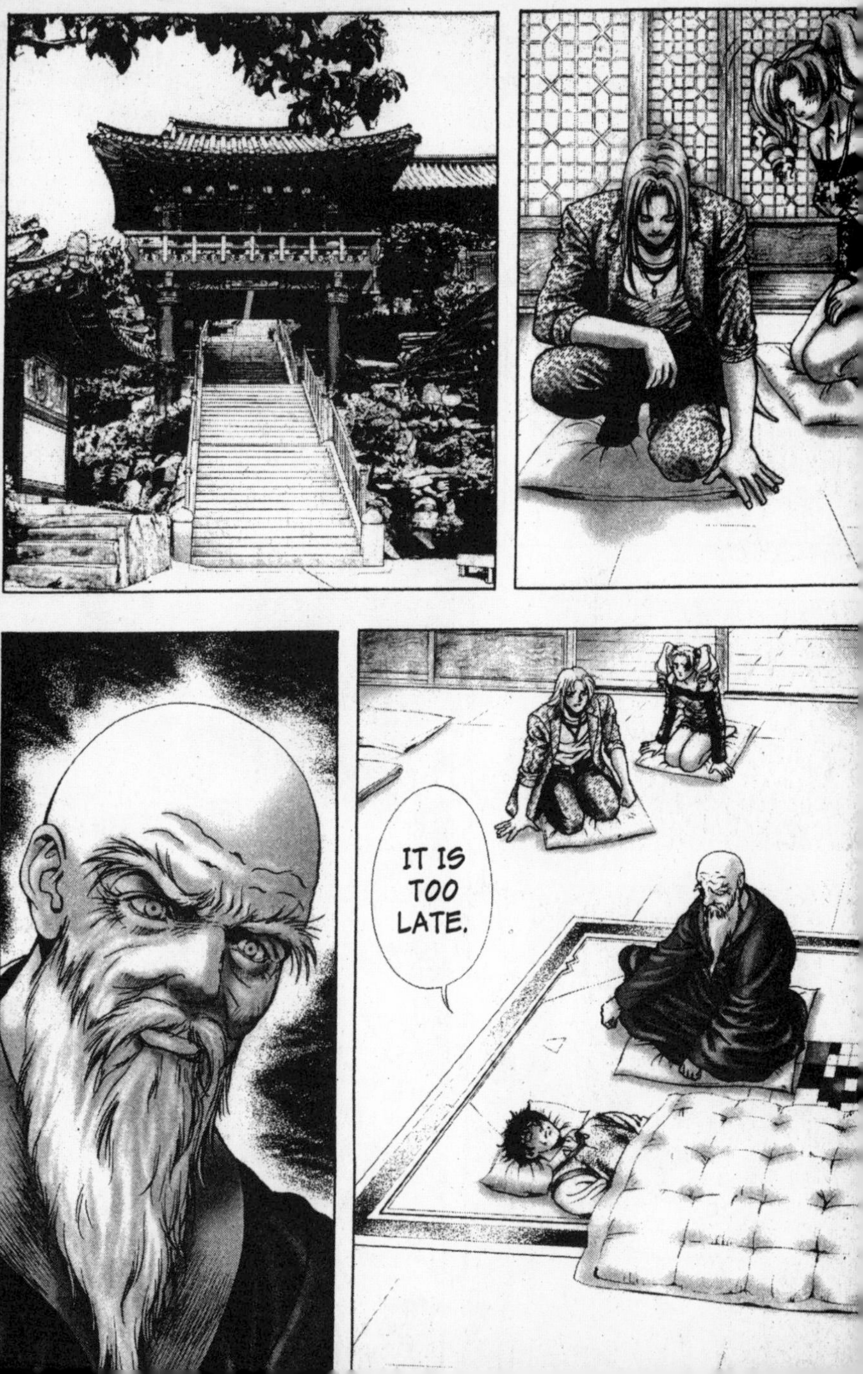
IT IS TOO LATE.

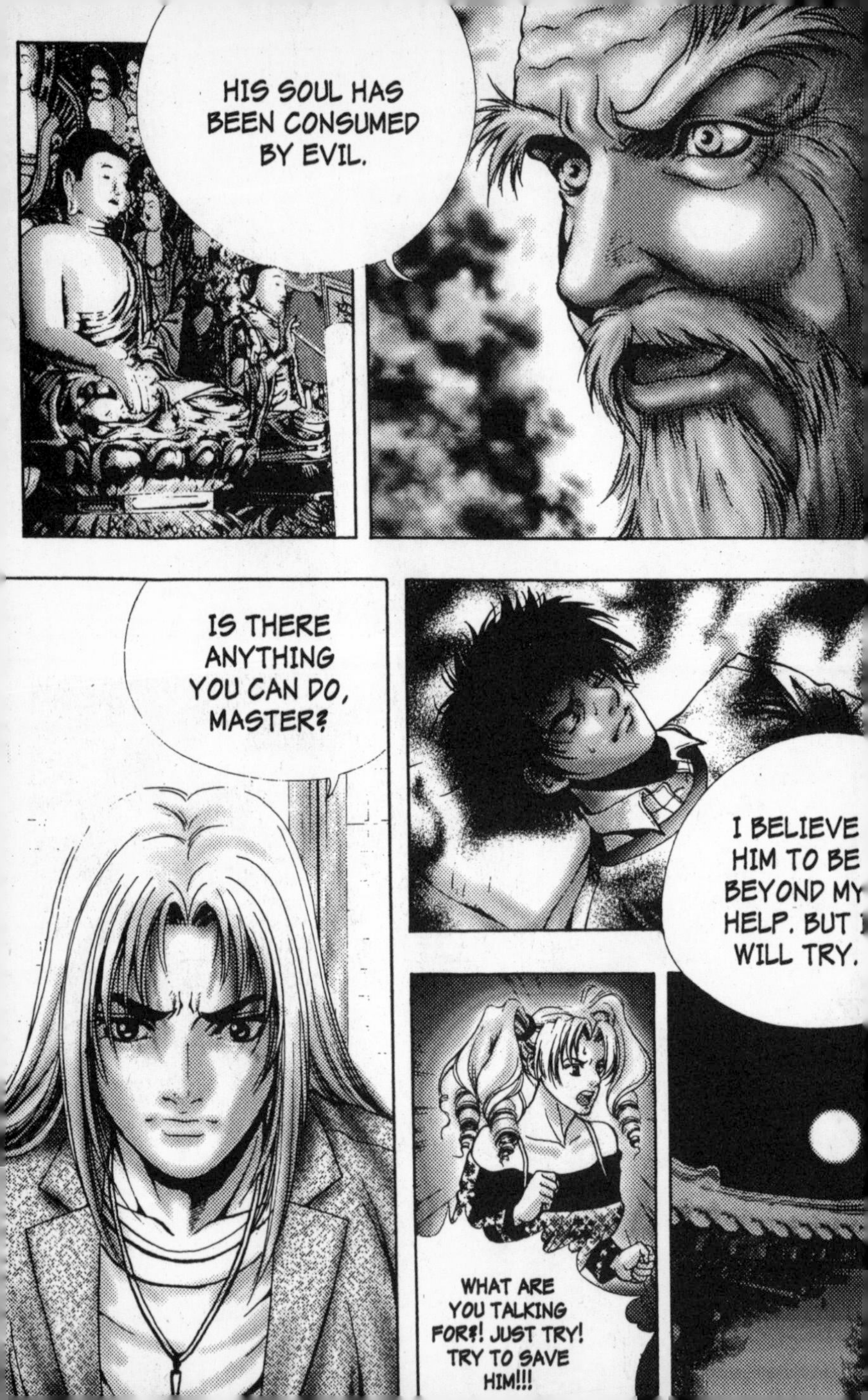
HIS SOUL HAS BEEN CONSUMED BY EVIL.
IS THERE ANYTHING YOU CAN DO, MASTER?
I BELIEVE HIM TO BE BEYOND MY HELP. BUT WILL TRY.
WHAT ARE YOU TALKING FOR?! JUST TRY! TRY TO SAVE HIM!!!

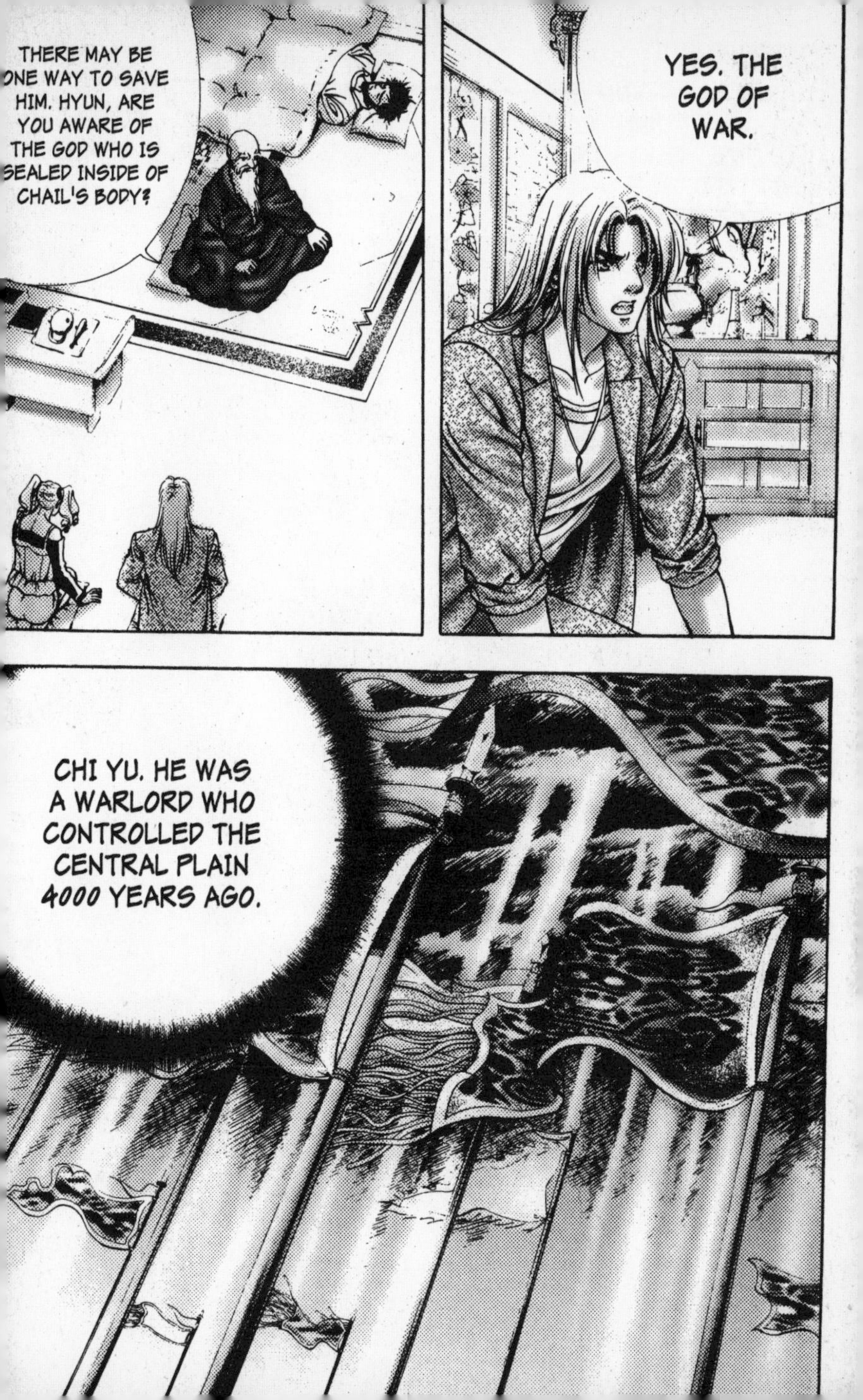
YES. THE GOD OF WAR.
THERE MAY BE ONE WAY TO SAVE HIM. HYUN, ARE YOU AWARE OF THE GOD WHO IS SEALED INSIDE OF CHAIL'S BODY?
CHI YU. HE WAS A WARLORD WHO CONTROLLED THE CENTRAL PLAIN 4000 YEARS AGO.

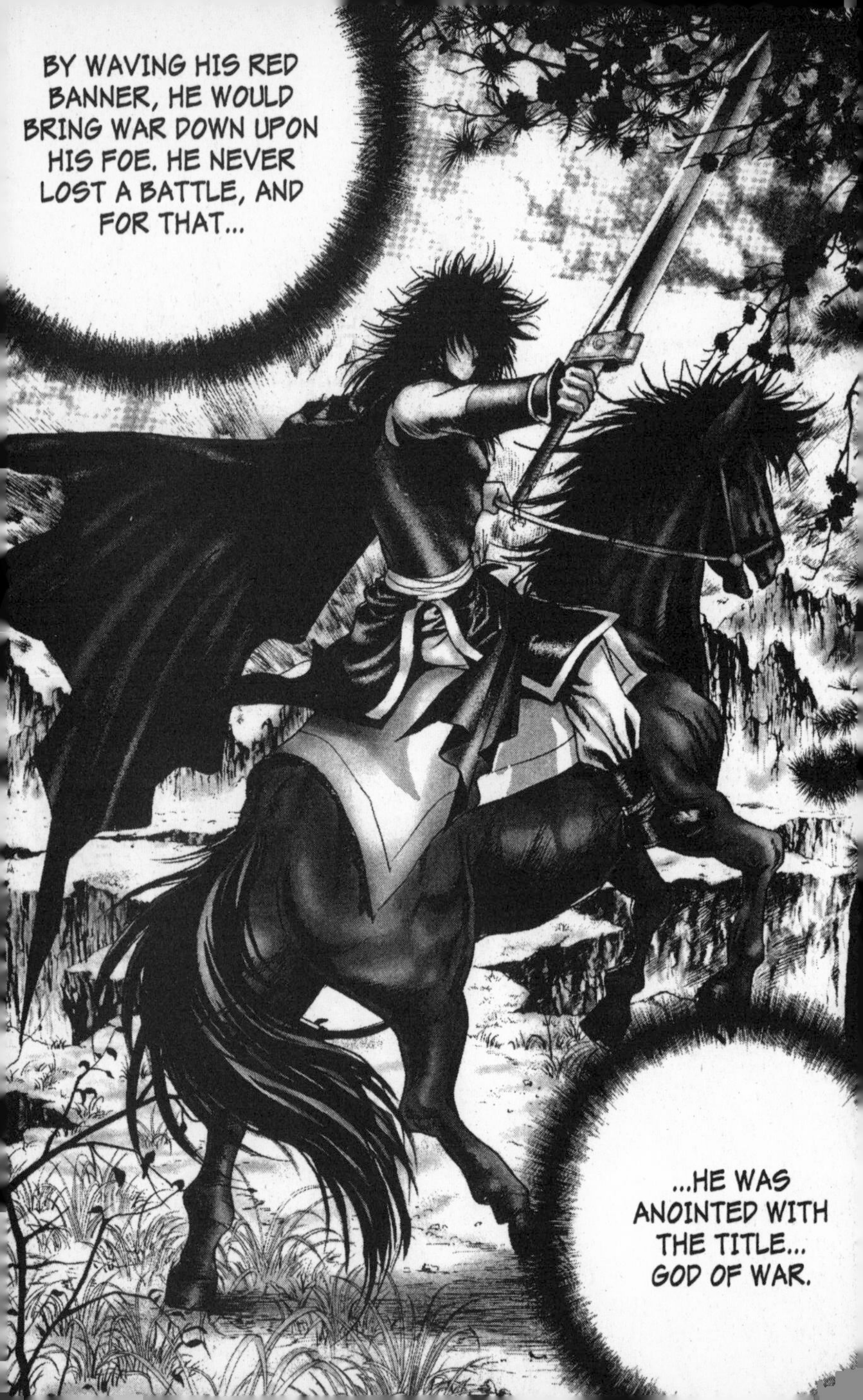
BY WAVING HIS RED BANNER, HE WOULD BRING WAR DOWN UPON HIS FOE. HE NEVER LOST A BATTLE, AND FOR THAT...
...HE WAS ANOINTED WITH THE TITLE... GOD OF WAR.

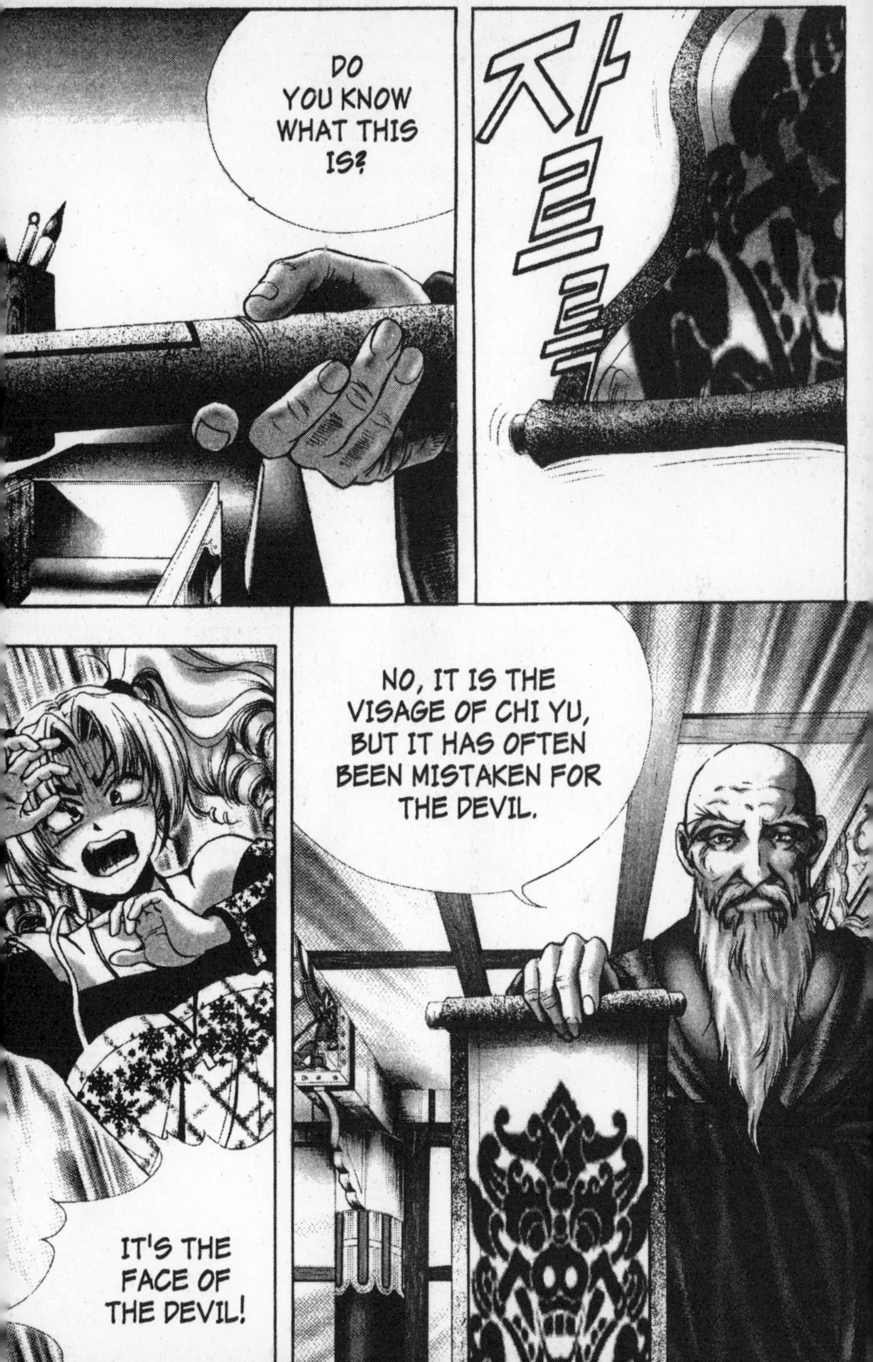
DO YOU KNOW WHAT THIS IS?
자르륵
IT'S THE FACE OF THE DEVIL!
NO, IT IS THE VISAGE OF CHI YU, BUT IT HAS OFTEN BEEN MISTAKEN FOR THE DEVIL.

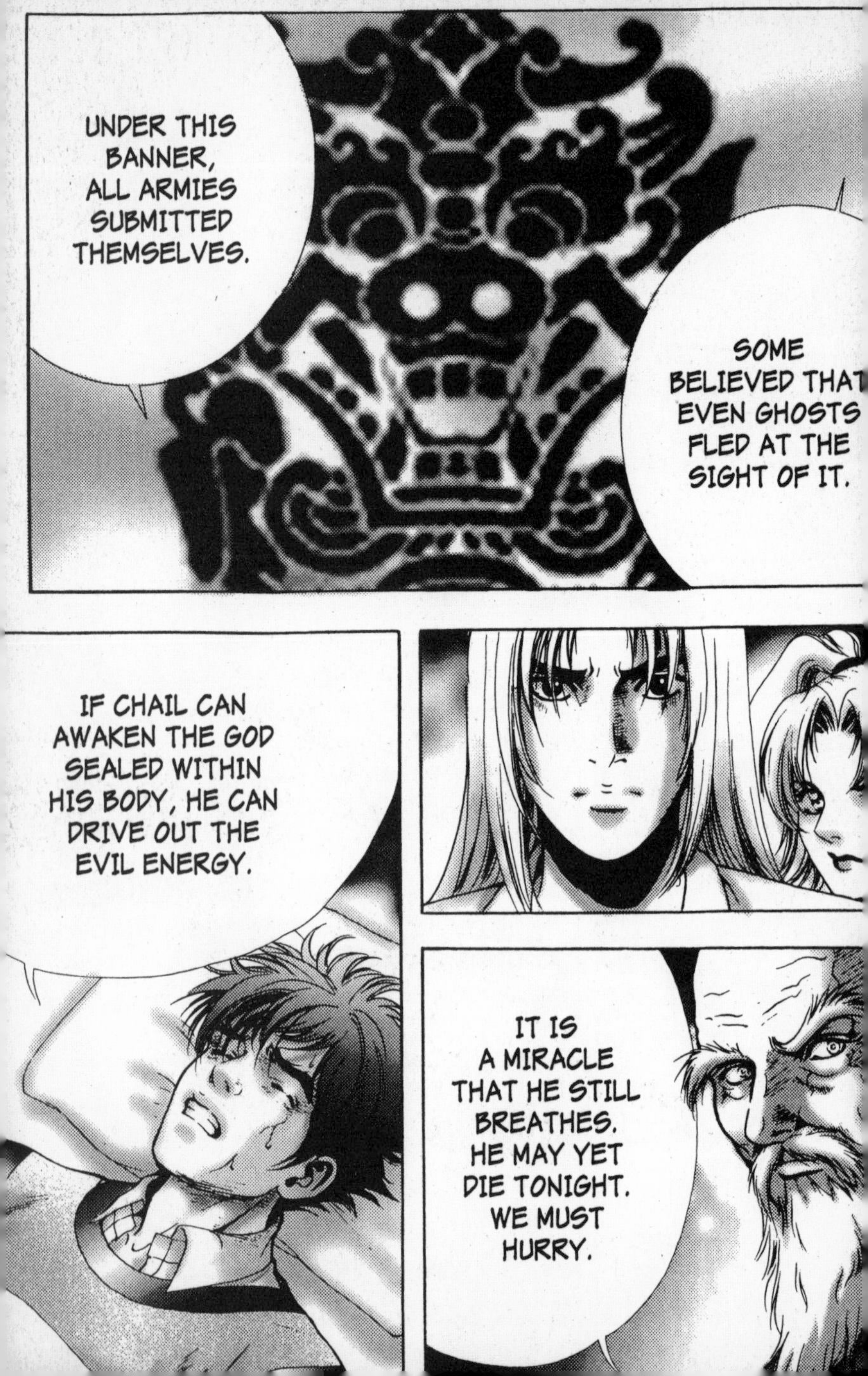
UNDER THIS BANNER, ALL ARMIES SUBMITTED THEMSELVES.
SOME BELIEVED THAT EVEN GHOSTS FLED AT THE SIGHT OF IT.
IF CHAIL CAN AWAKEN THE GOD SEALED WITHIN HIS BODY, HE CAN DRIVE OUT THE EVIL ENERGY.
IT IS A MIRACLE THAT HE STILL BREATHES. HE MAY YET DIE TONIGHT. WE MUST HURRY.

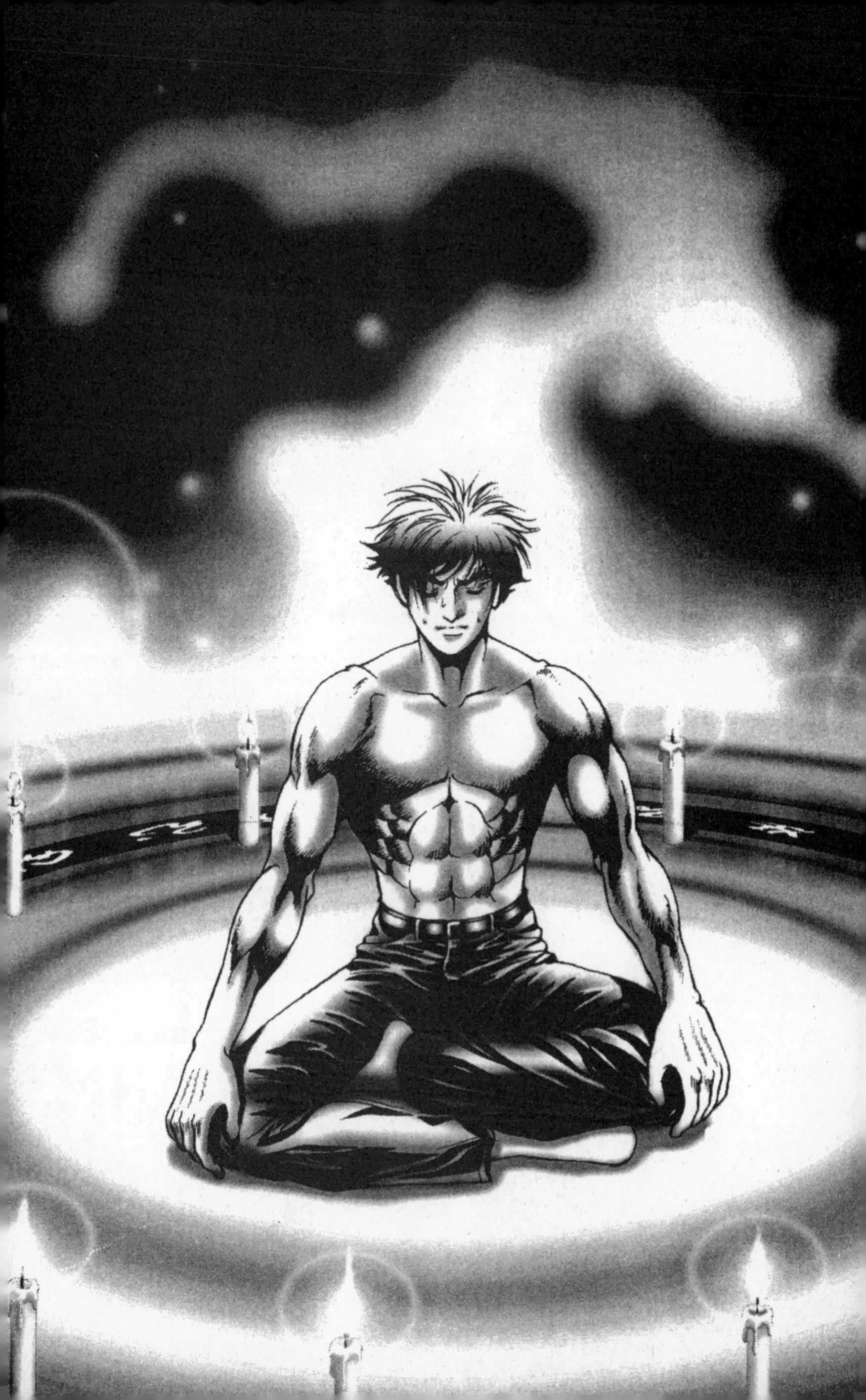

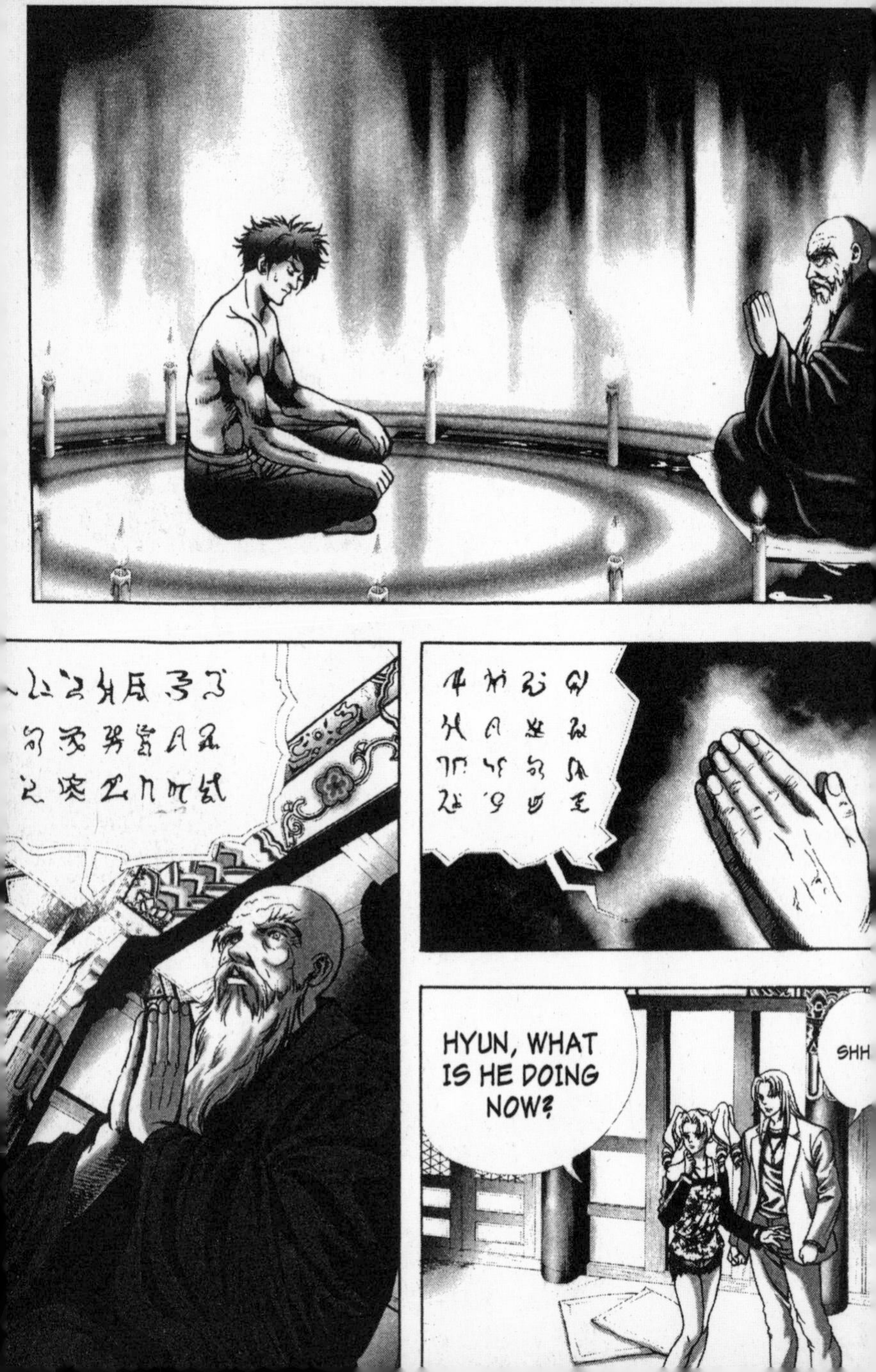
HYUN, WHAT IS HE DOING NOW?
SHH

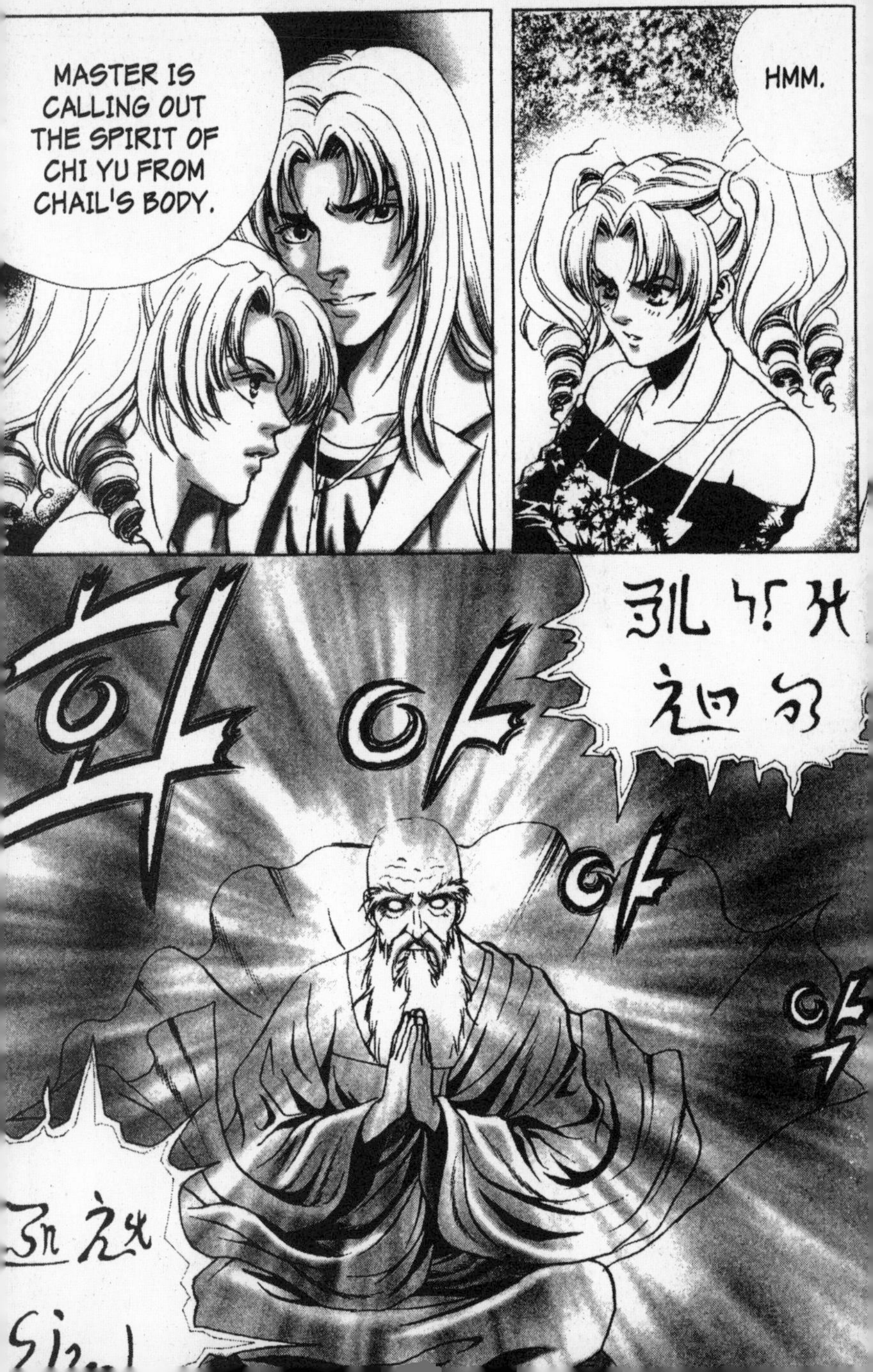
MASTER IS CALLING OUT THE SPIRIT OF CHI YU FROM CHAIL'S BODY.
HMM.

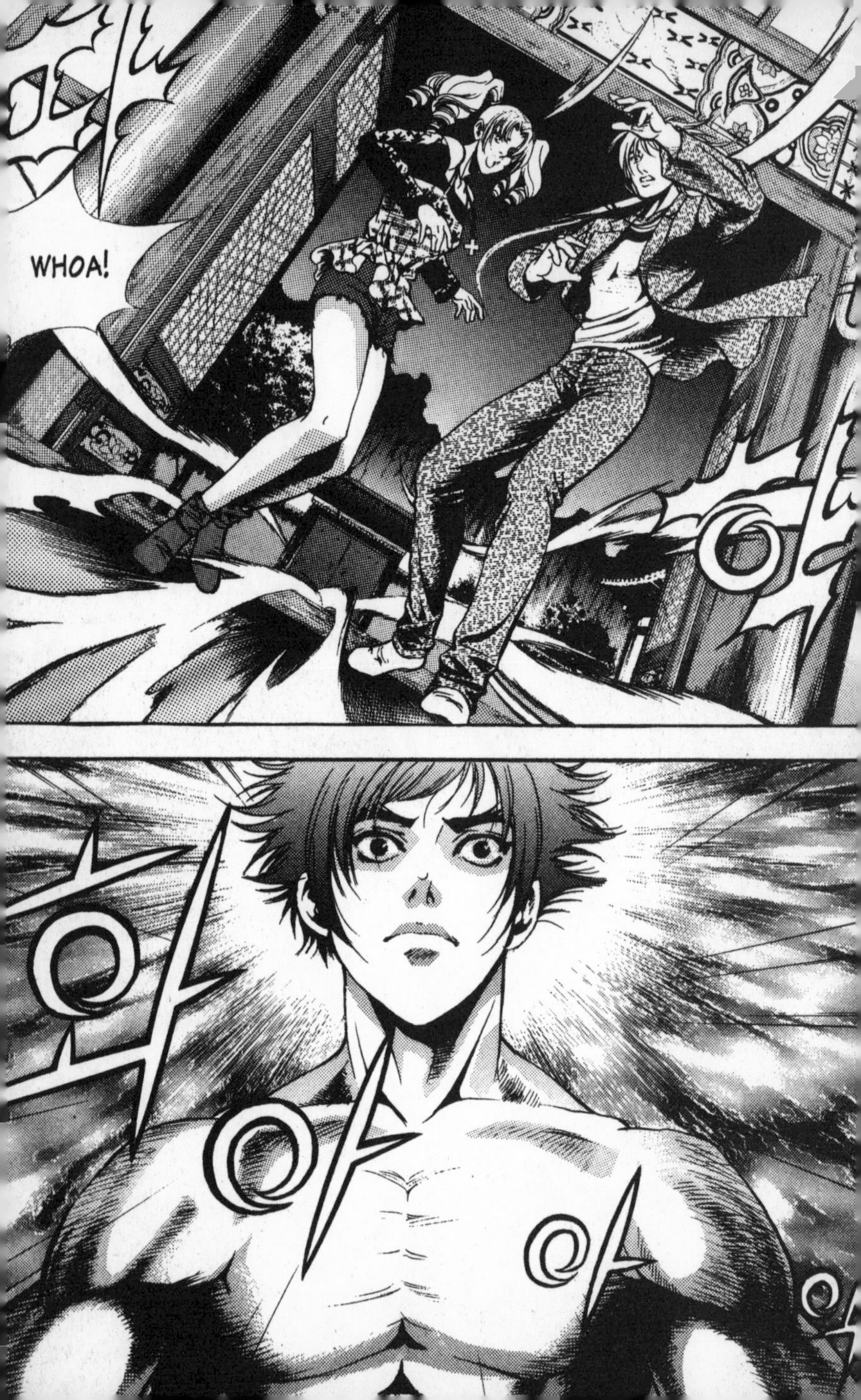
WHOA!

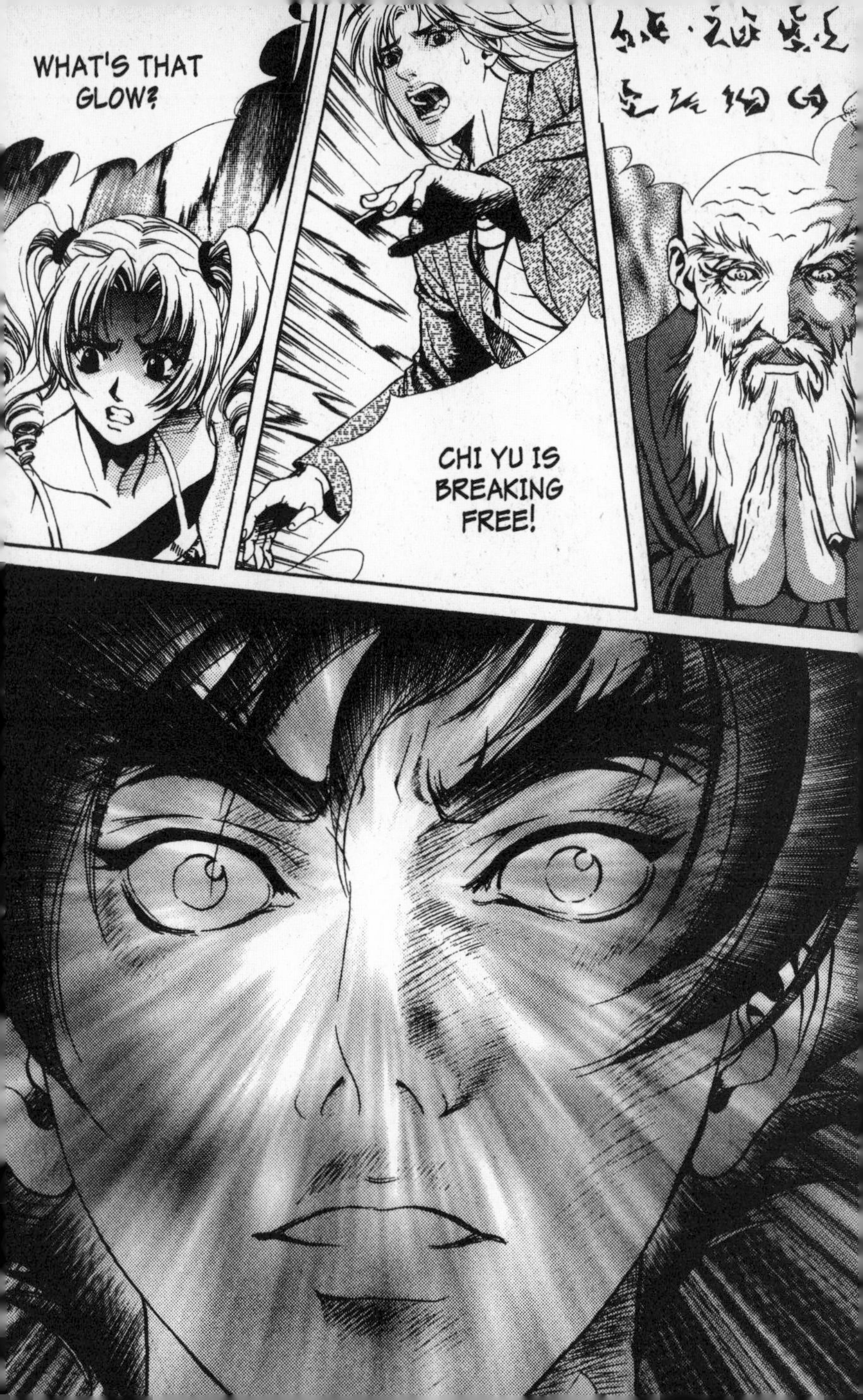
CHI YU IS BREAKING FREE!
WHAT'S THAT GLOW?

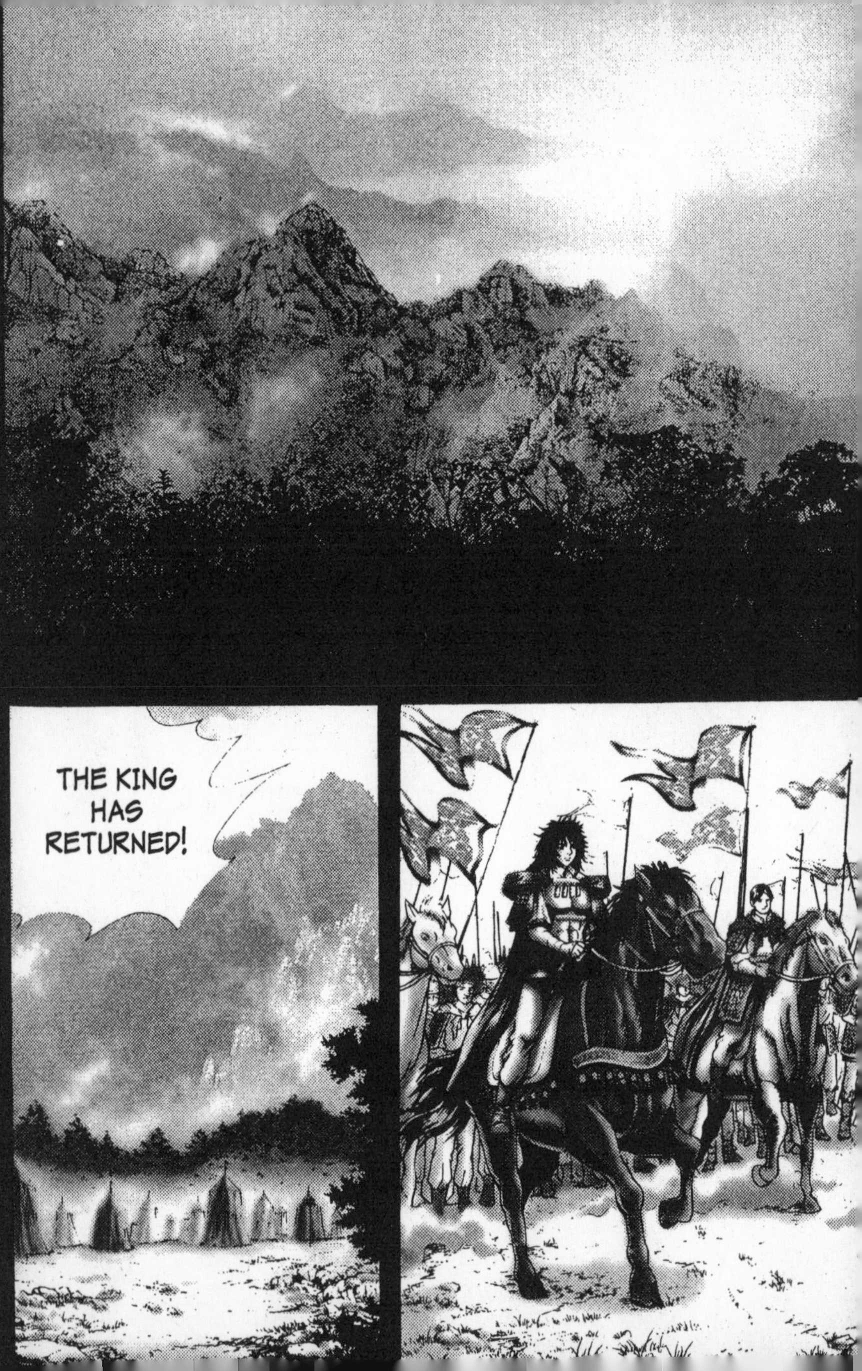
THE KING HAS RETURNED!

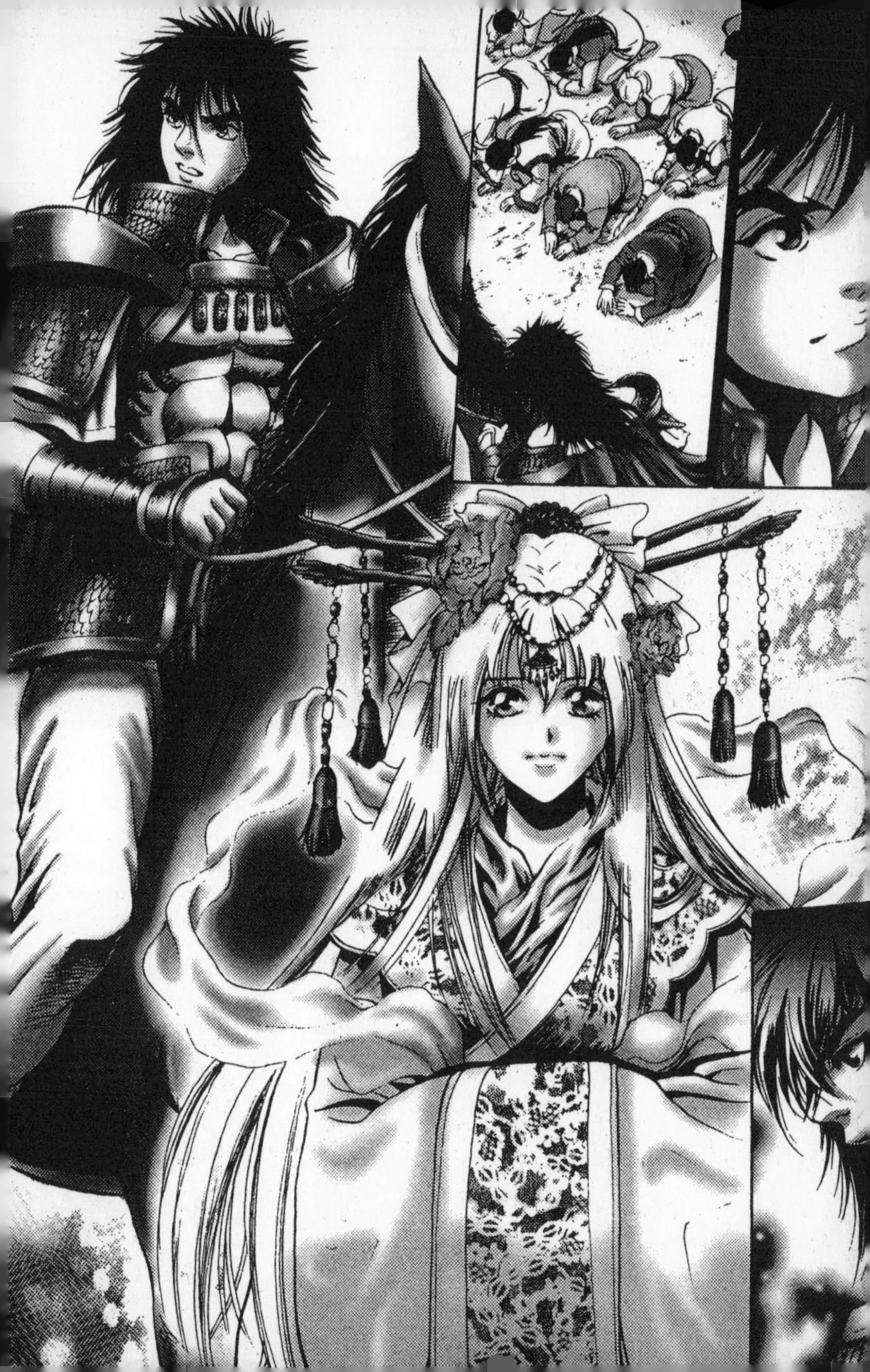

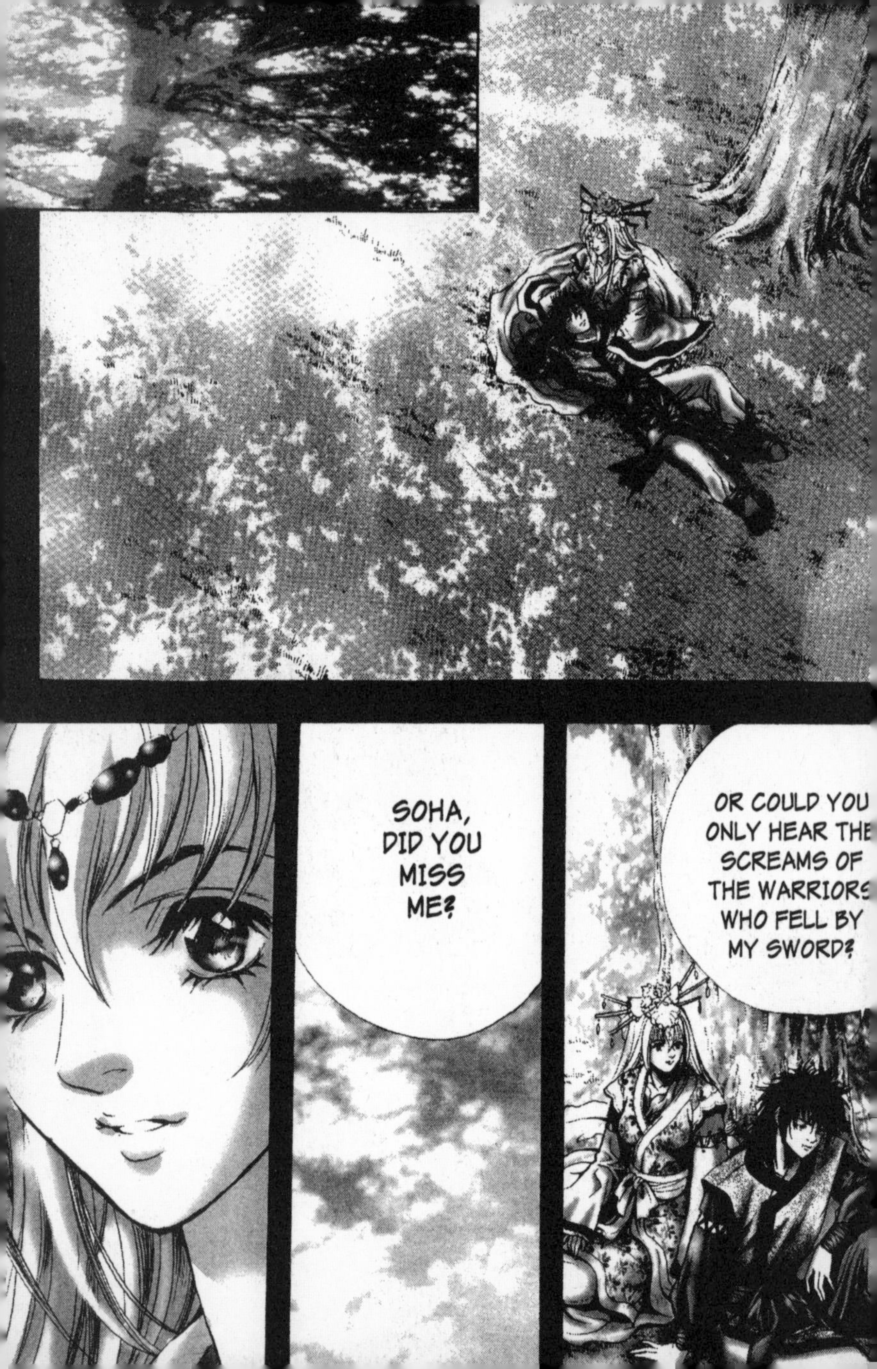
SOHA, DID YOU MISS ME?
OR COULD YOU ONLY HEAR THE SCREAMS OF THE WARRIORS WHO FELL BY MY SWORD?

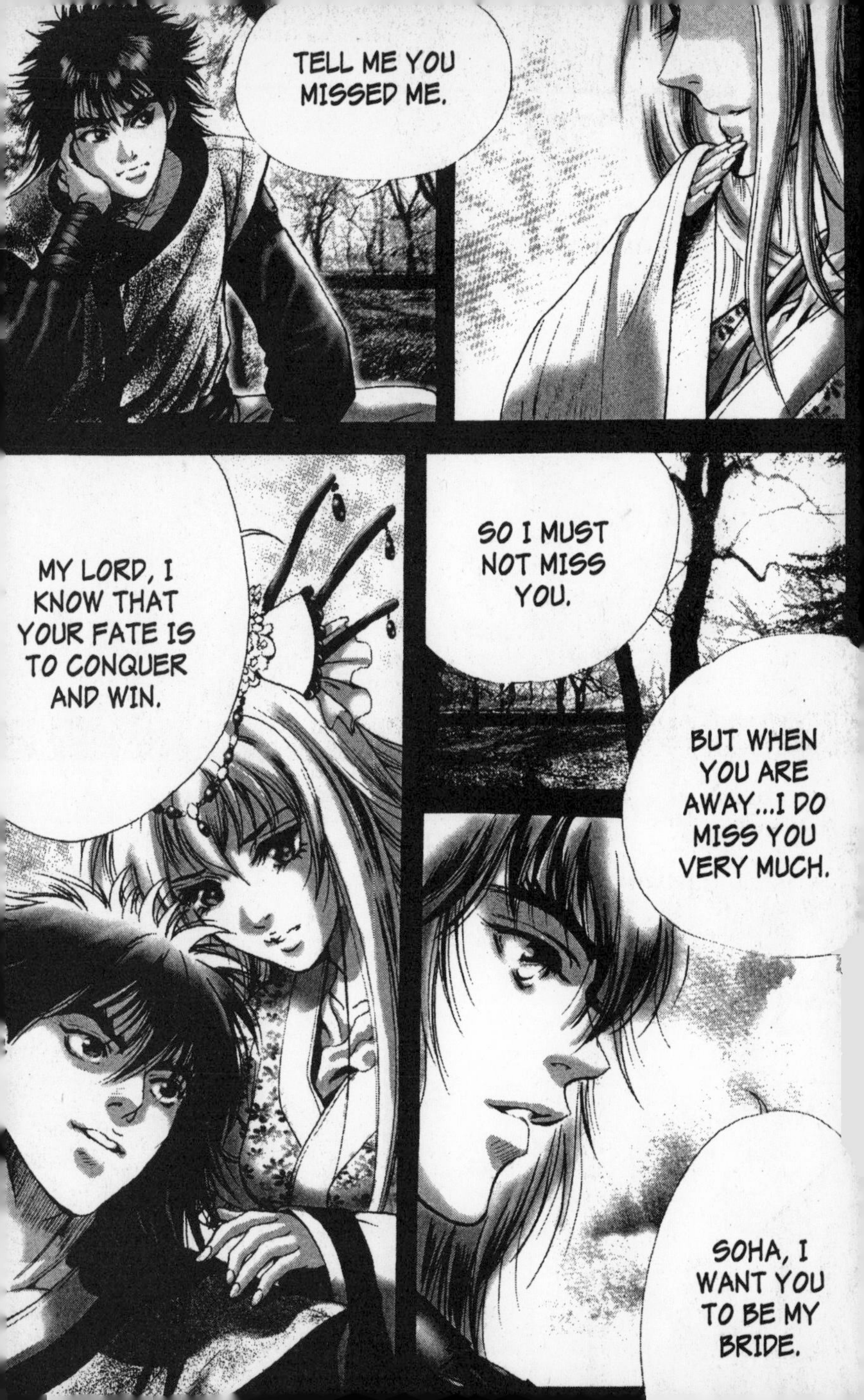
TELL ME YOU MISSED ME.
MY LORD, I KNOW THAT YOUR FATE IS TO CONQUER AND WIN.
SO I MUST NOT MISS YOU.
BUT WHEN YOU ARE AWAY...I DO MISS YOU VERY MUCH.
SOHA, I WANT YOU TO BE MY BRIDE.

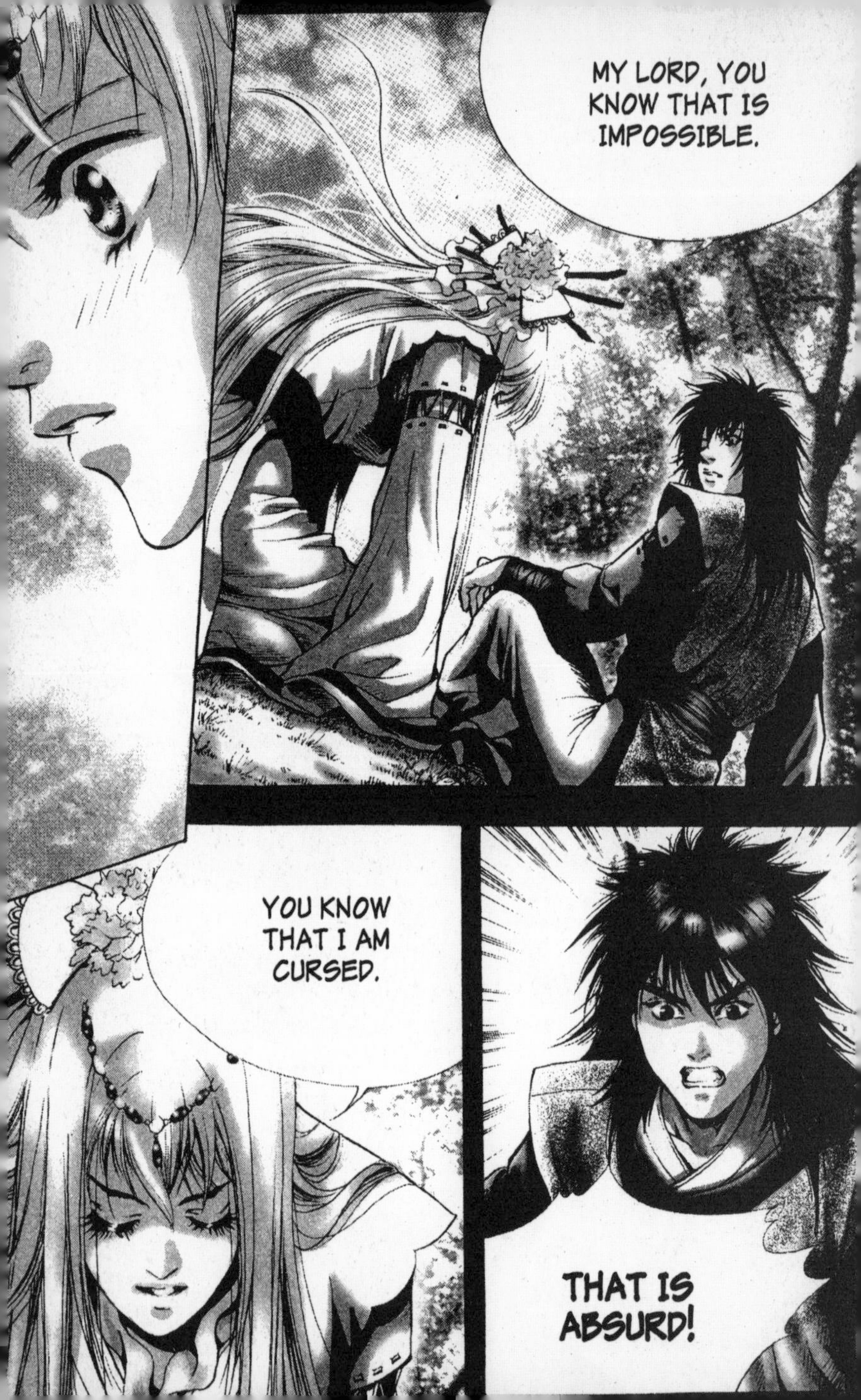
MY LORD, YOU KNOW THAT IS IMPOSSIBLE.
YOU KNOW THAT I AM CURSED.
THAT IS ABSURD!

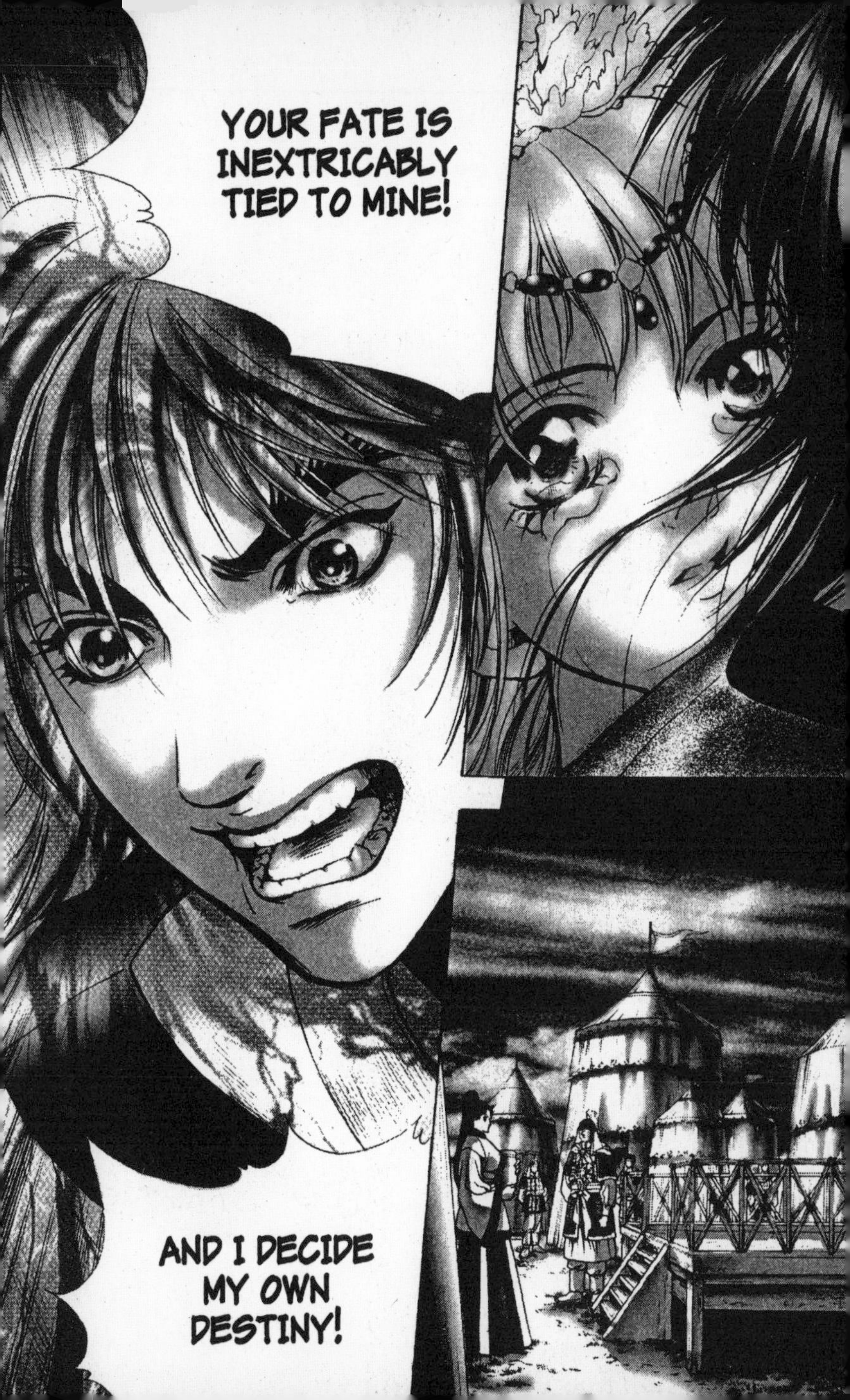
YOUR FATE IS INEXTRICABLY TIED TO MINE!
AND I DECIDE MY OWN DESTINY!

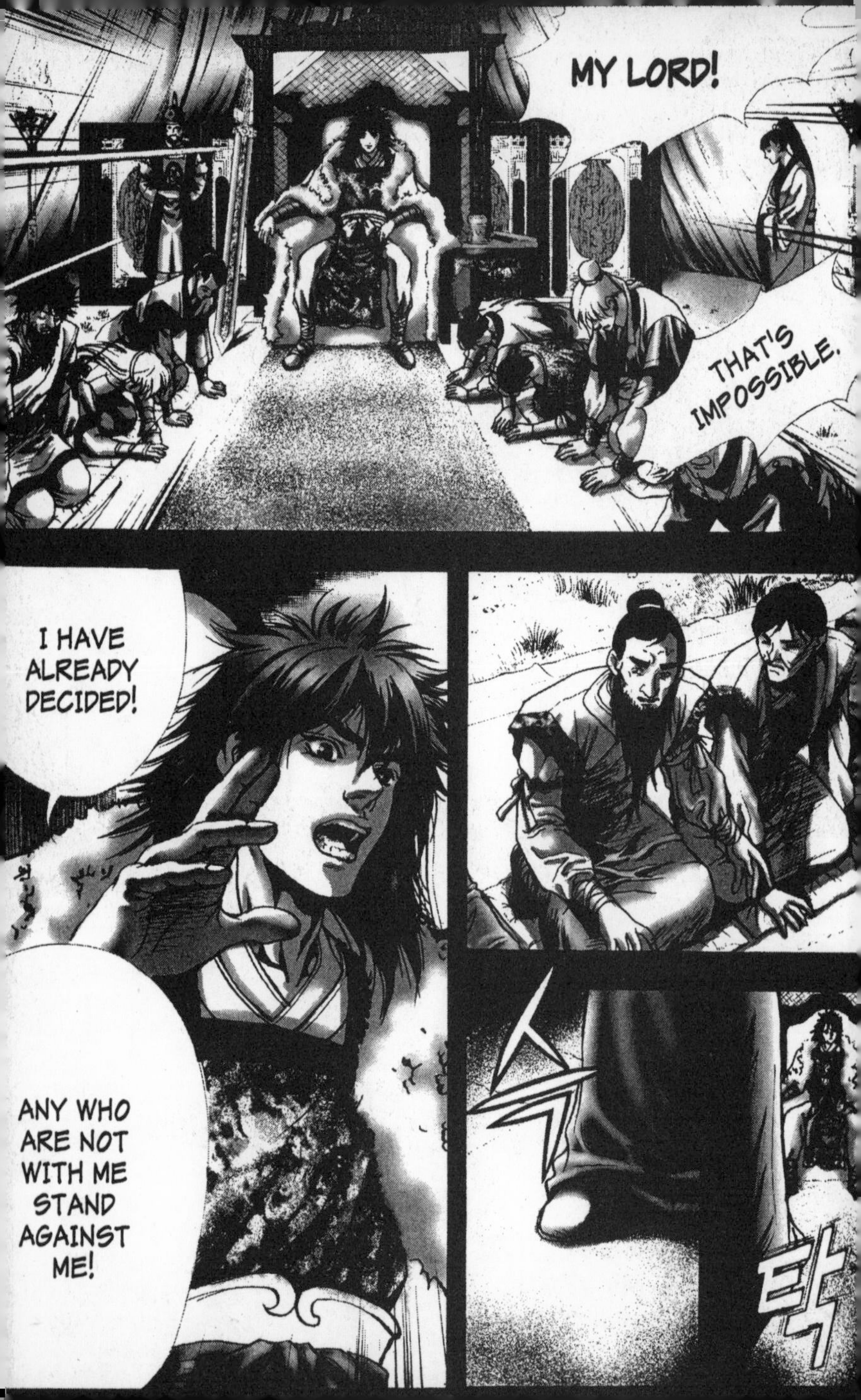
MY LORD!
THAT'S IMPOSSIBLE.
I HAVE ALREADY DECIDED!
ANY WHO ARE NOT WITH ME STAND AGAINST ME!
탁

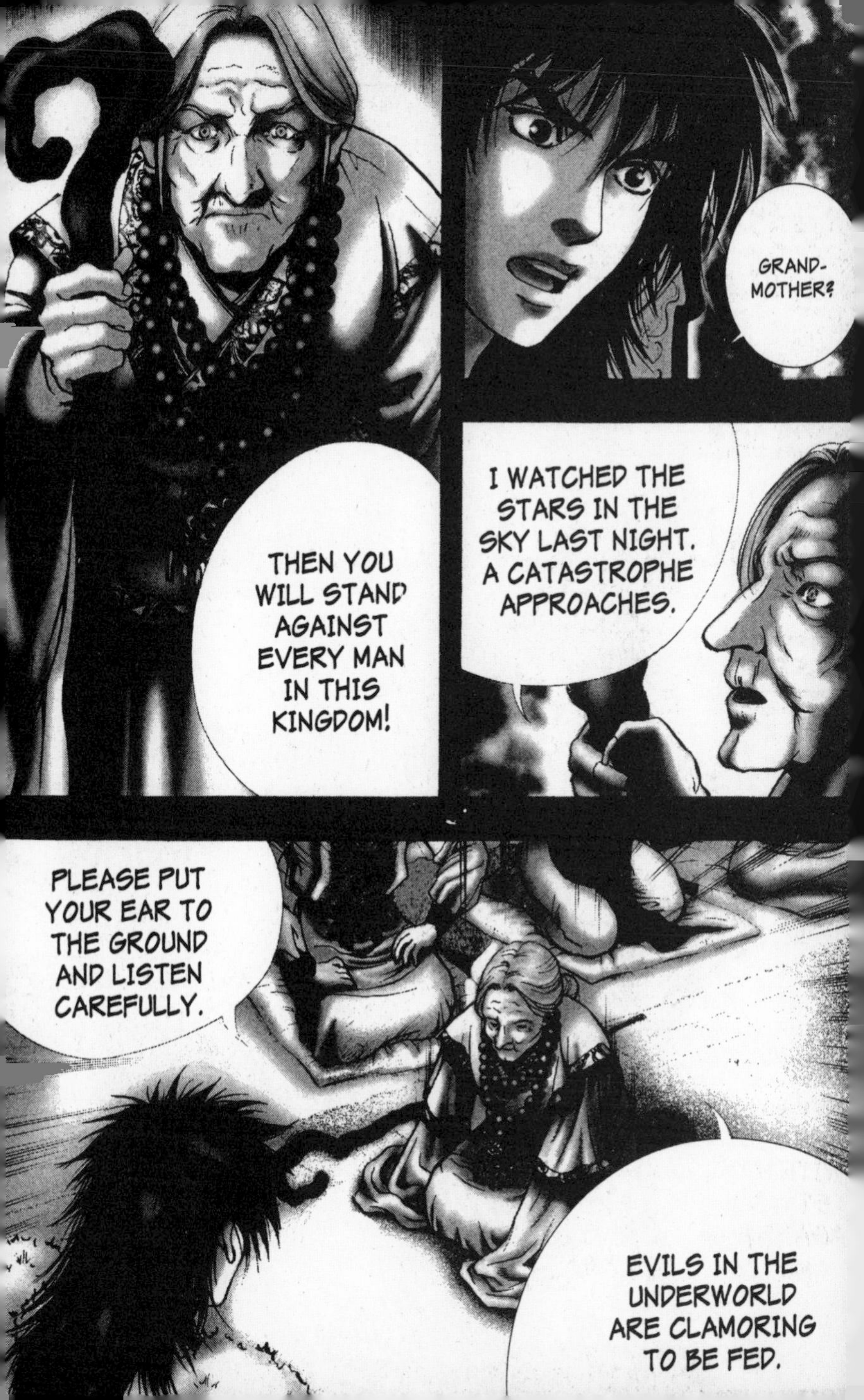
GRAND-MOTHER?
I WATCHED THE STARS IN THE SKY LAST NIGHT. A CATASTROPHE APPROACHES.
THEN YOU WILL STAND AGAINST EVERY MAN IN THIS KINGDOM!
PLEASE PUT YOUR EAR TO THE GROUND AND LISTEN CAREFULLY.
EVILS IN THE UNDERWORLD ARE CLAMORING TO BE FED.

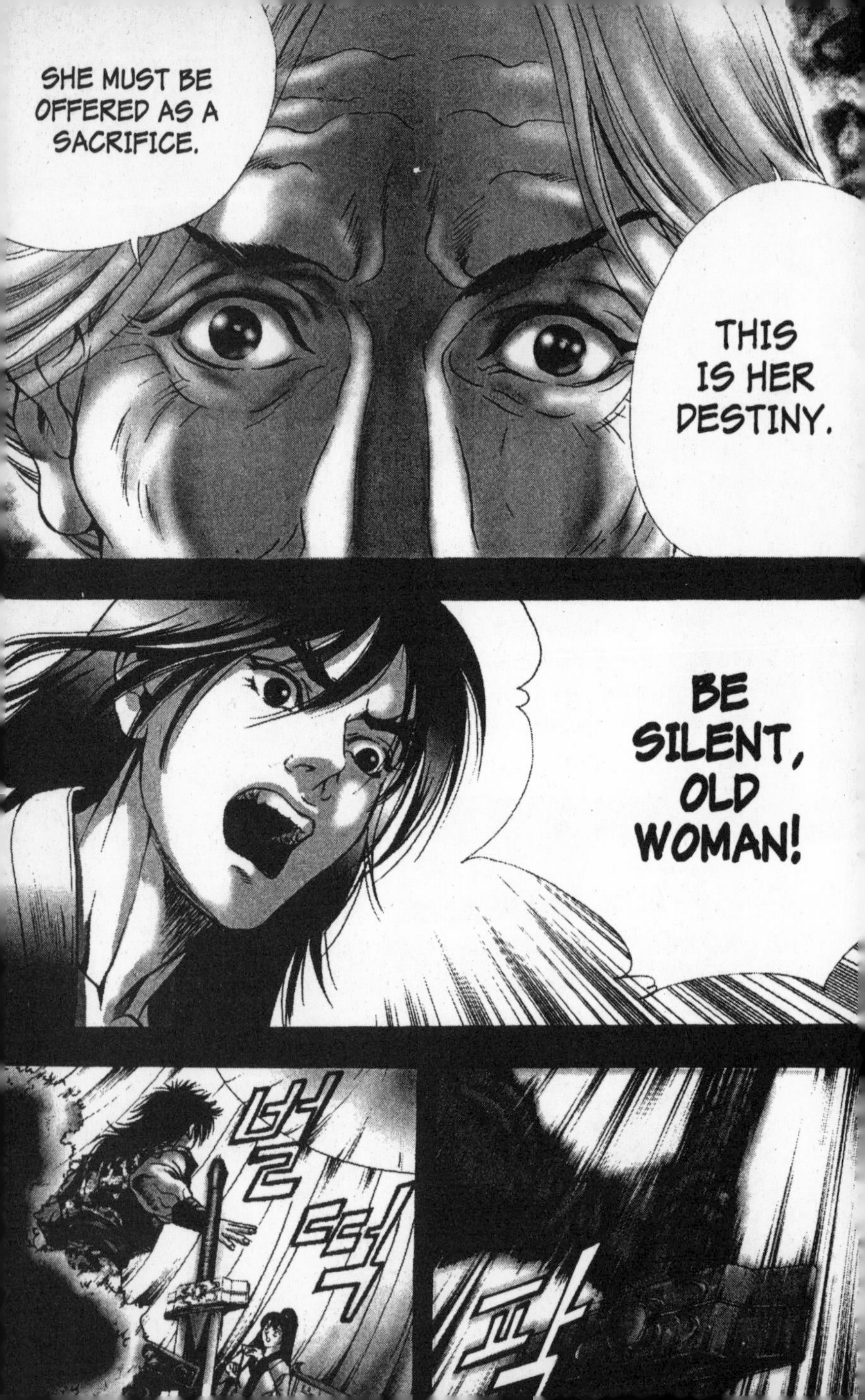
SHE MUST BE OFFERED AS A SACRIFICE.
THIS IS HER DESTINY.
BE SILENT, OLD WOMAN!

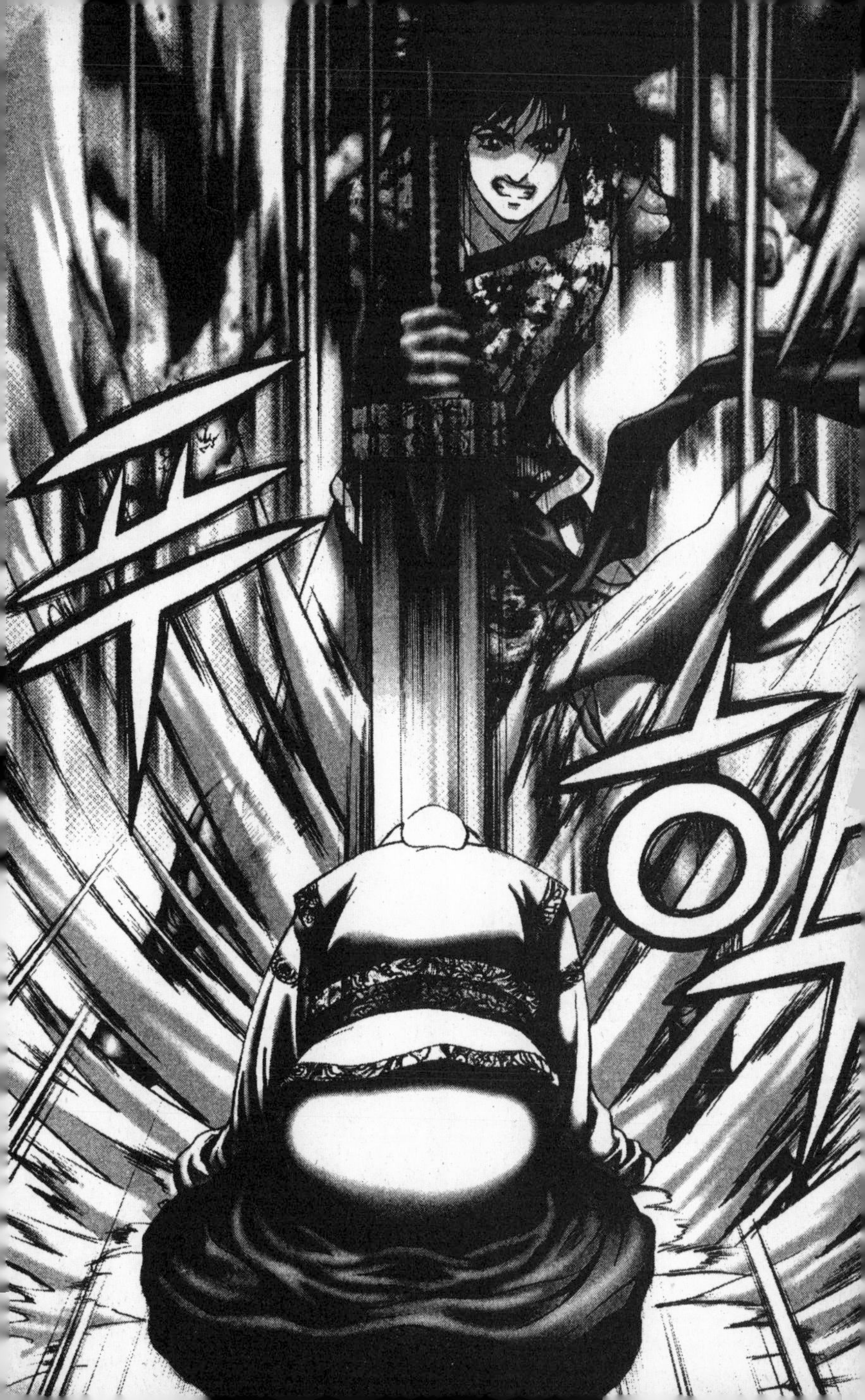

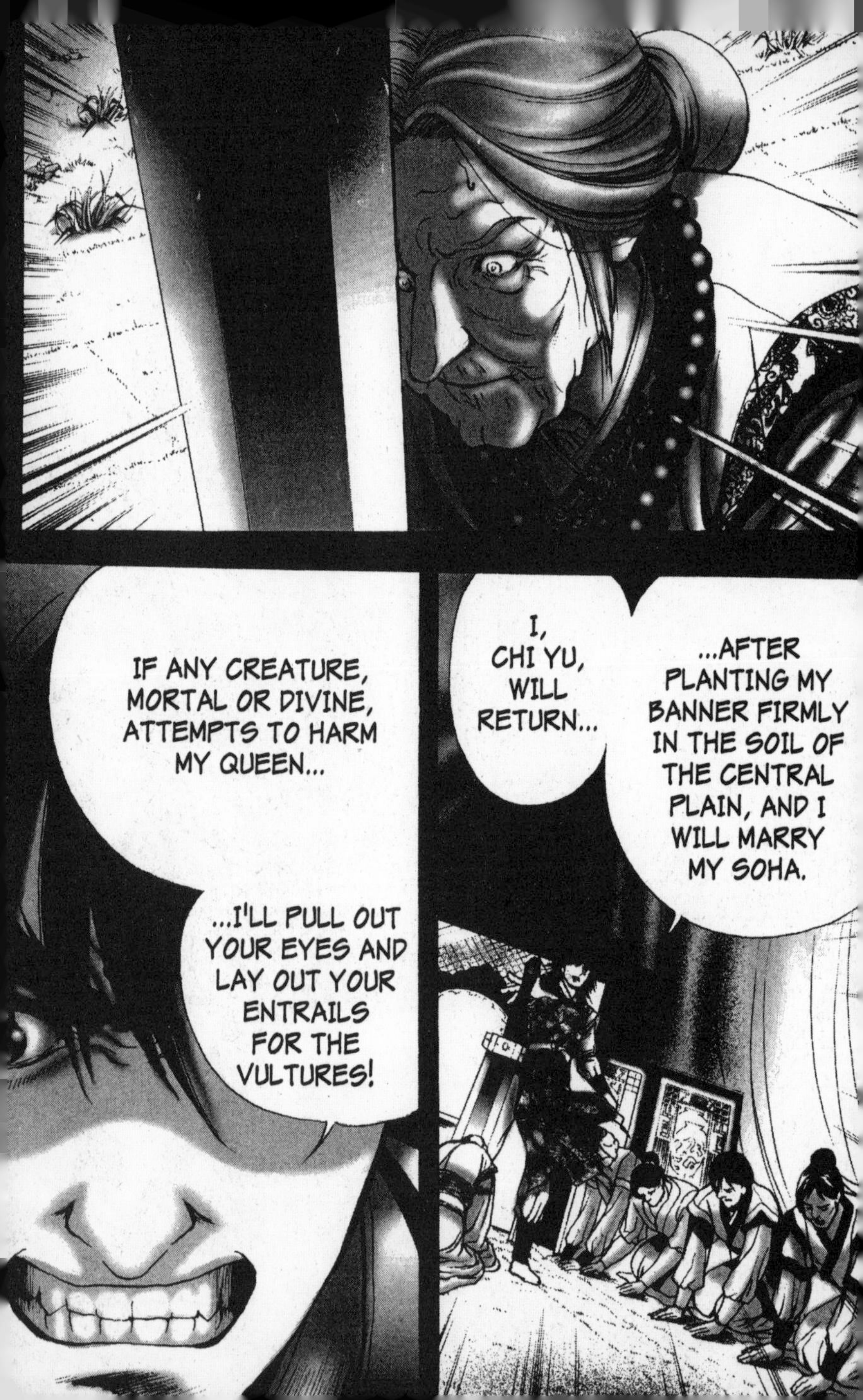
I, CHI YU, WILL RETURN...
...AFTER PLANTING MY BANNER FIRMLY IN THE SOIL OF THE CENTRAL PLAIN, AND I WILL MARRY MY SOHA.
IF ANY CREATURE, MORTAL OR DIVINE, ATTEMPTS TO HARM MY QUEEN...
...I'LL PULL OUT YOUR EYES AND LAY OUT YOUR ENTRAILS FOR THE VULTURES!

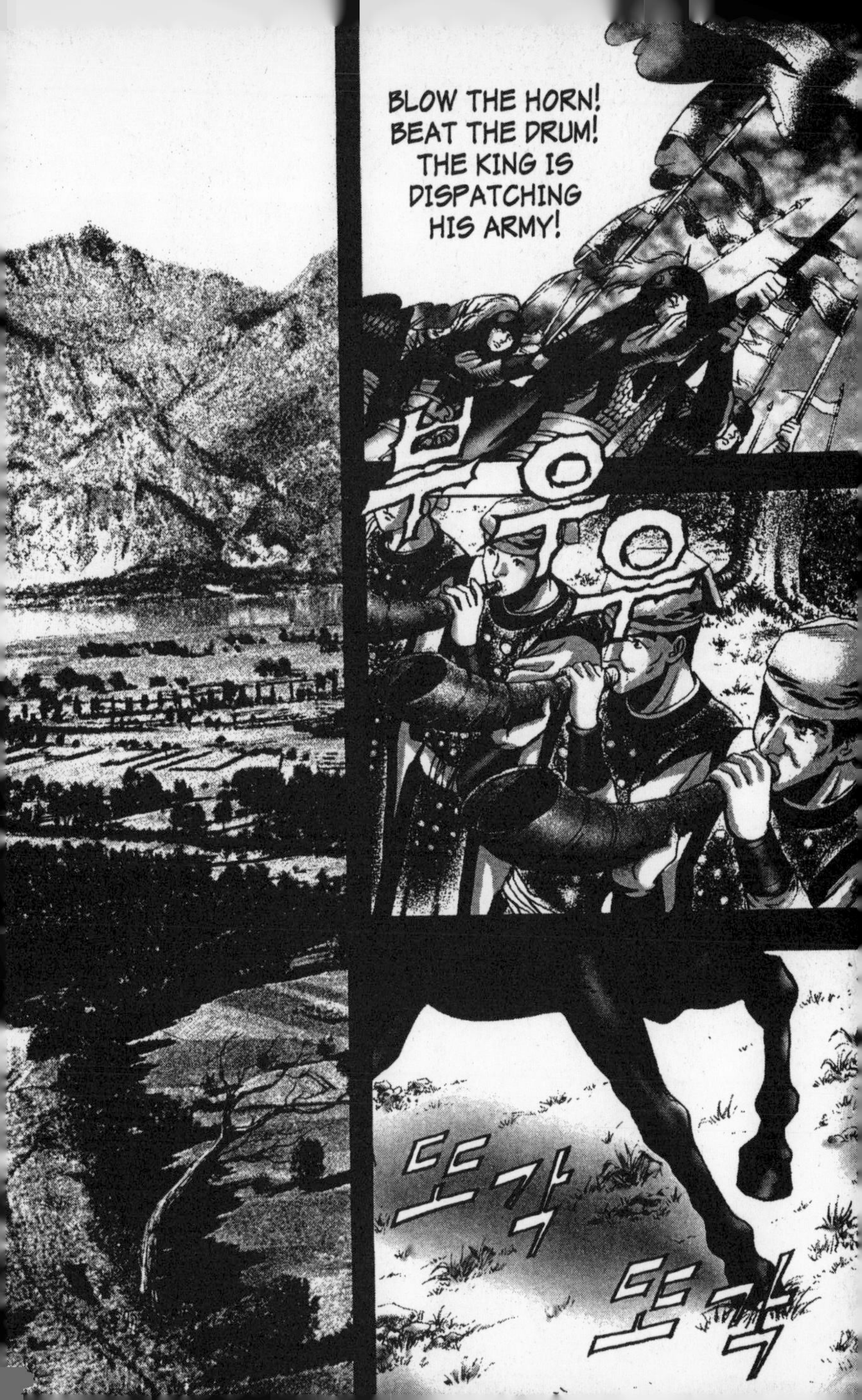
BLOW THE HORN! BEAT THE DRUM! THE KING IS DISPATCHING HIS ARMY!
또각
또각

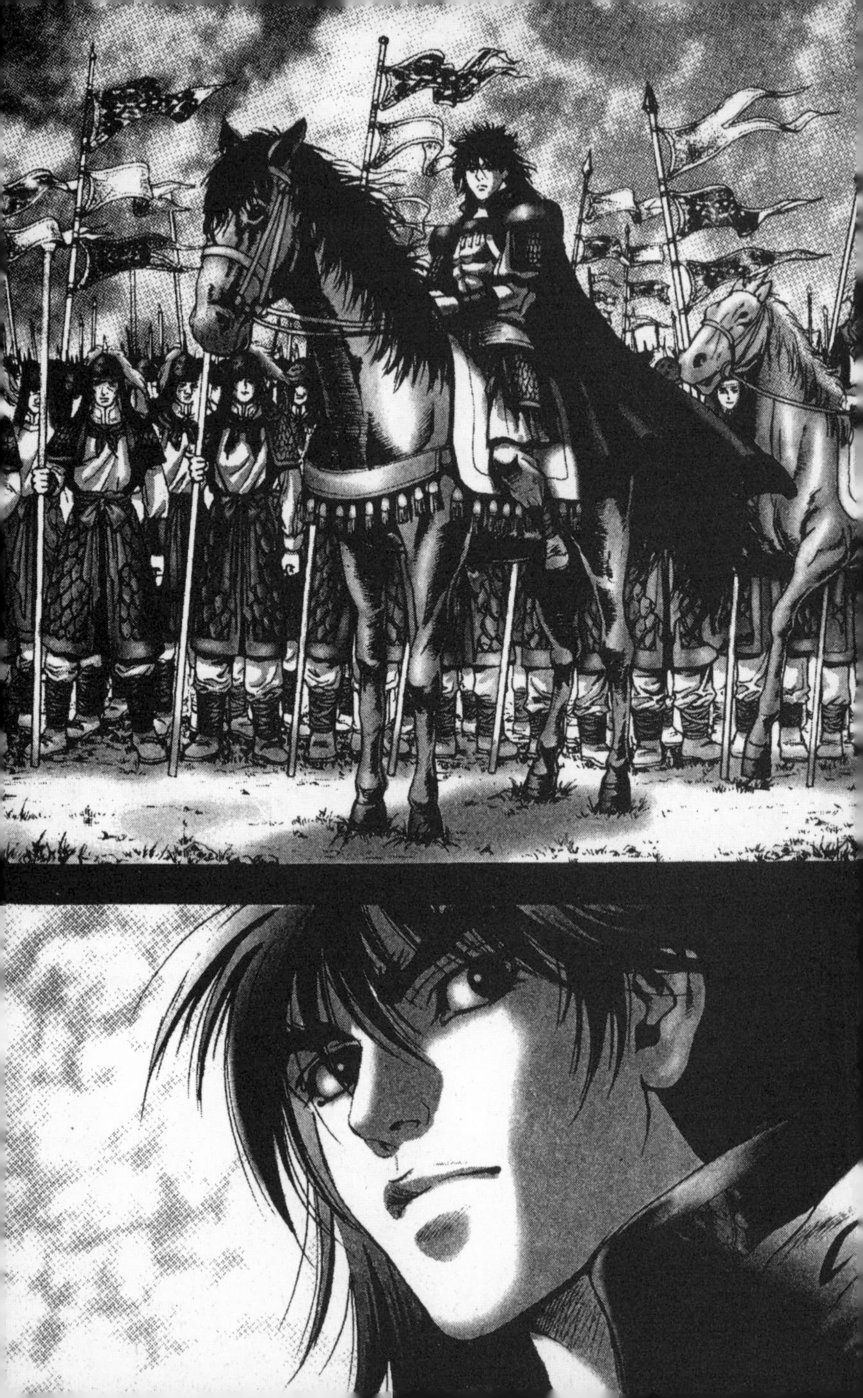

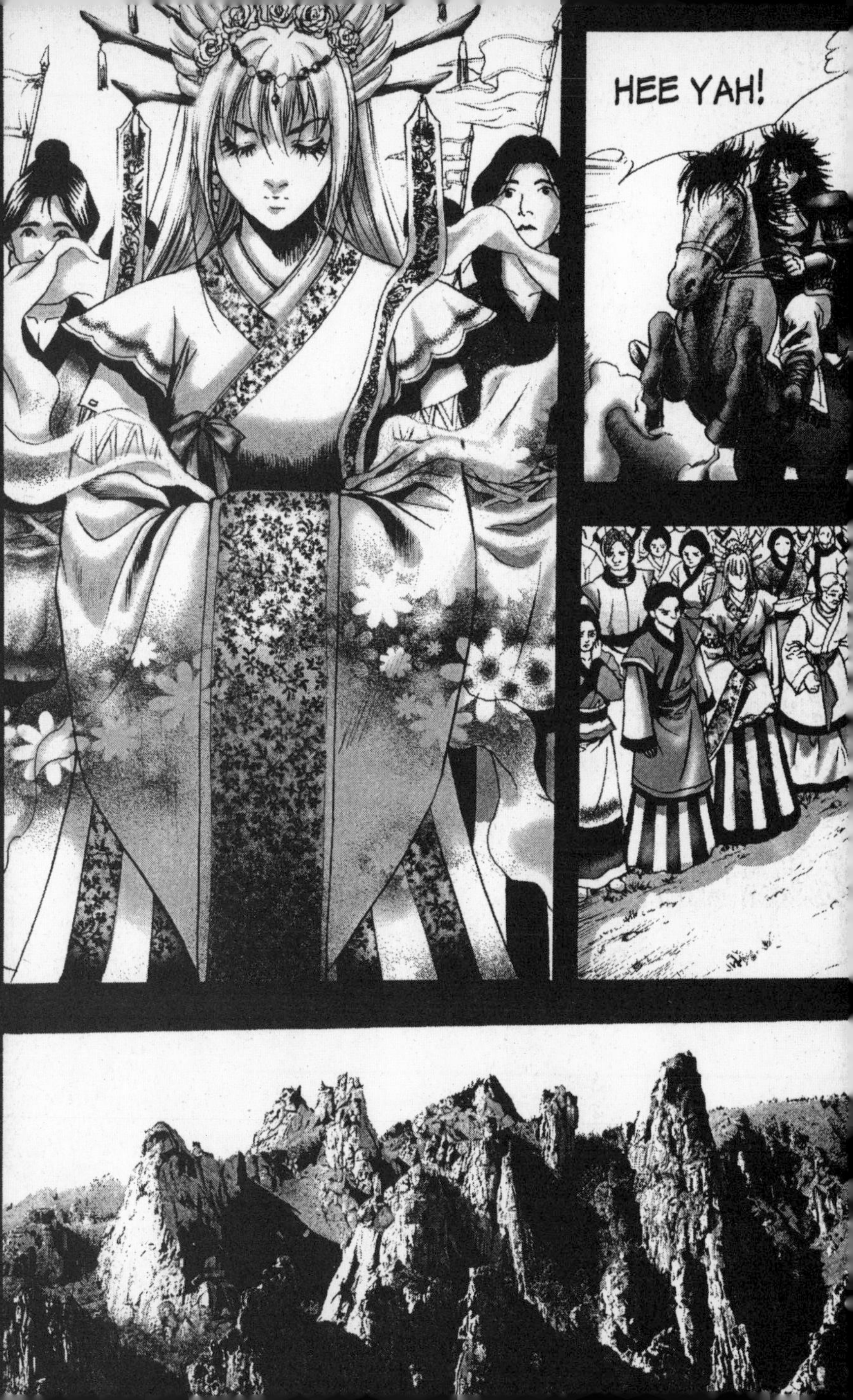
HEE YAH!

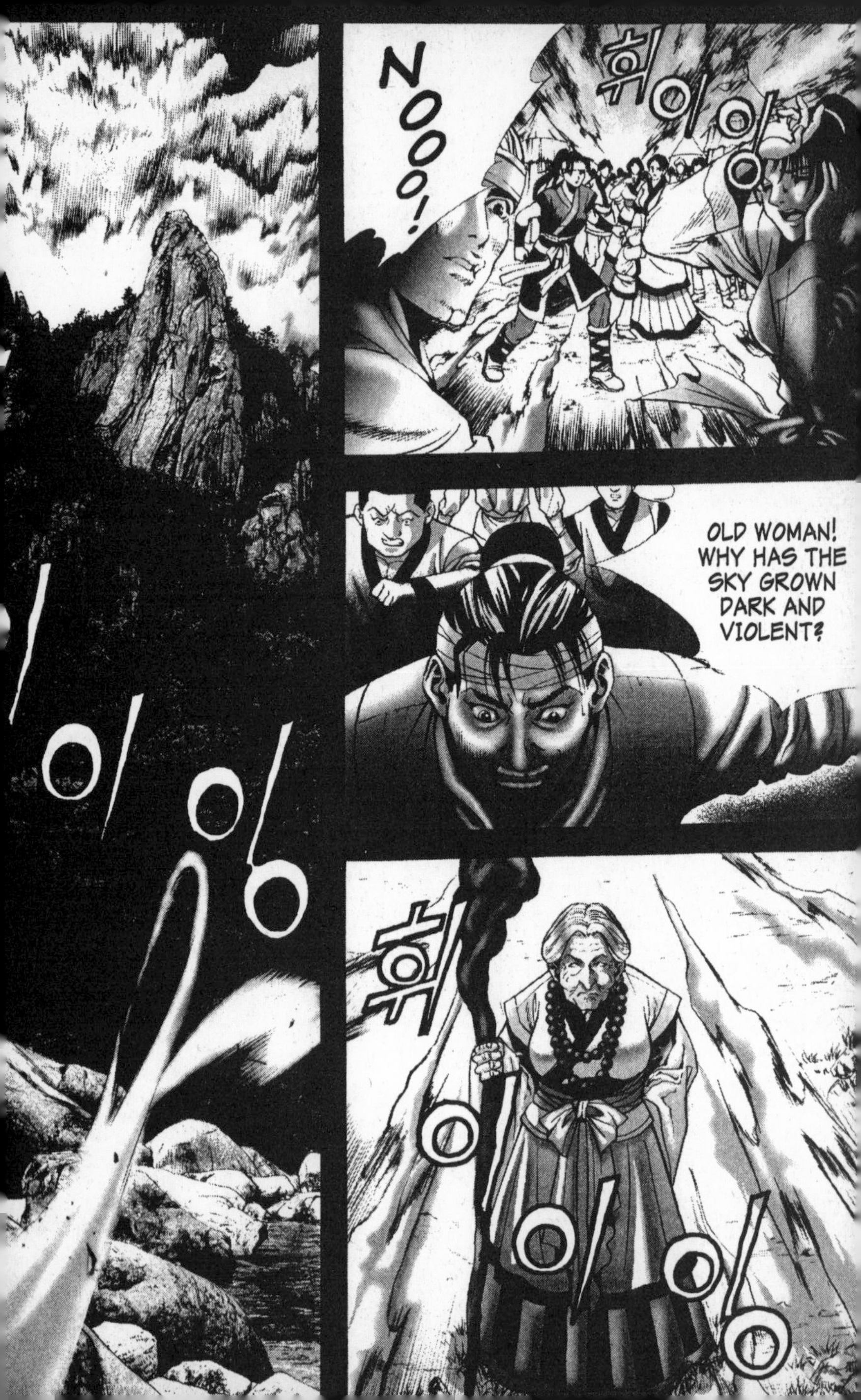

NOOOO!
휘이잉
OLD WOMAN! WHY HAS THE SKY GROWN DARK AND VIOLENT?
후

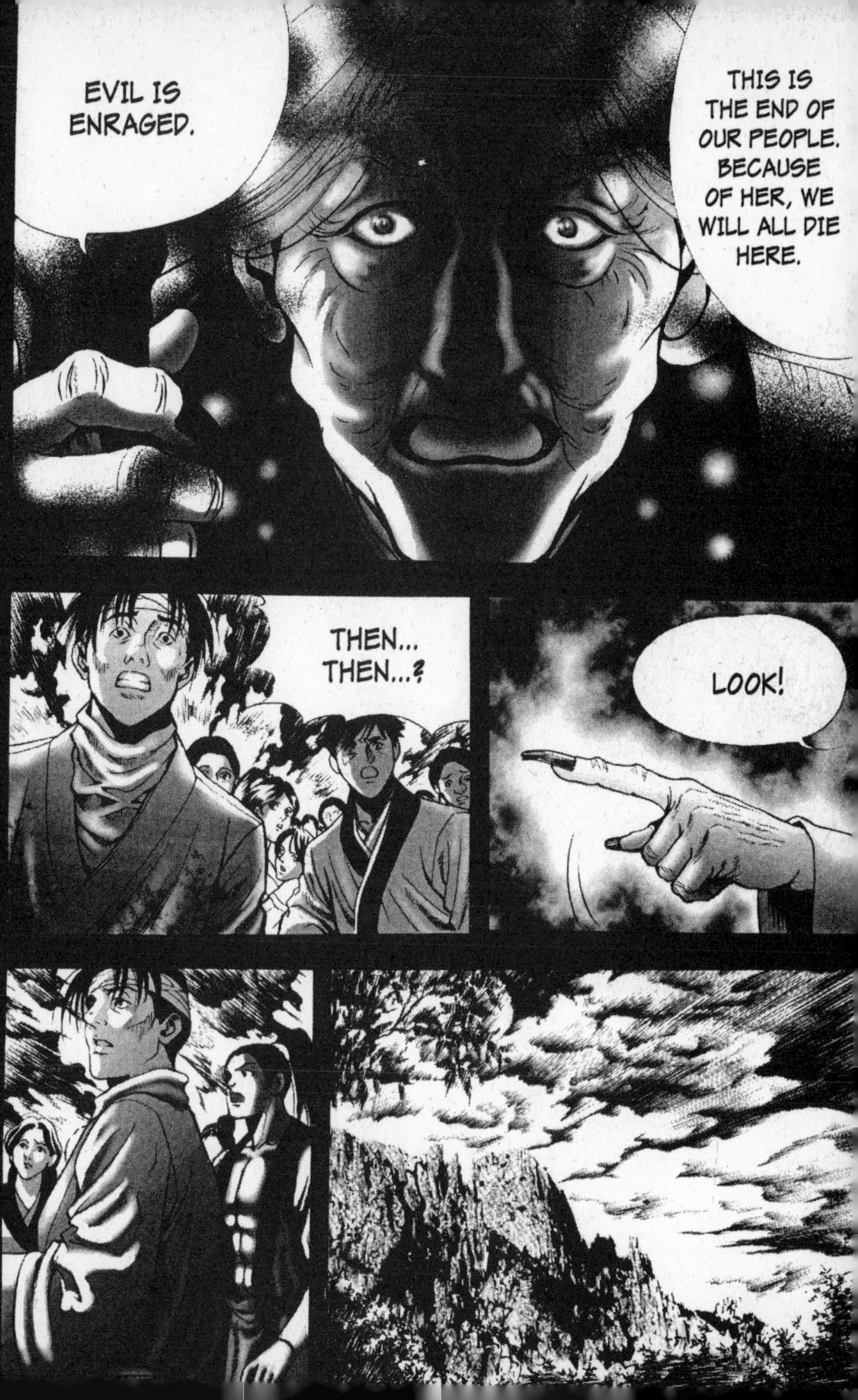
THIS IS THE END OF OUR PEOPLE. BECAUSE OF HER, WE WILL ALL DIE HERE.
EVIL IS ENRAGED.
LOOK!
THEN... THEN...?

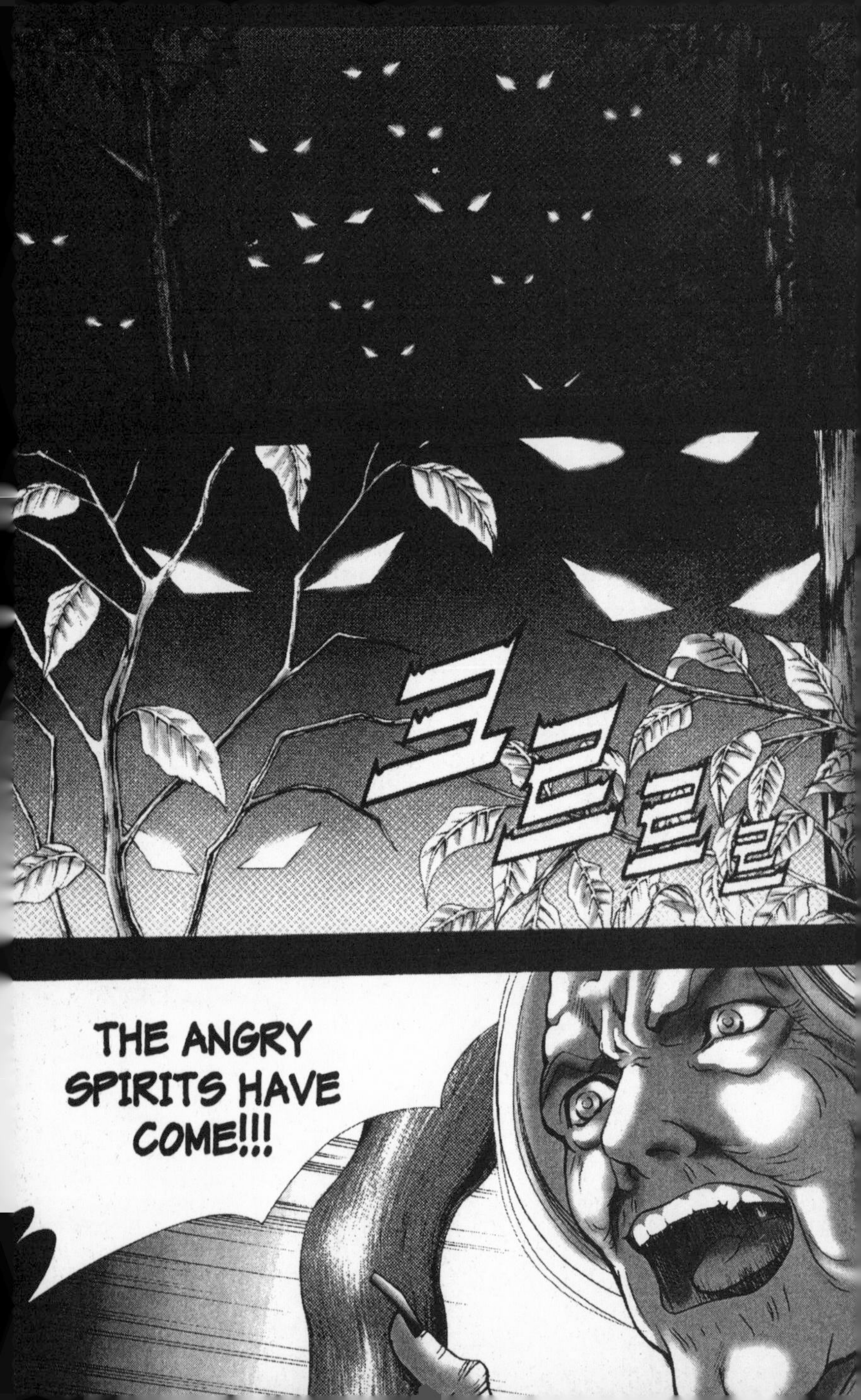
THE ANGRY SPIRITS HAVE COME!!!

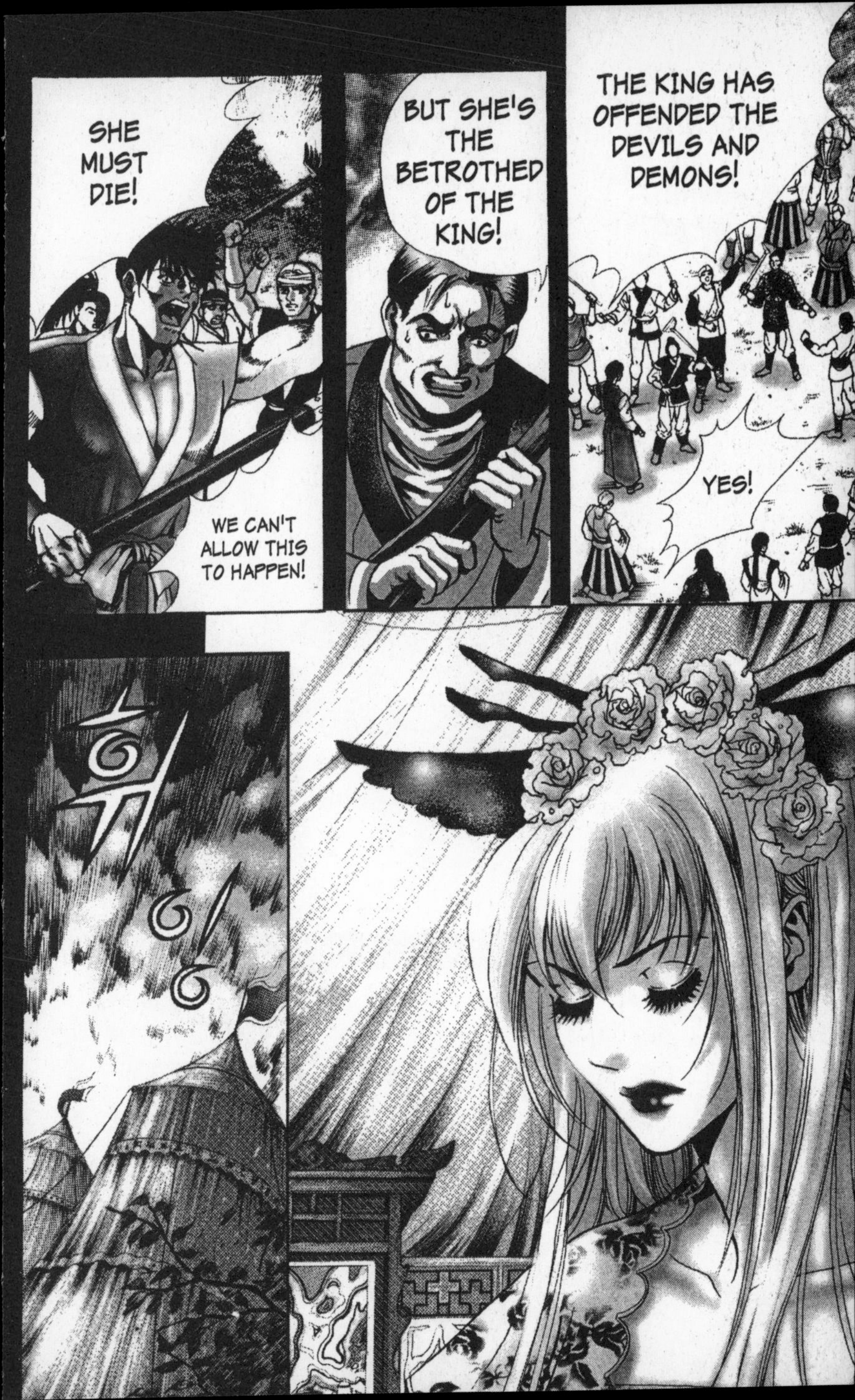
THE KING HAS OFFENDED THE DEVILS AND DEMONS!
YES!
BUT SHE'S THE BETROTHED OF THE KING!
SHE MUST DIE!
WE CAN'T ALLOW THIS TO HAPPEN!

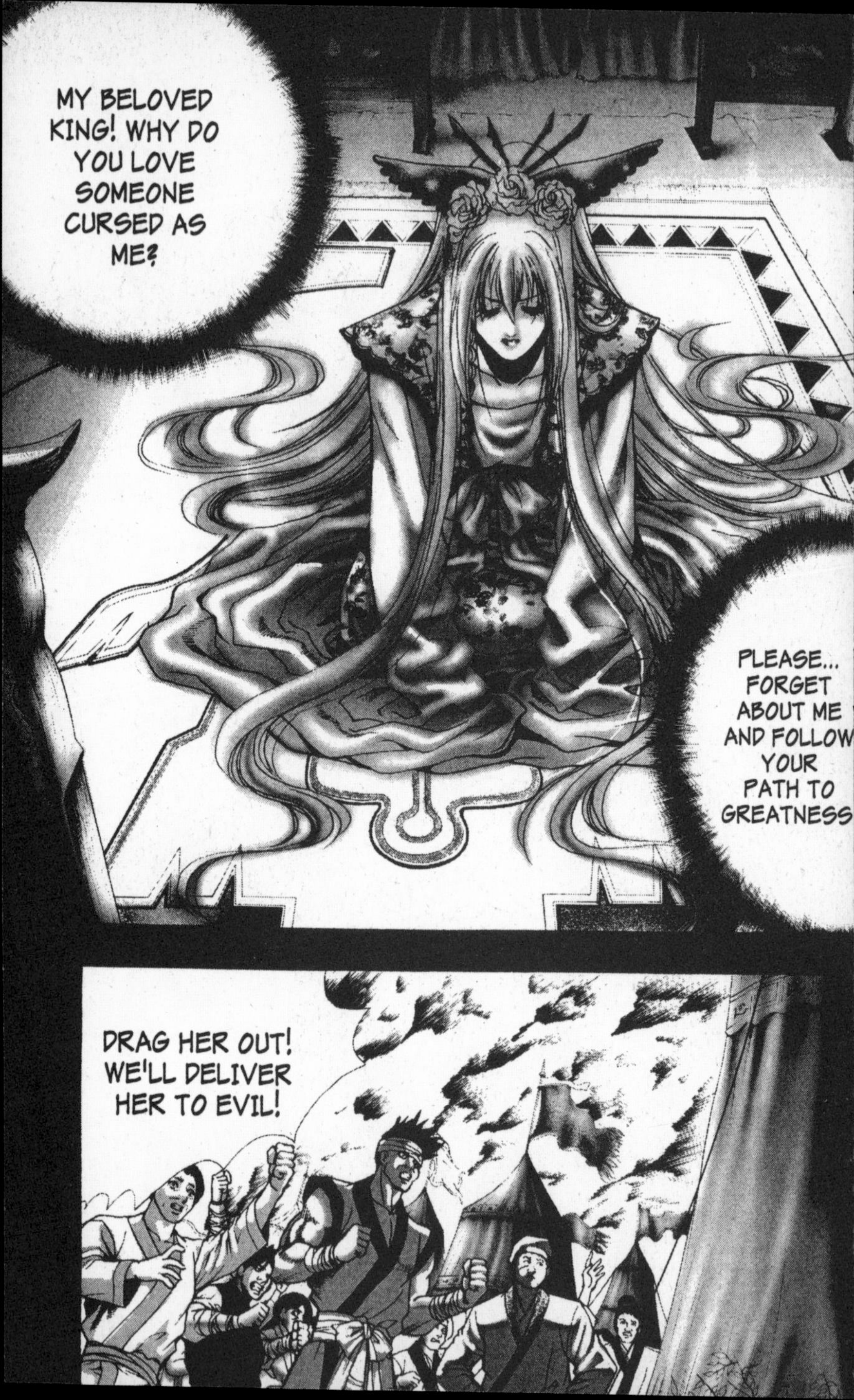
MY BELOVED KING! WHY DO YOU LOVE SOMEONE CURSED AS ME?
PLEASE... FORGET ABOUT ME AND FOLLOW YOUR PATH TO GREATNESS
DRAG HER OUT! WE'LL DELIVER HER TO EVIL!

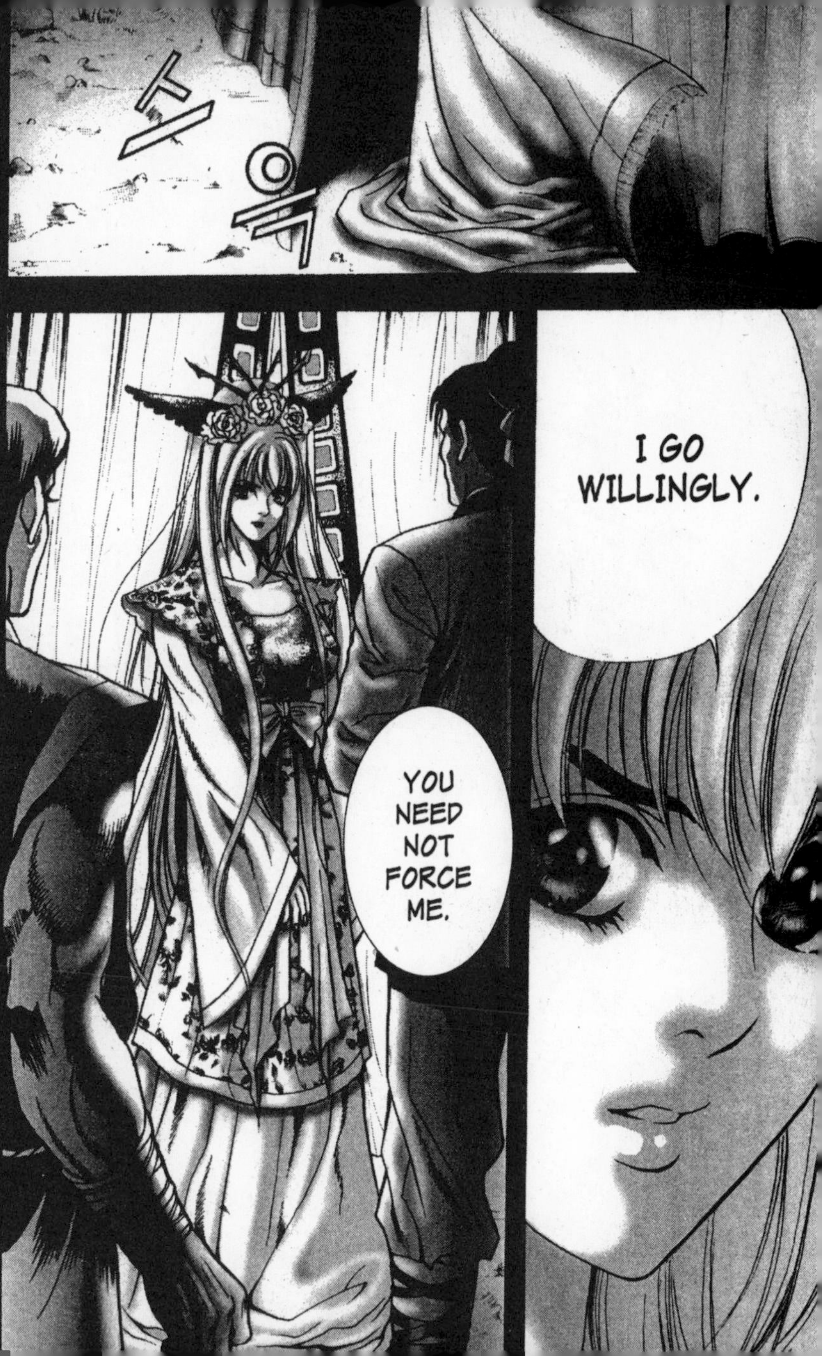
I GO WILLINGLY.
YOU NEED NOT FORCE ME.

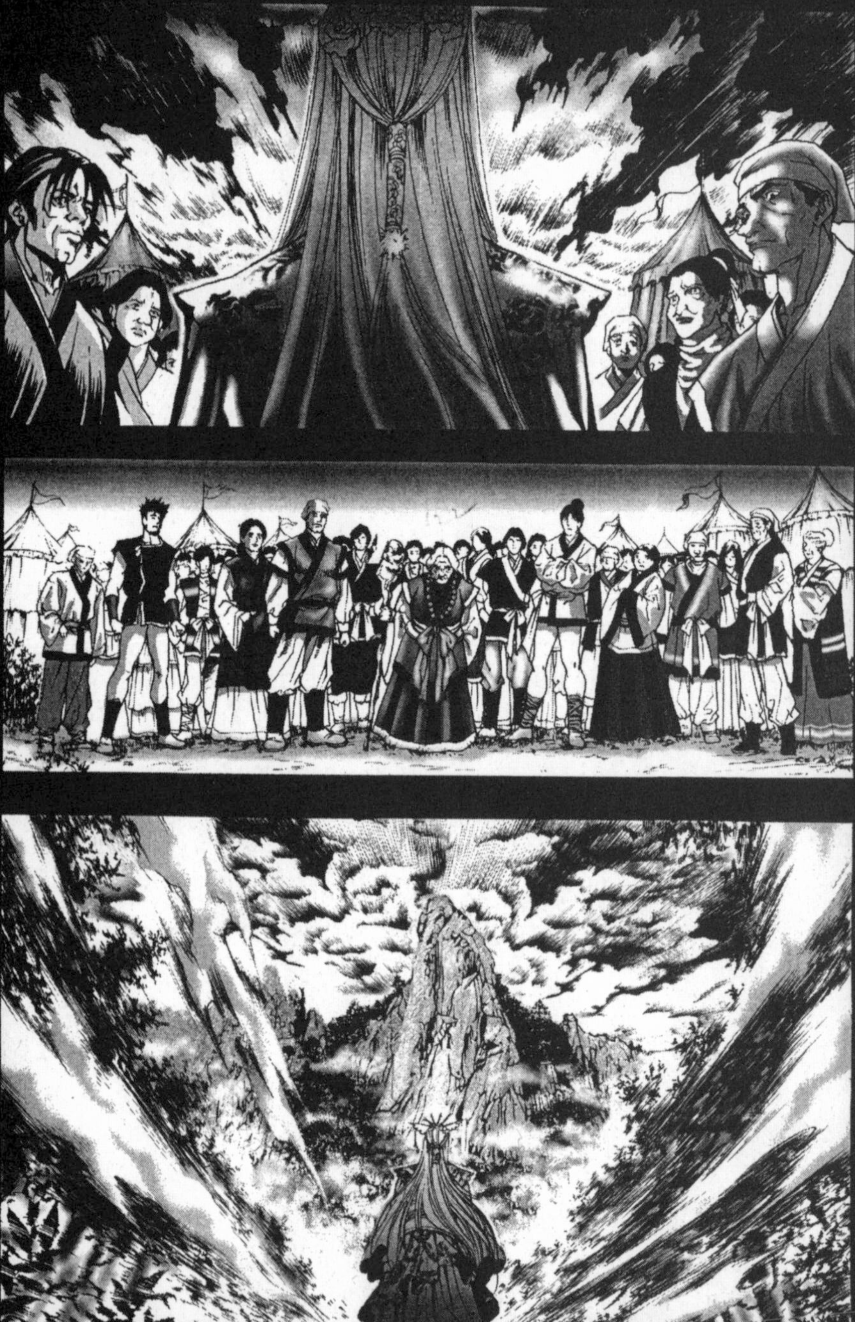

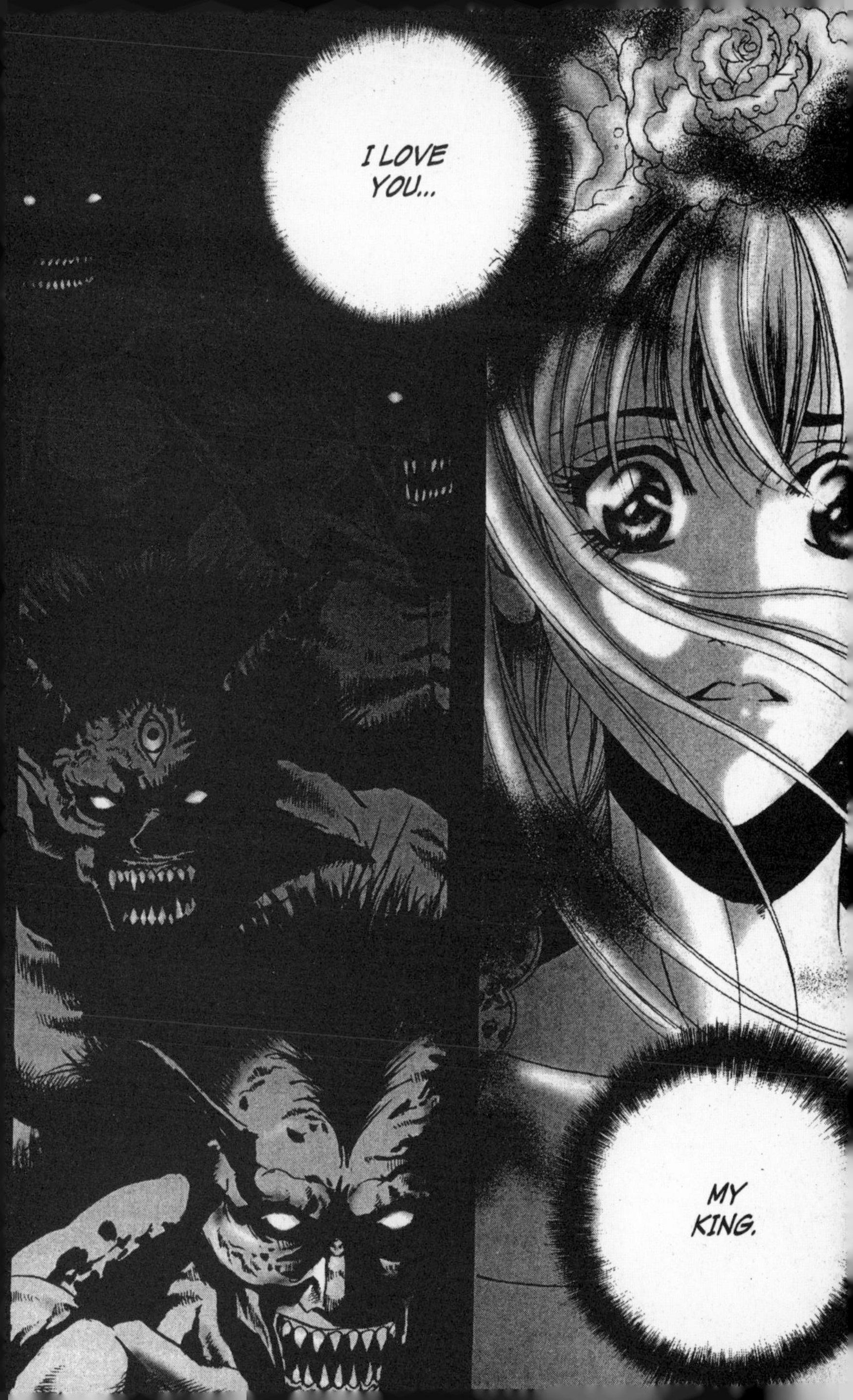
I LOVE YOU...
MY KING.

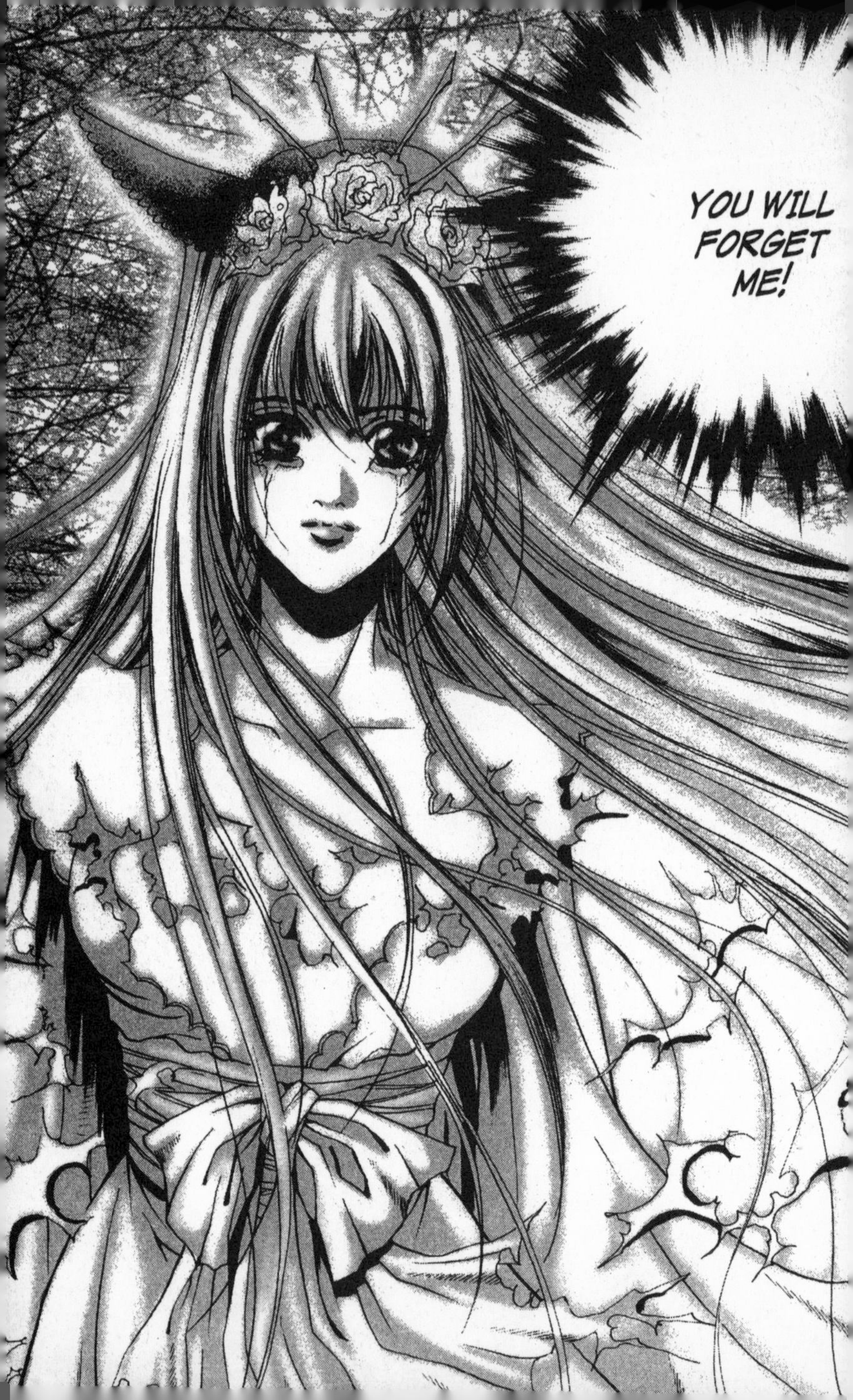
YOU WILL FORGET ME!

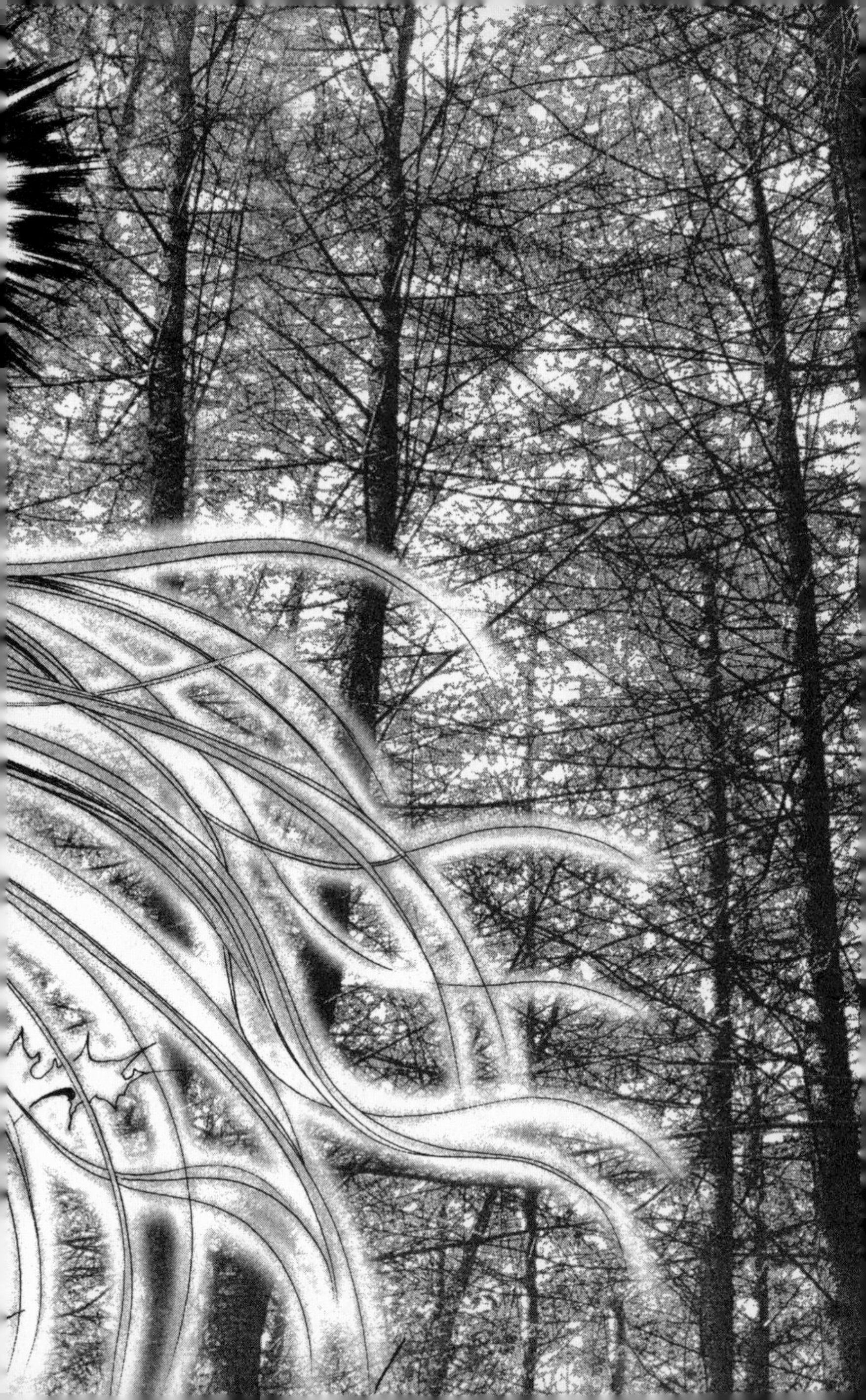

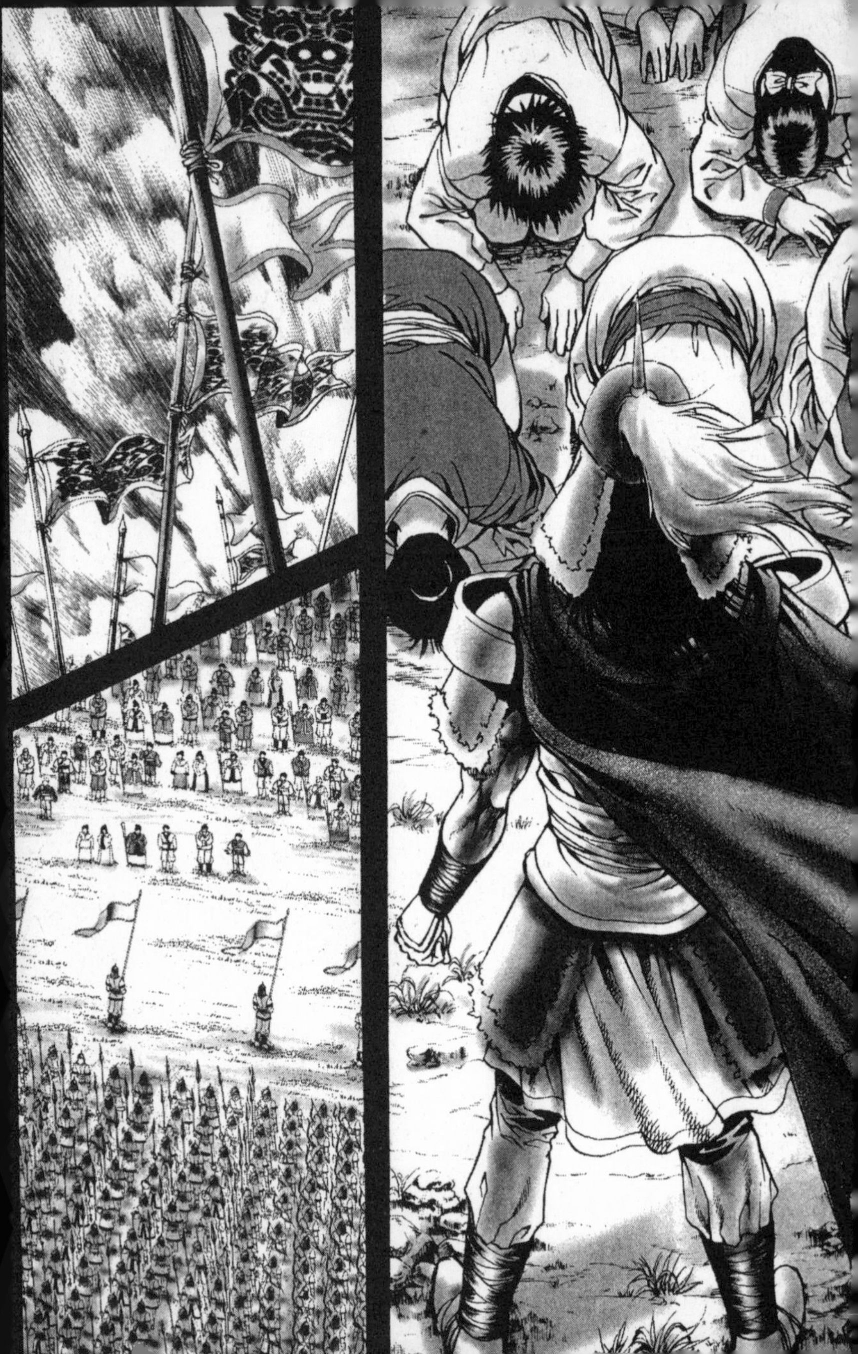

SHE SAVED THE ENTIRE KINGDOM, MY LORD.

SHE WENT OF HER OWN WILL.

SILENCE!

HER FATE IS TO BE THE SACRIFICE FOR EVIL. EVIL SPAWNS FROM HER WOMB ALONE.

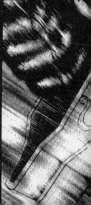

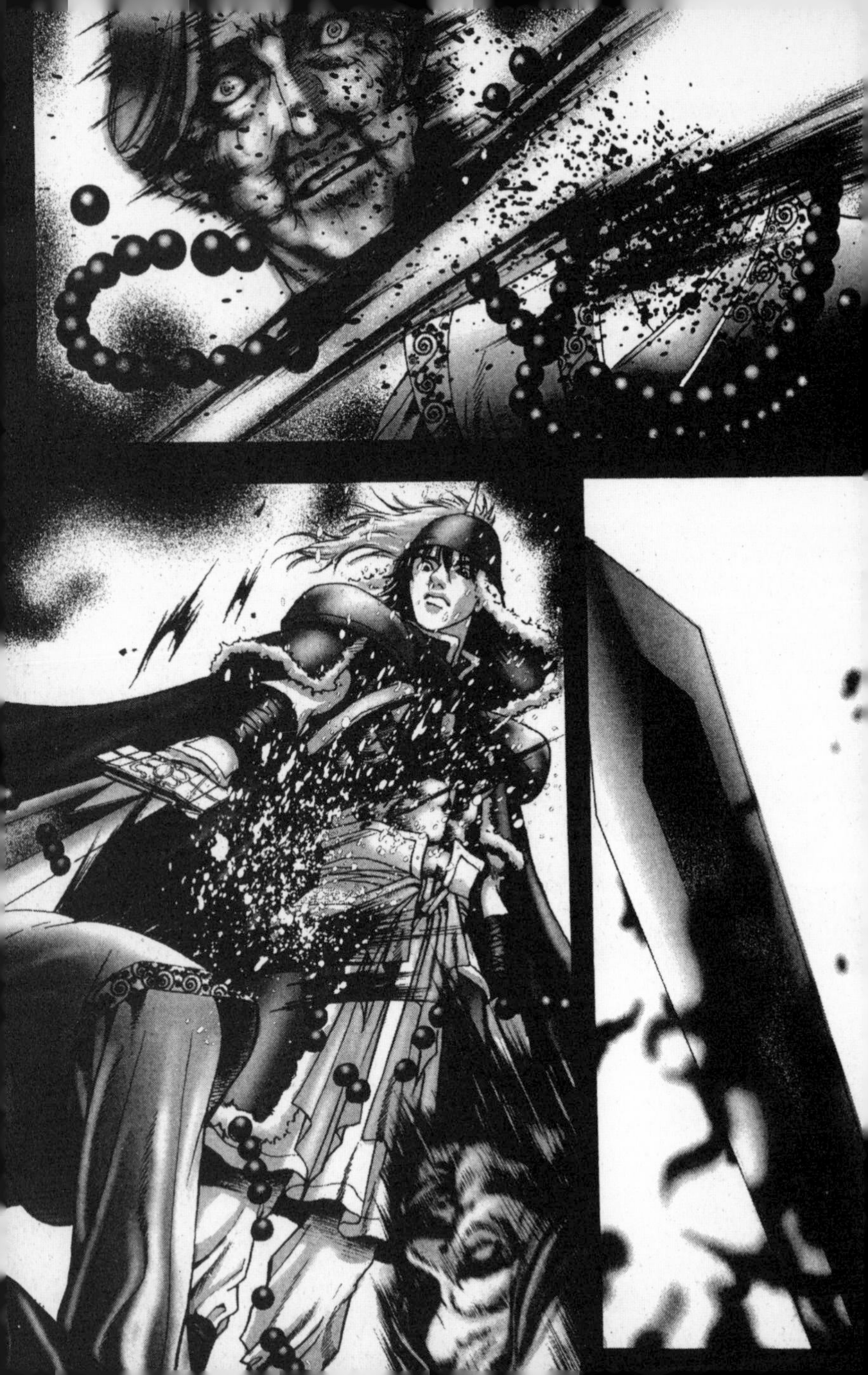

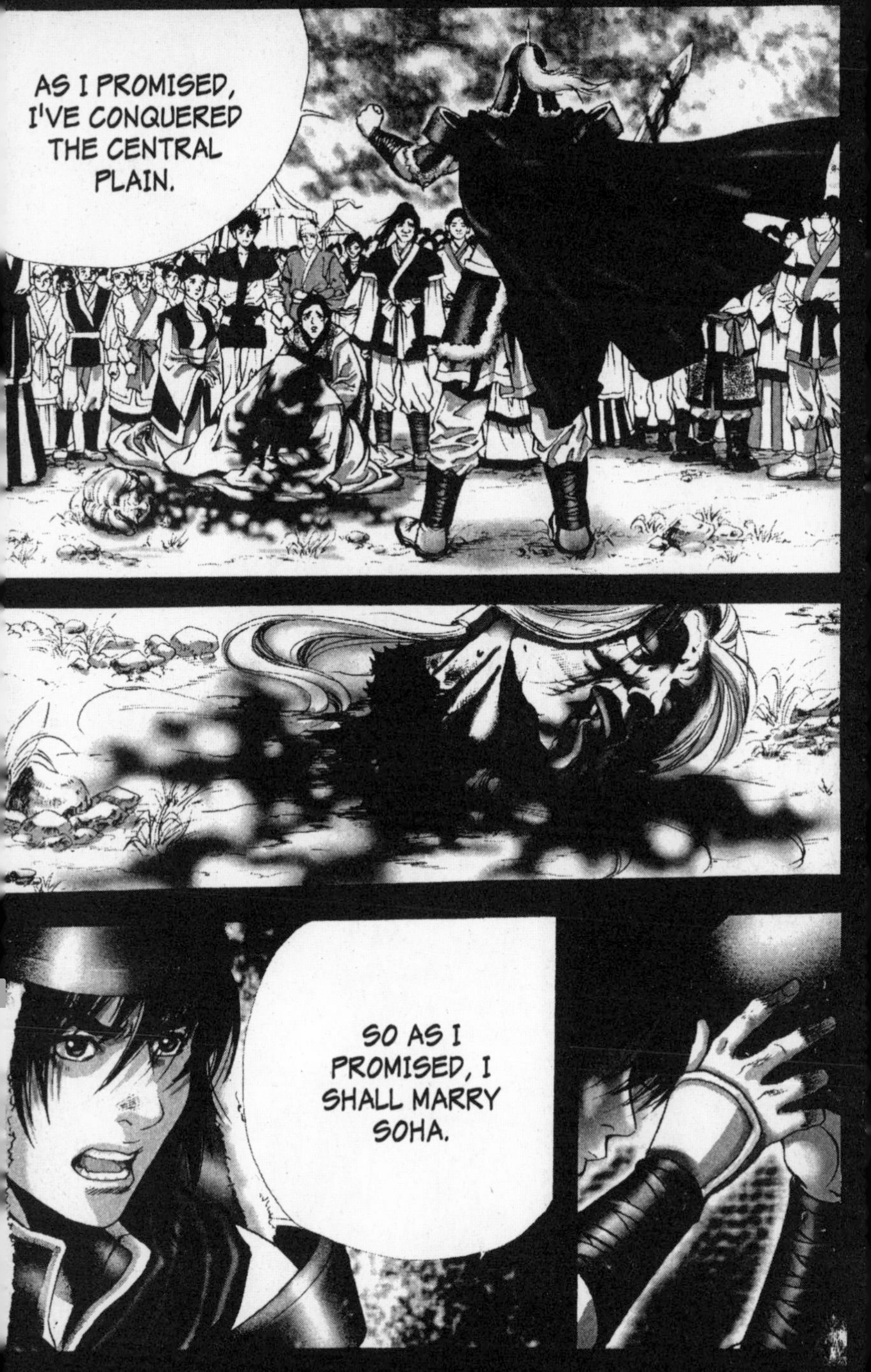
AS I PROMISED, I'VE CONQUERED THE CENTRAL PLAIN.
SO AS I PROMISED, I SHALL MARRY SOHA.

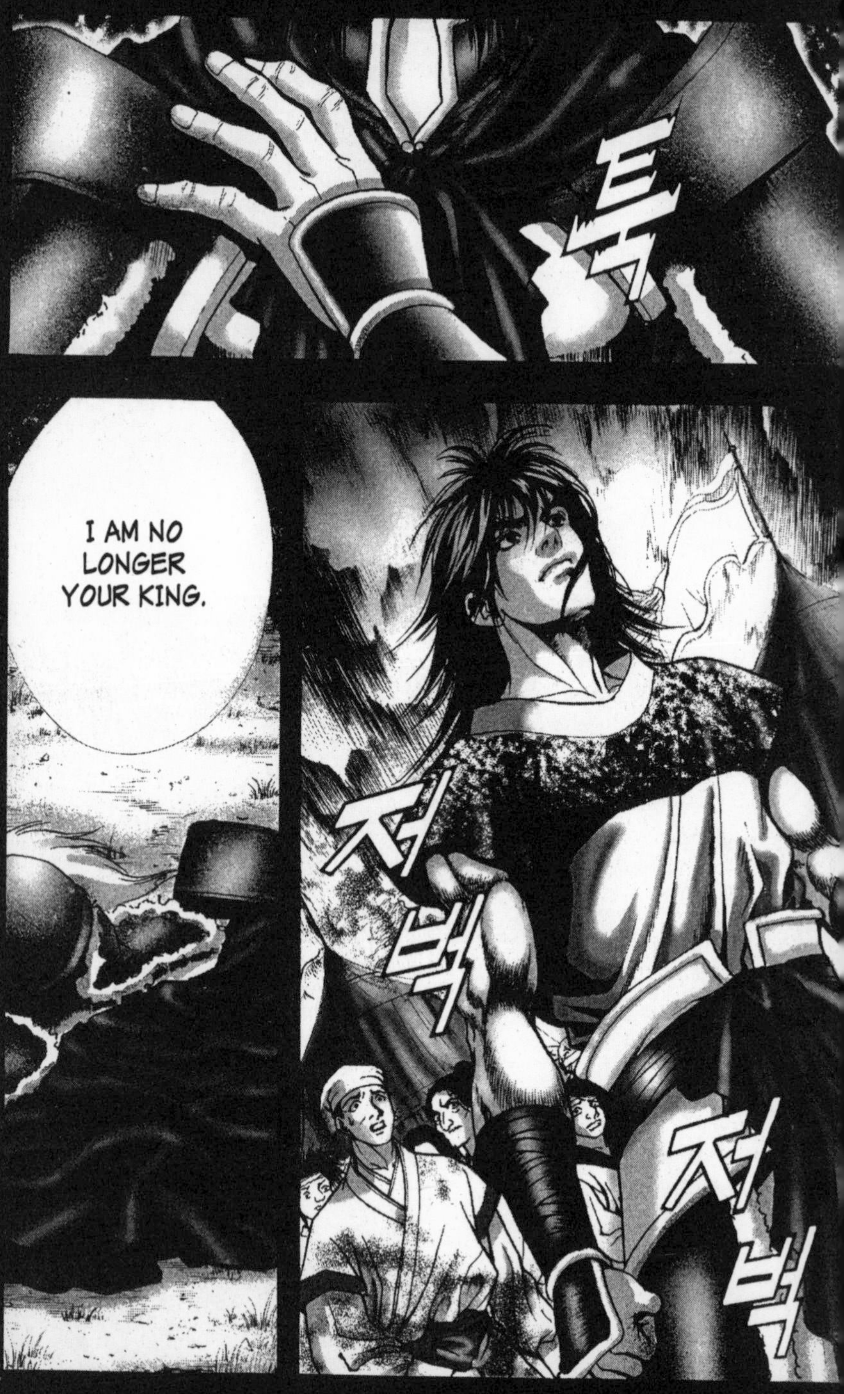
I AM NO LONGER YOUR KING.
저벅
저벅

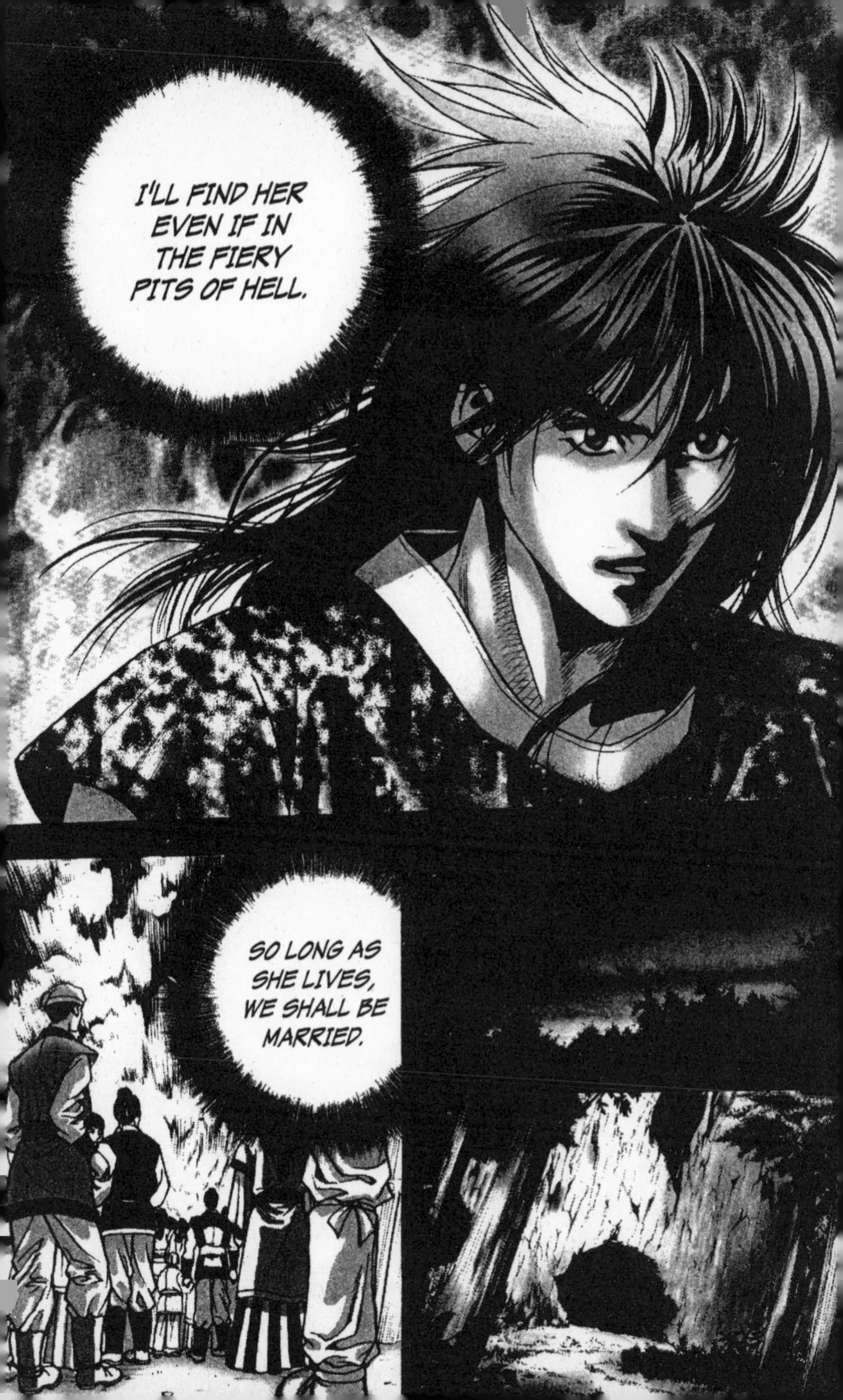
I'LL FIND HER EVEN IF IN THE FIERY PITS OF HELL.
SO LONG AS SHE LIVES, WE SHALL BE MARRIED.

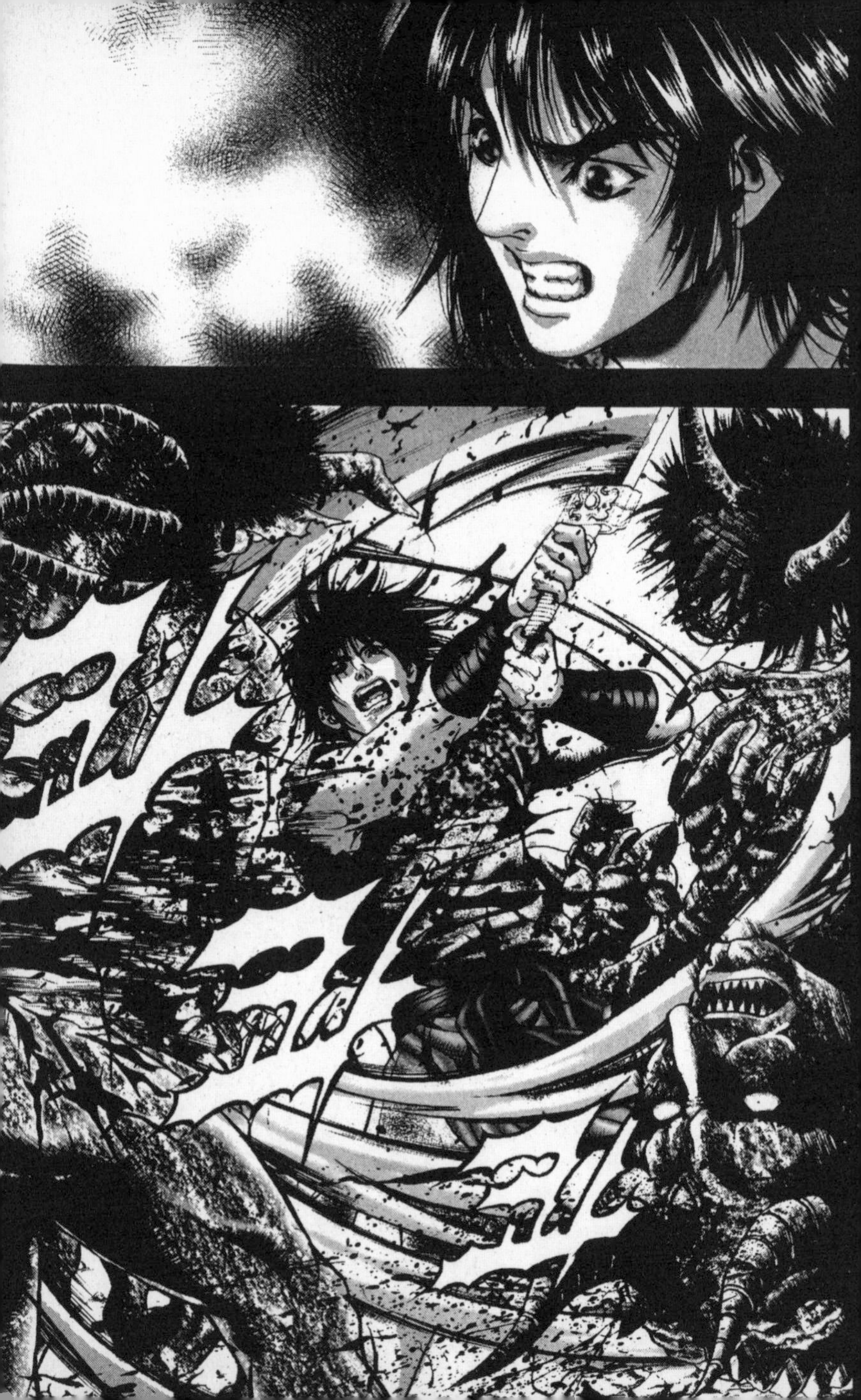

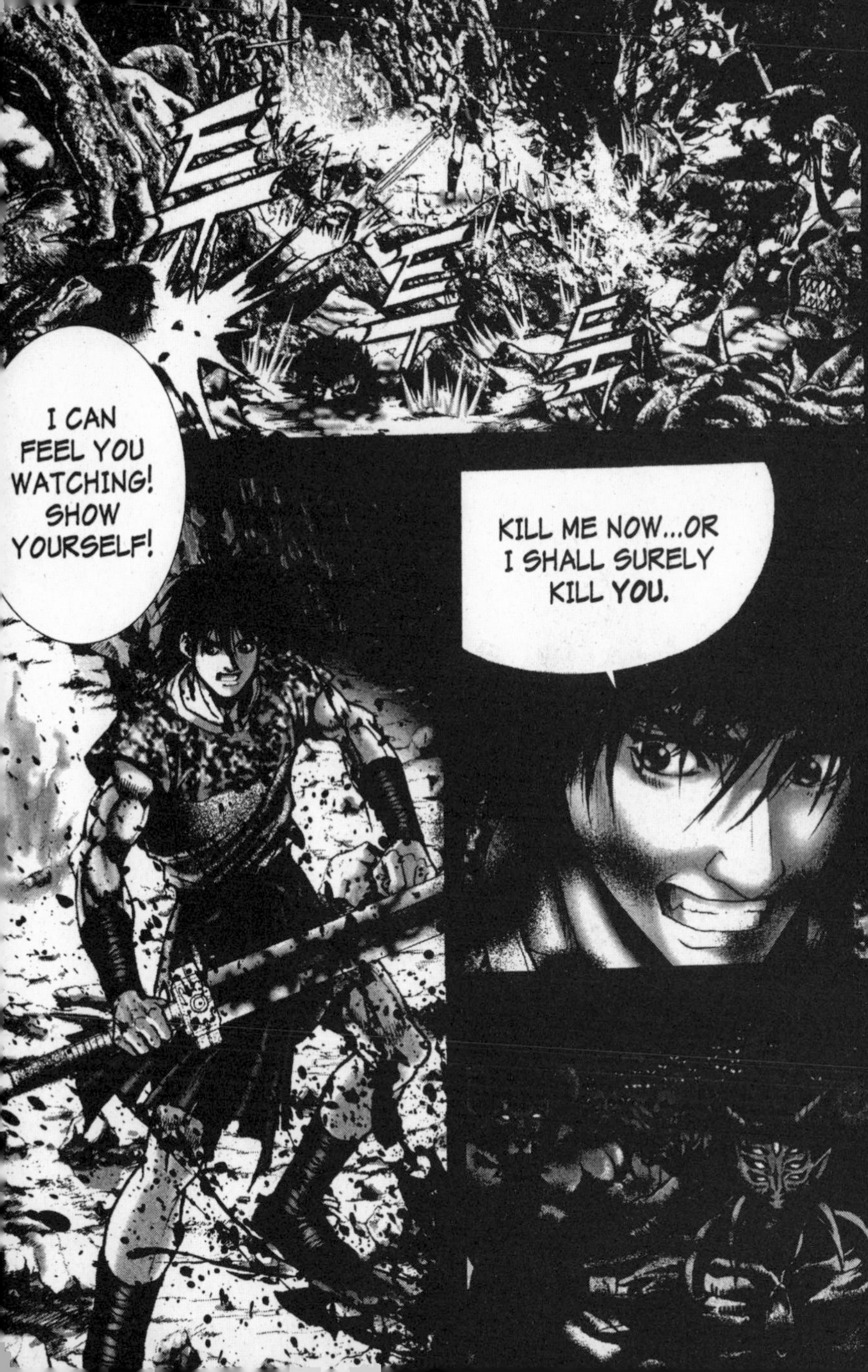
I CAN FEEL YOU WATCHING! SHOW YOURSELF!
KILL ME NOW...OR I SHALL SURELY KILL YOU.

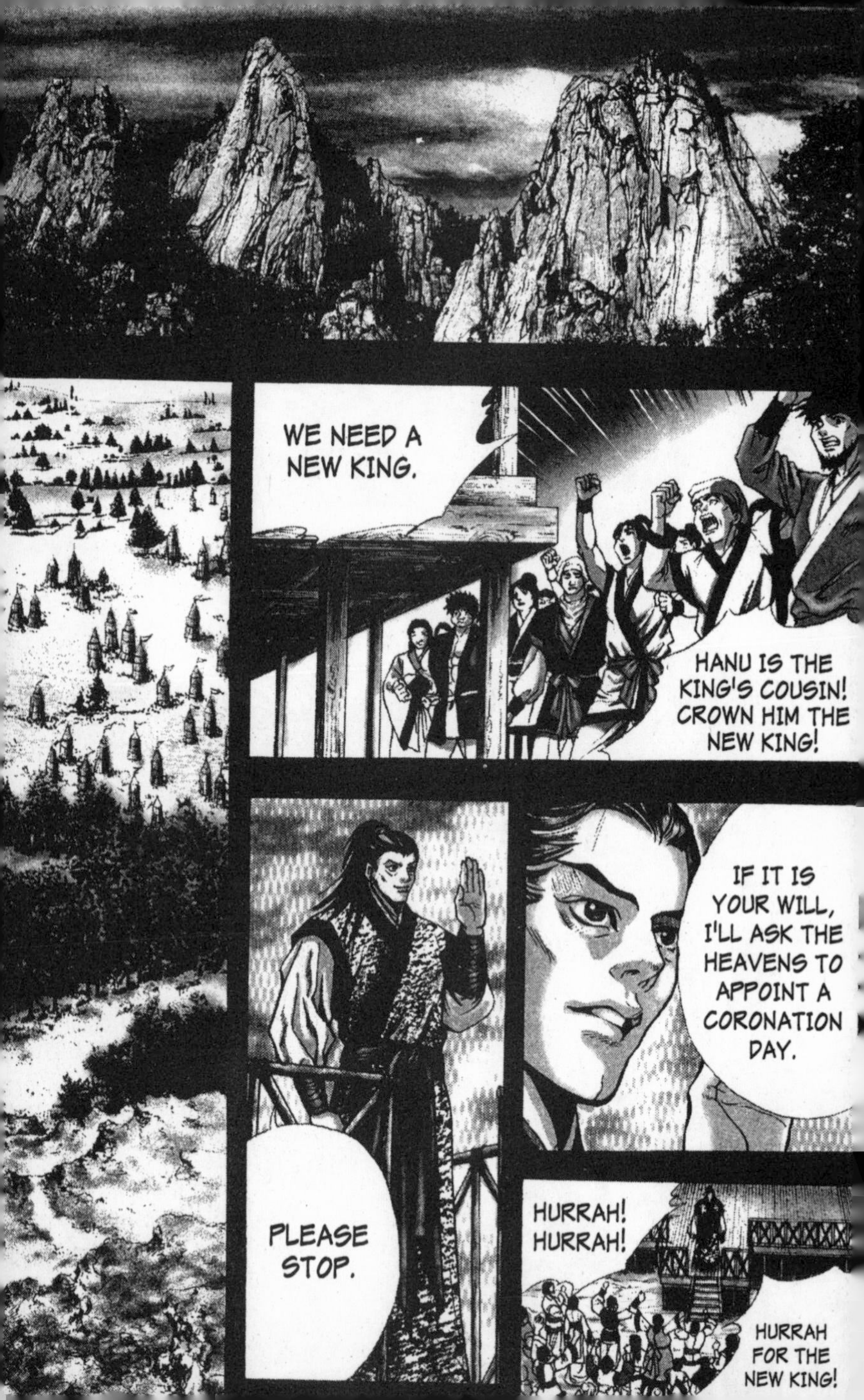
WE NEED A NEW KING.
HANU IS THE KING'S COUSIN! CROWN HIM THE NEW KING!
IF IT IS YOUR WILL, I'LL ASK THE HEAVENS TO APPOINT A CORONATION DAY.
PLEASE STOP.
HURRAH! HURRAH!
HURRAH FOR THE NEW KING!

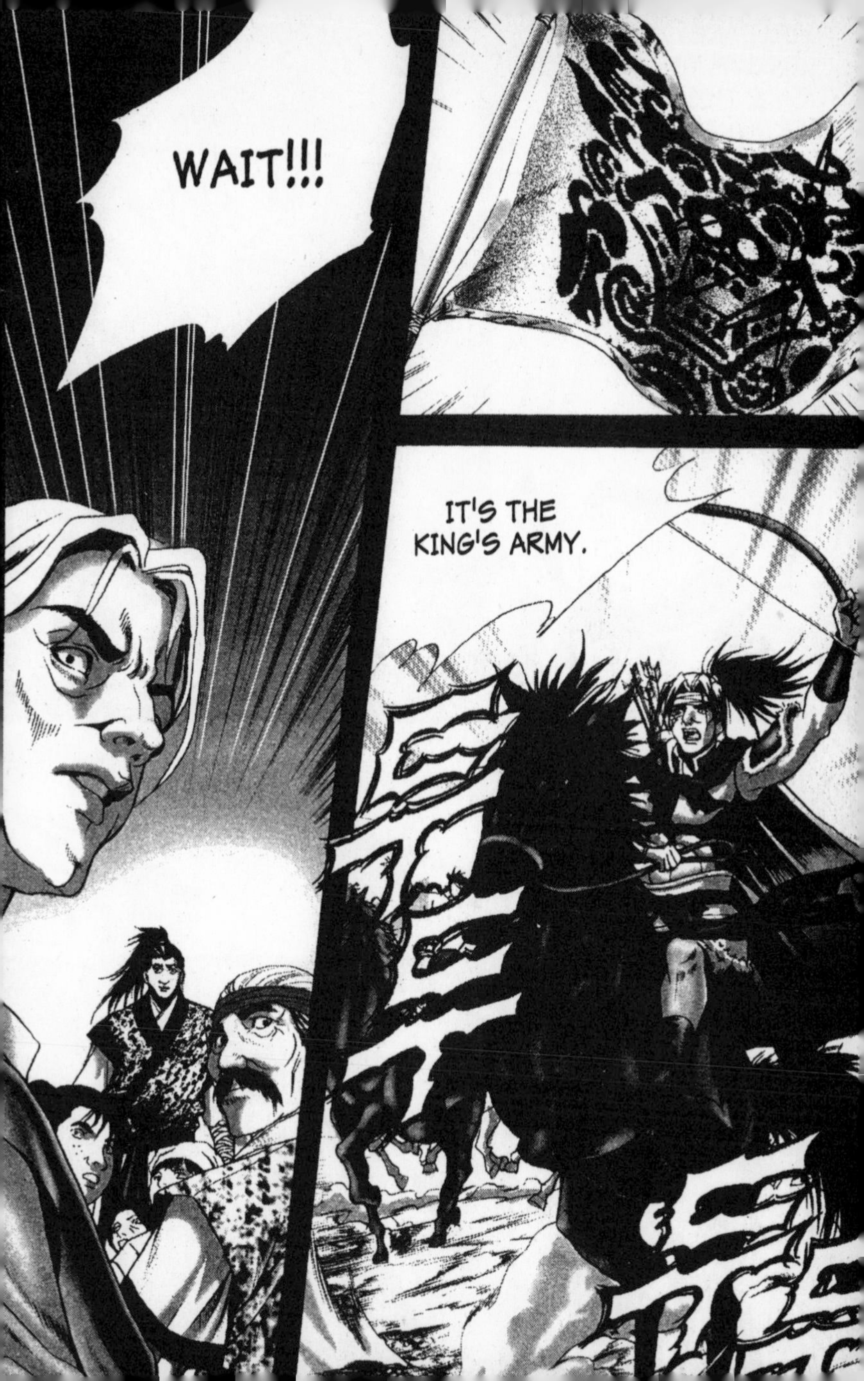
WAIT!!!
IT'S THE KING'S ARMY.

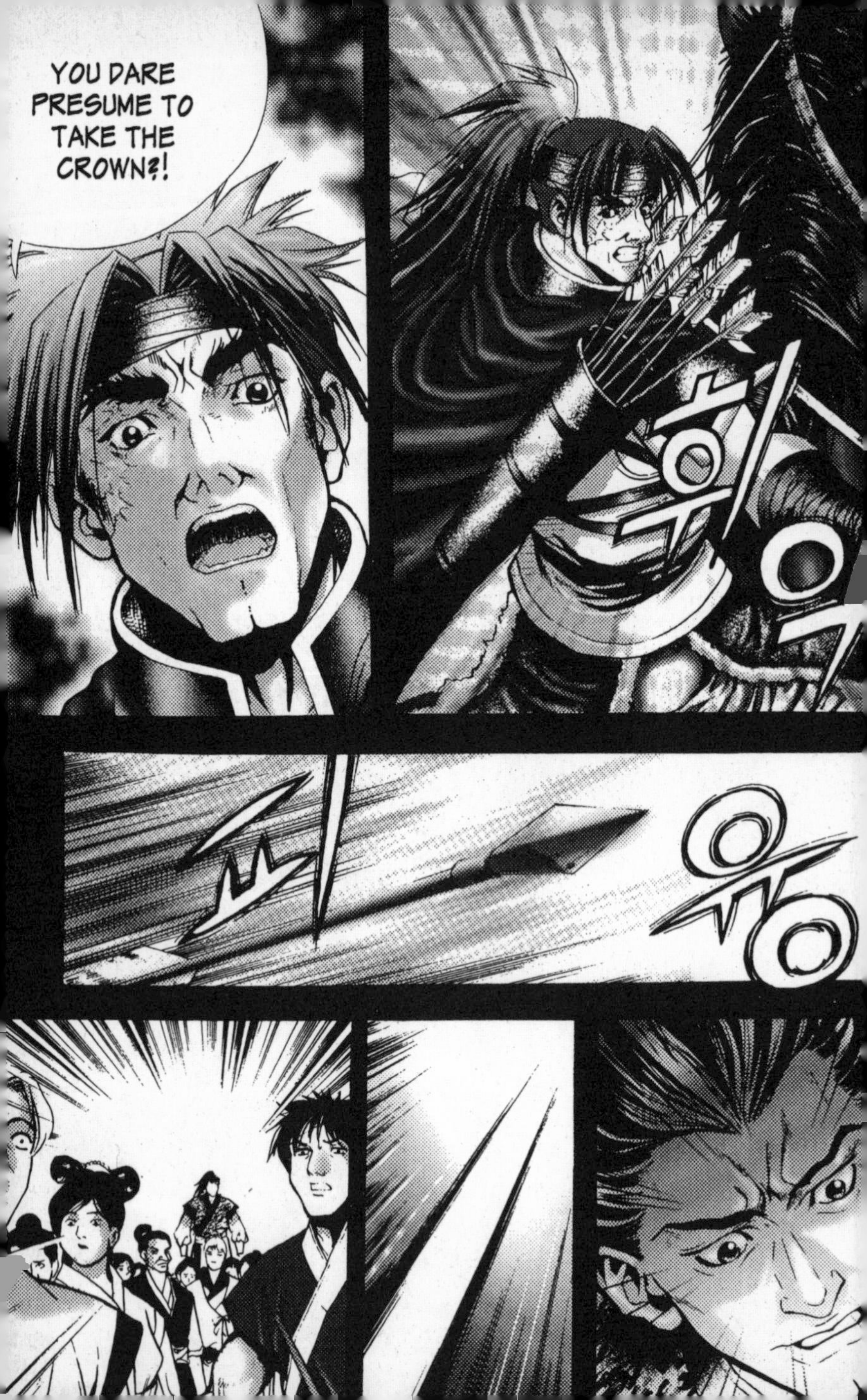
YOU DARE PRESUME TO TAKE THE CROWN?!

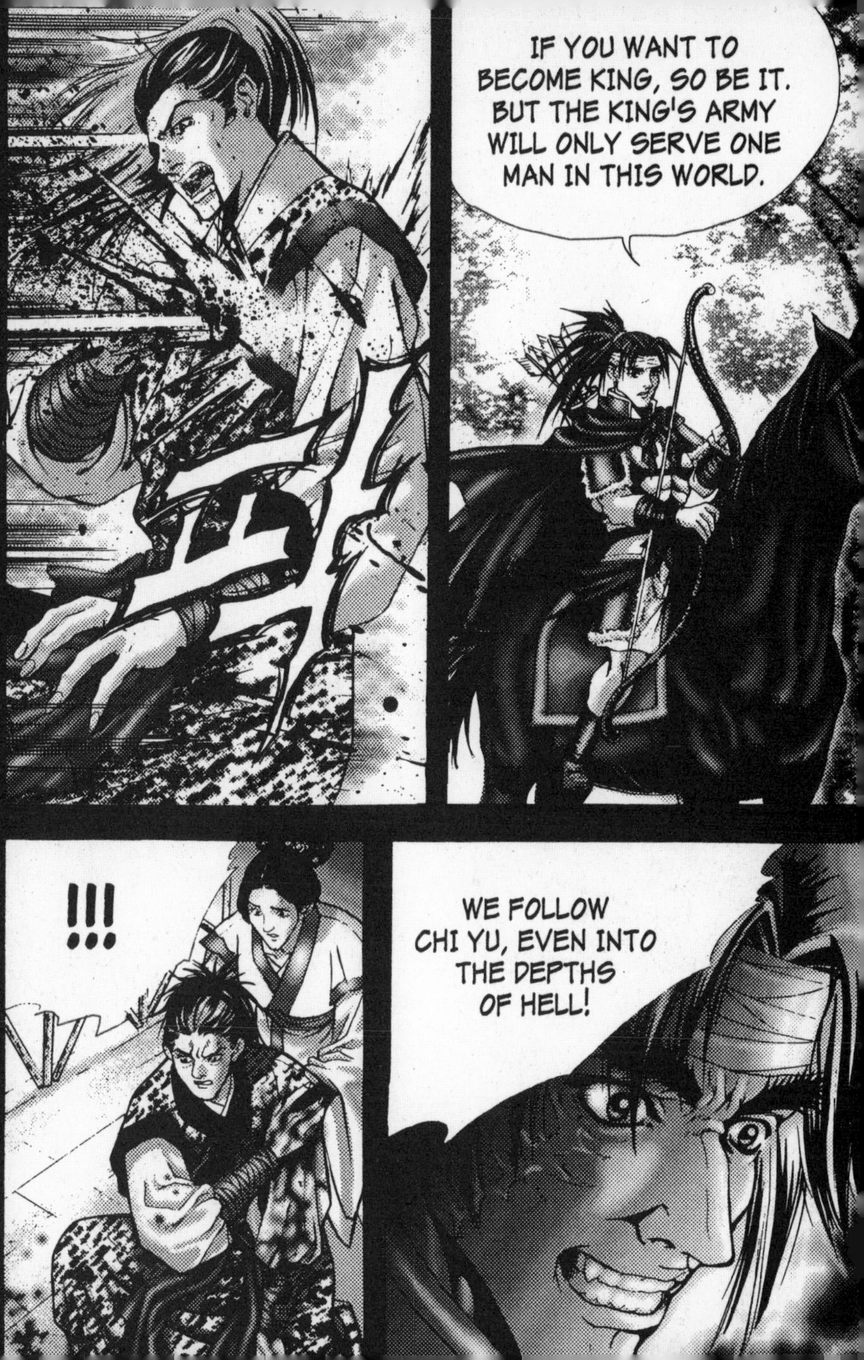
IF YOU WANT TO BECOME KING, SO BE IT. BUT THE KING'S ARMY WILL ONLY SERVE ONE MAN IN THIS WORLD.
!!!
WE FOLLOW CHI YU, EVEN INTO THE DEPTHS OF HELL!

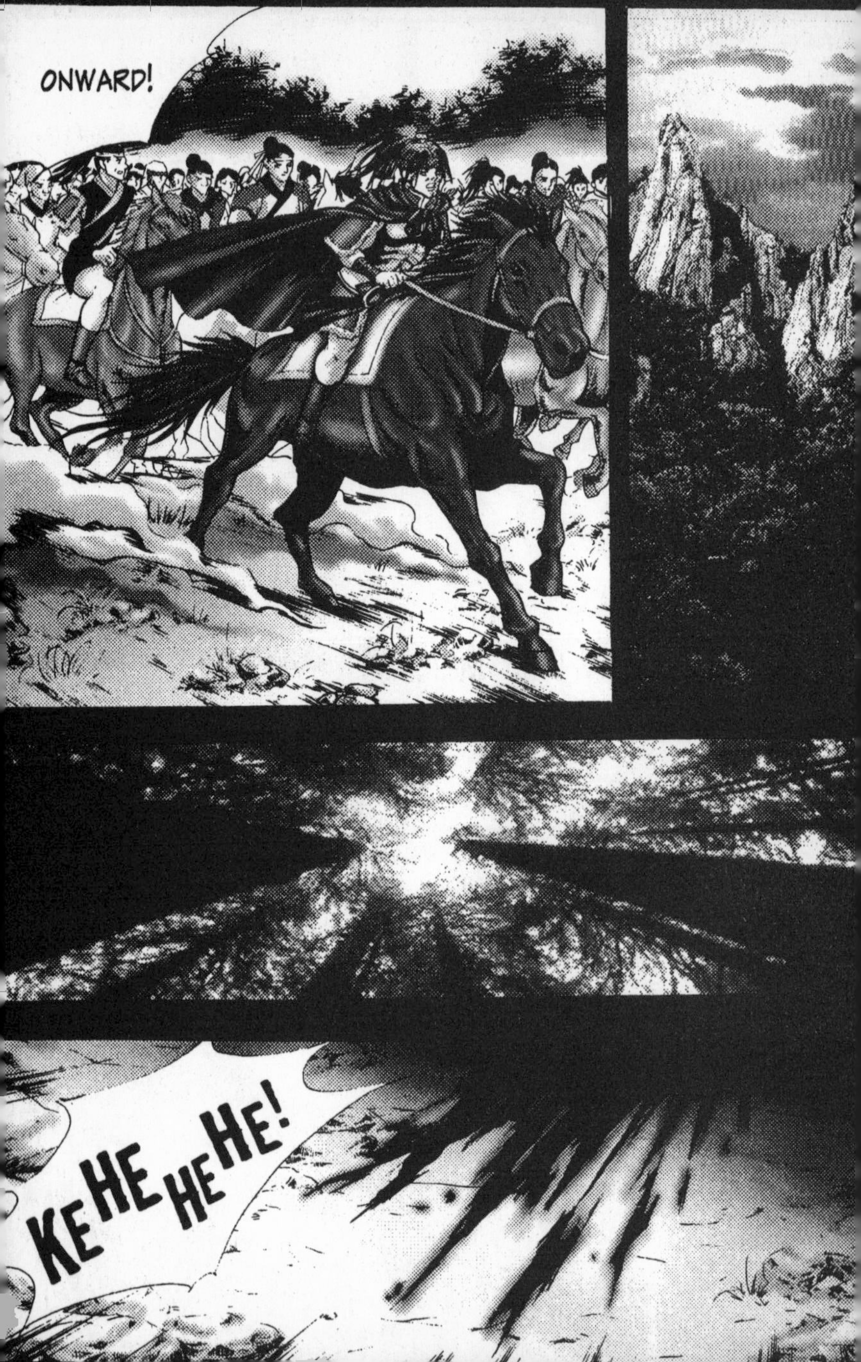
ONWARD!
KE HE HE HE!

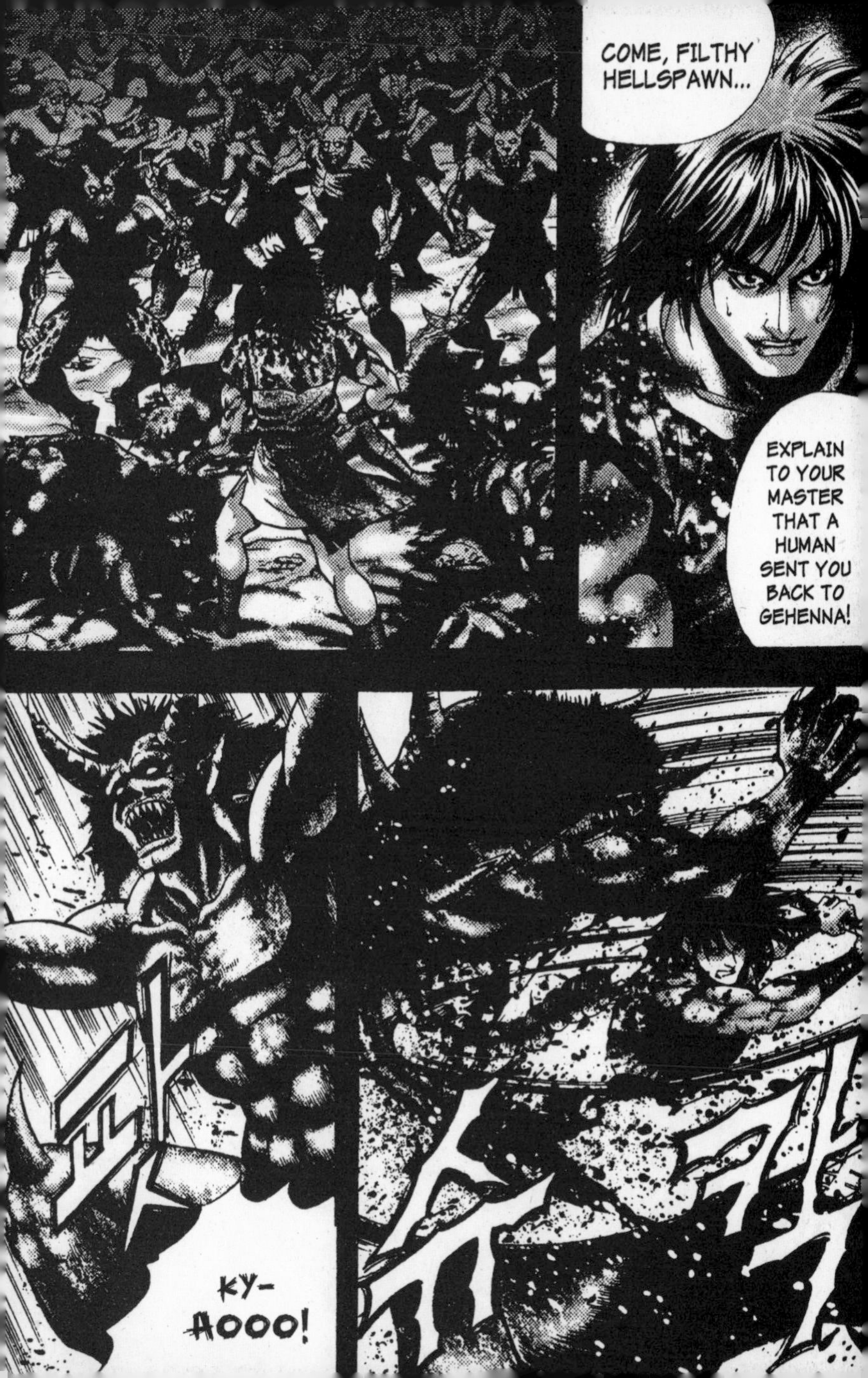
COME, FILTHY HELLSPAWN...
EXPLAIN TO YOUR MASTER THAT A HUMAN SENT YOU BACK TO GEHENNA!
KY-AOOO!

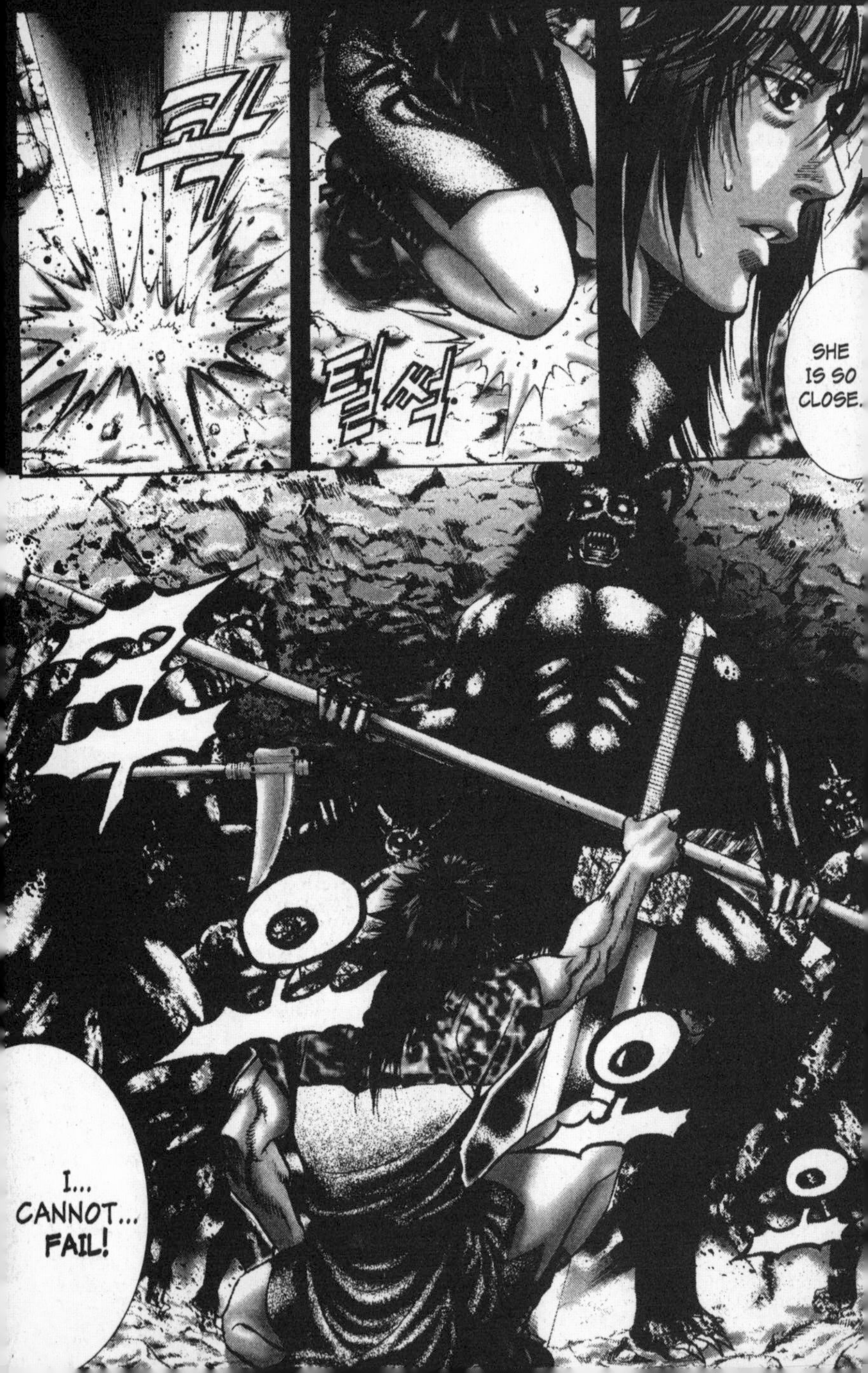
콱
털썩
SHE IS SO CLOSE.
I... CANNOT... FAIL!

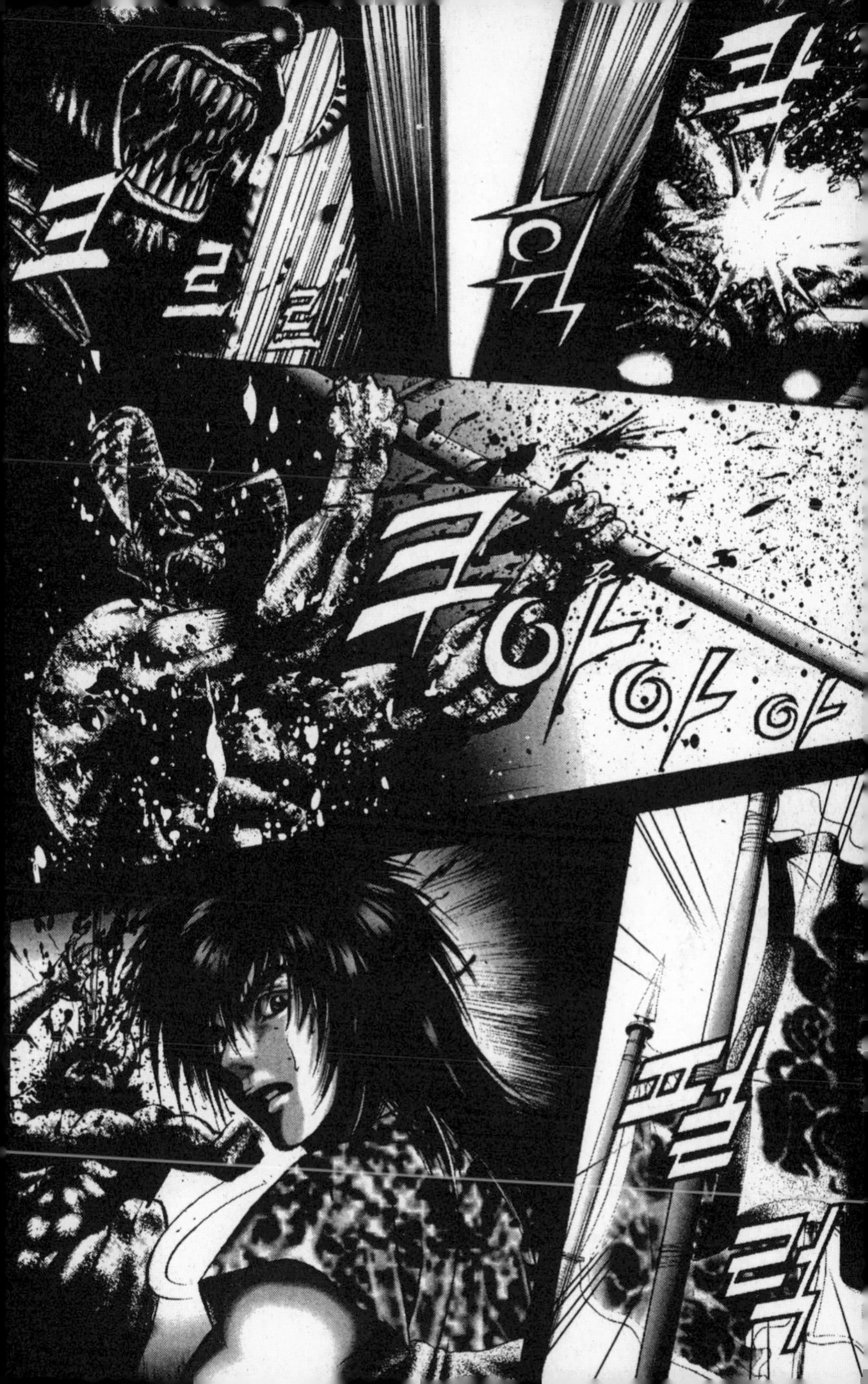
크르르
크아아아

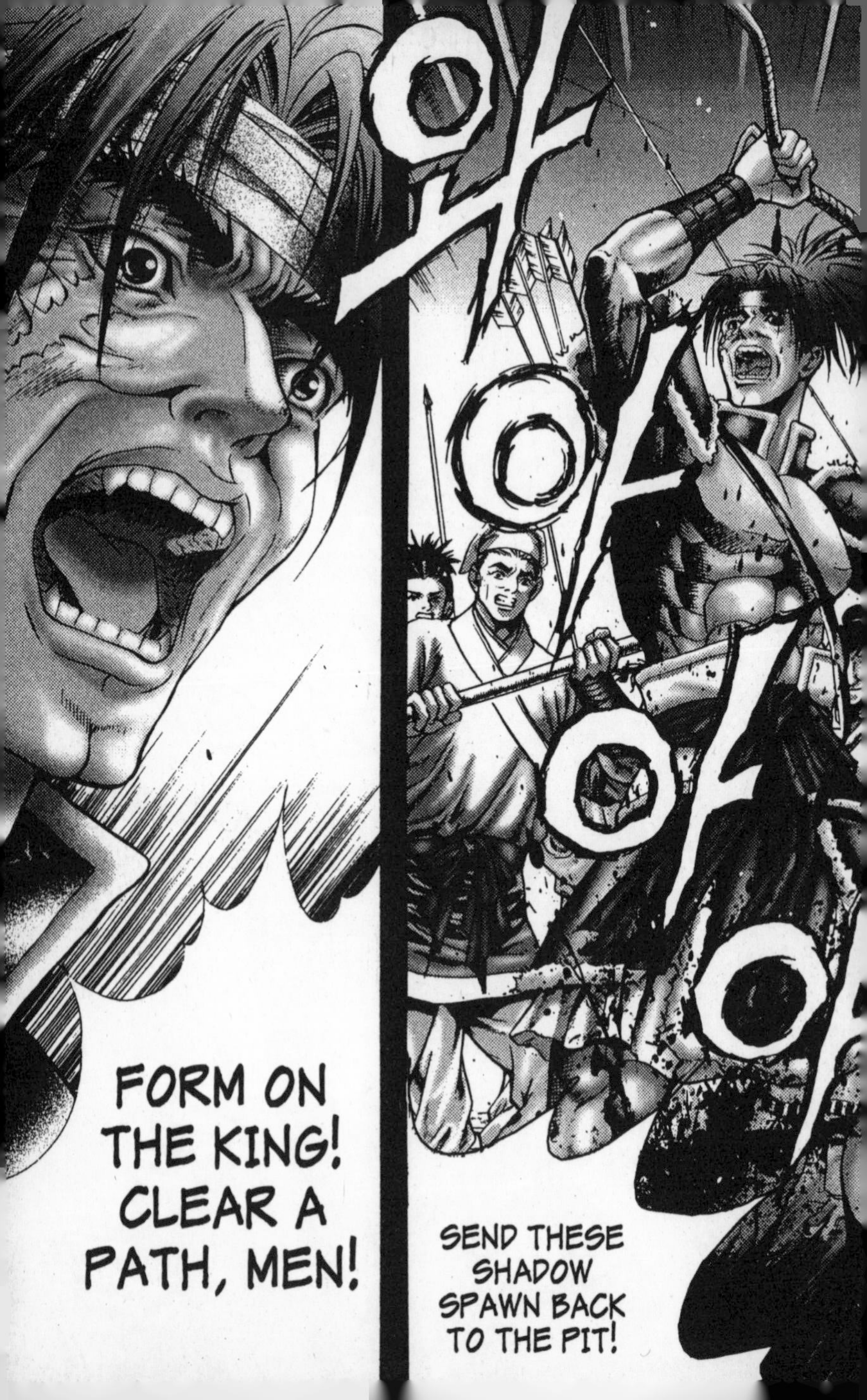
SEND THESE SHADOW SPAWN BACK TO THE PIT!
FORM ON THE KING! CLEAR A PATH, MEN!

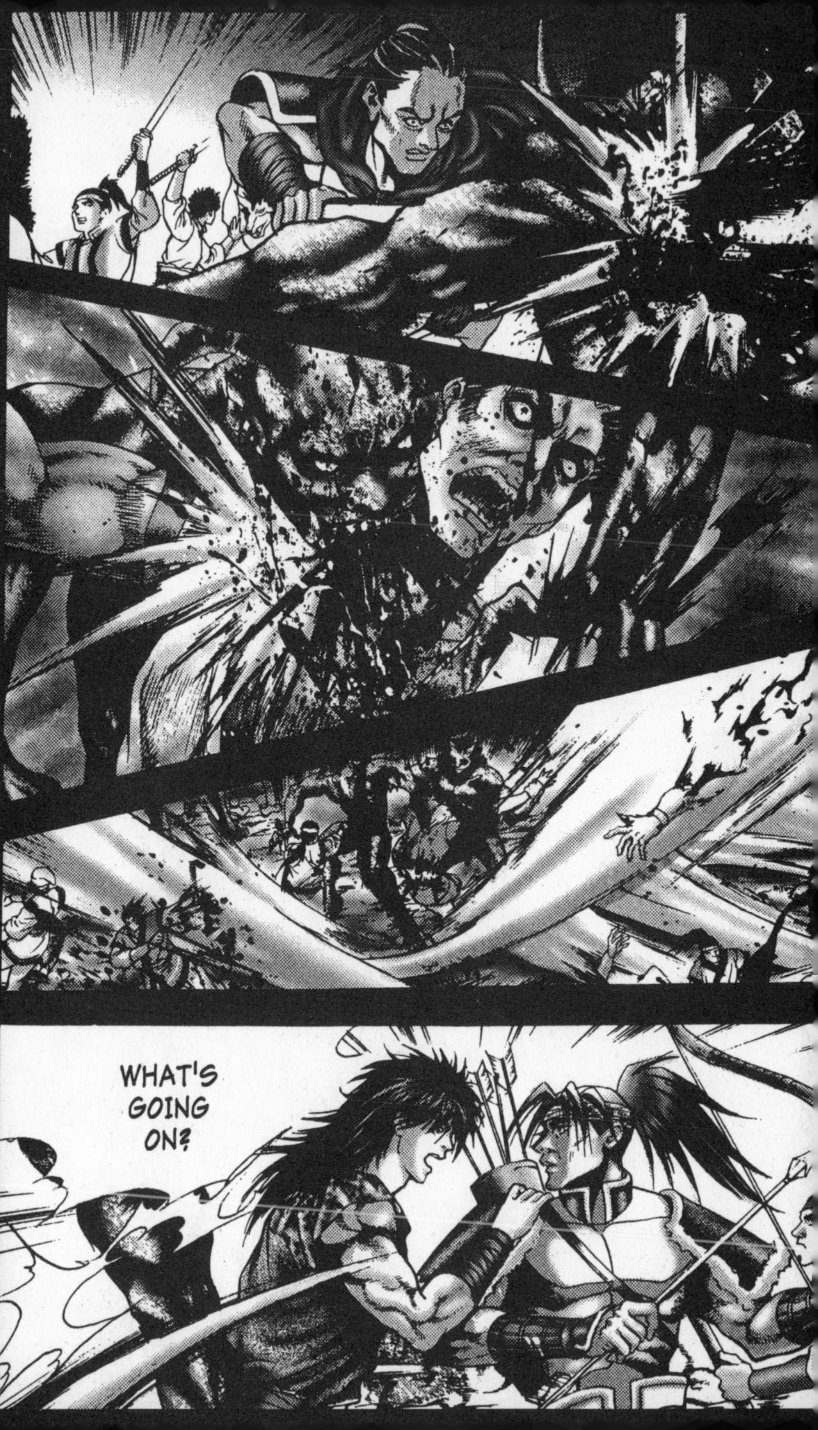
WHAT'S GOING ON?

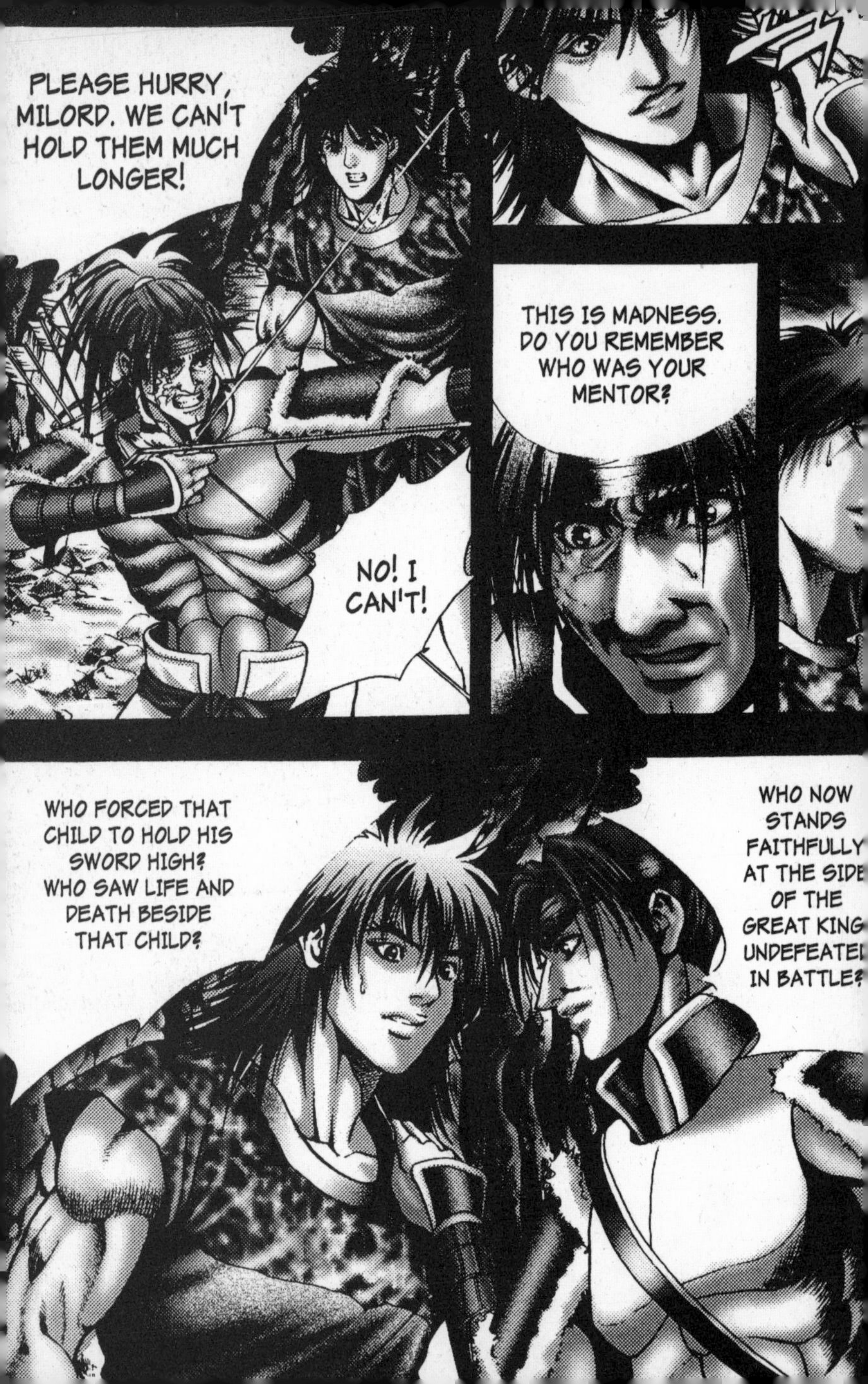
PLEASE HURRY, MILORD. WE CAN'T HOLD THEM MUCH LONGER!
NO! I CAN'T!
THIS IS MADNESS. DO YOU REMEMBER WHO WAS YOUR MENTOR?
WHO FORCED THAT CHILD TO HOLD HIS SWORD HIGH? WHO SAW LIFE AND DEATH BESIDE THAT CHILD?
WHO NOW STANDS FAITHFULLY AT THE SIDE OF THE GREAT KING UNDEFEATED IN BATTLE?

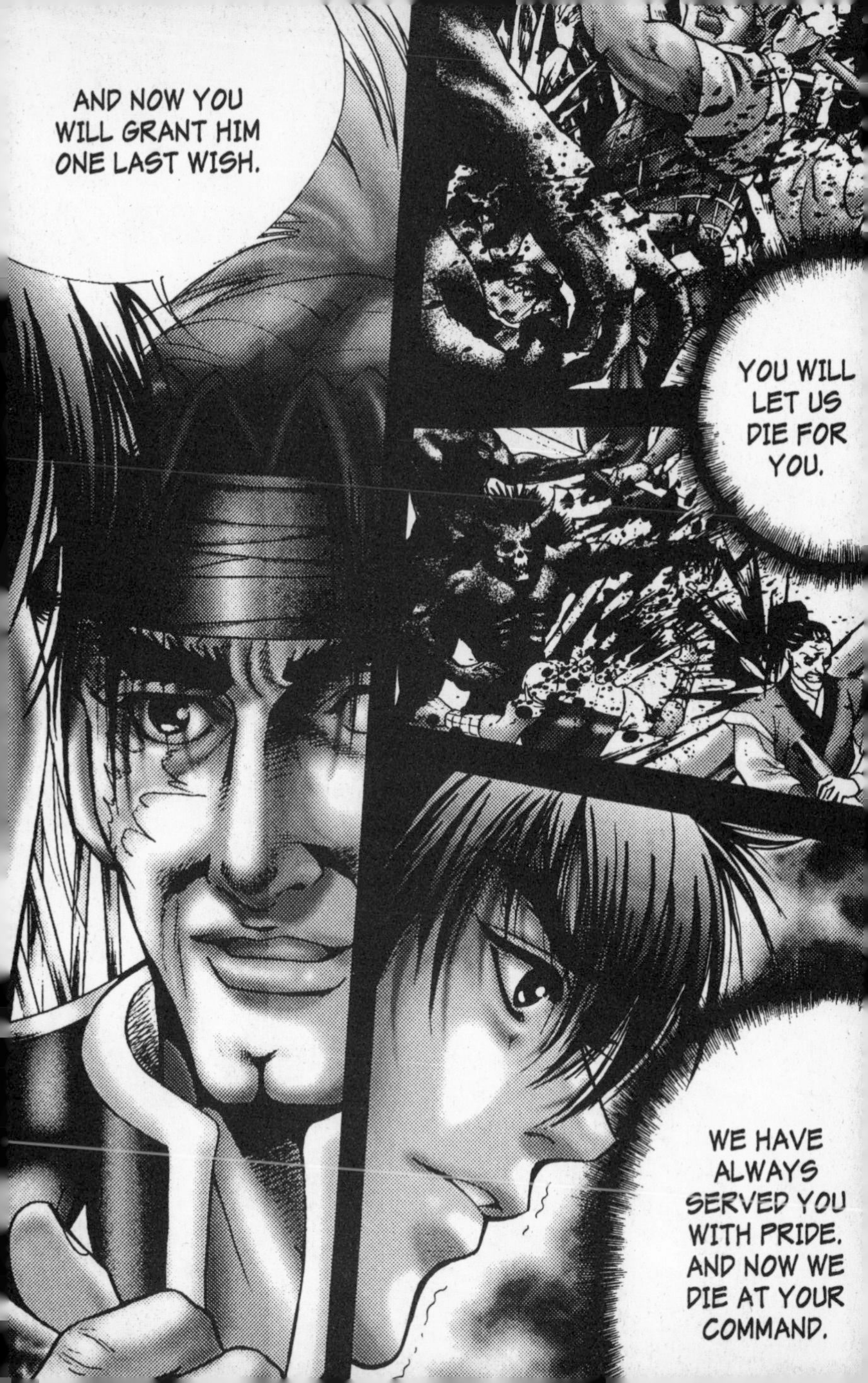
YOU WILL LET US DIE FOR YOU.
AND NOW YOU WILL GRANT HIM ONE LAST WISH.
WE HAVE ALWAYS SERVED YOU WITH PRIDE. AND NOW WE DIE AT YOUR COMMAND.

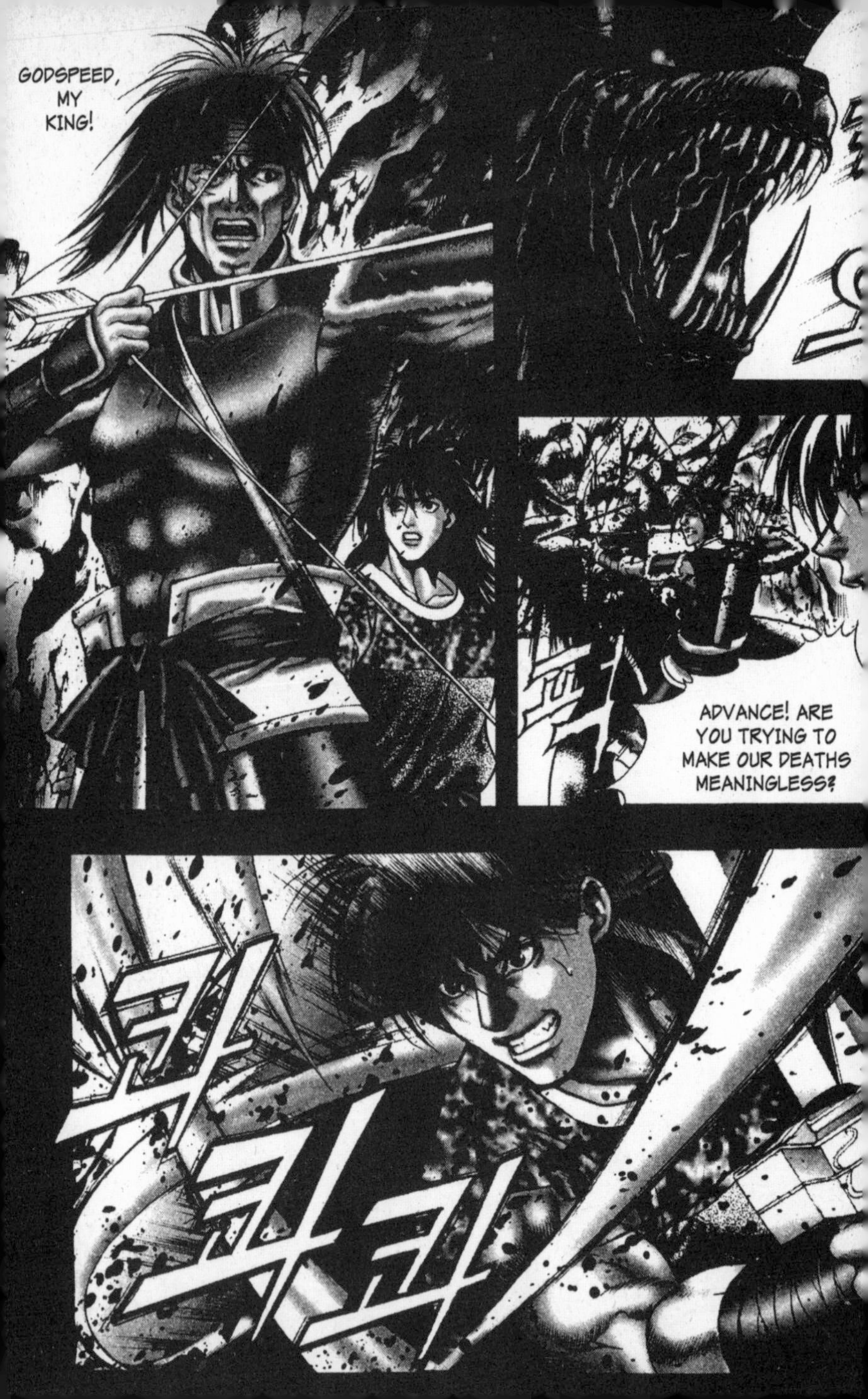
GODSPEED, MY KING!
ADVANCE! ARE YOU TRYING TO MAKE OUR DEATHS MEANINGLESS?

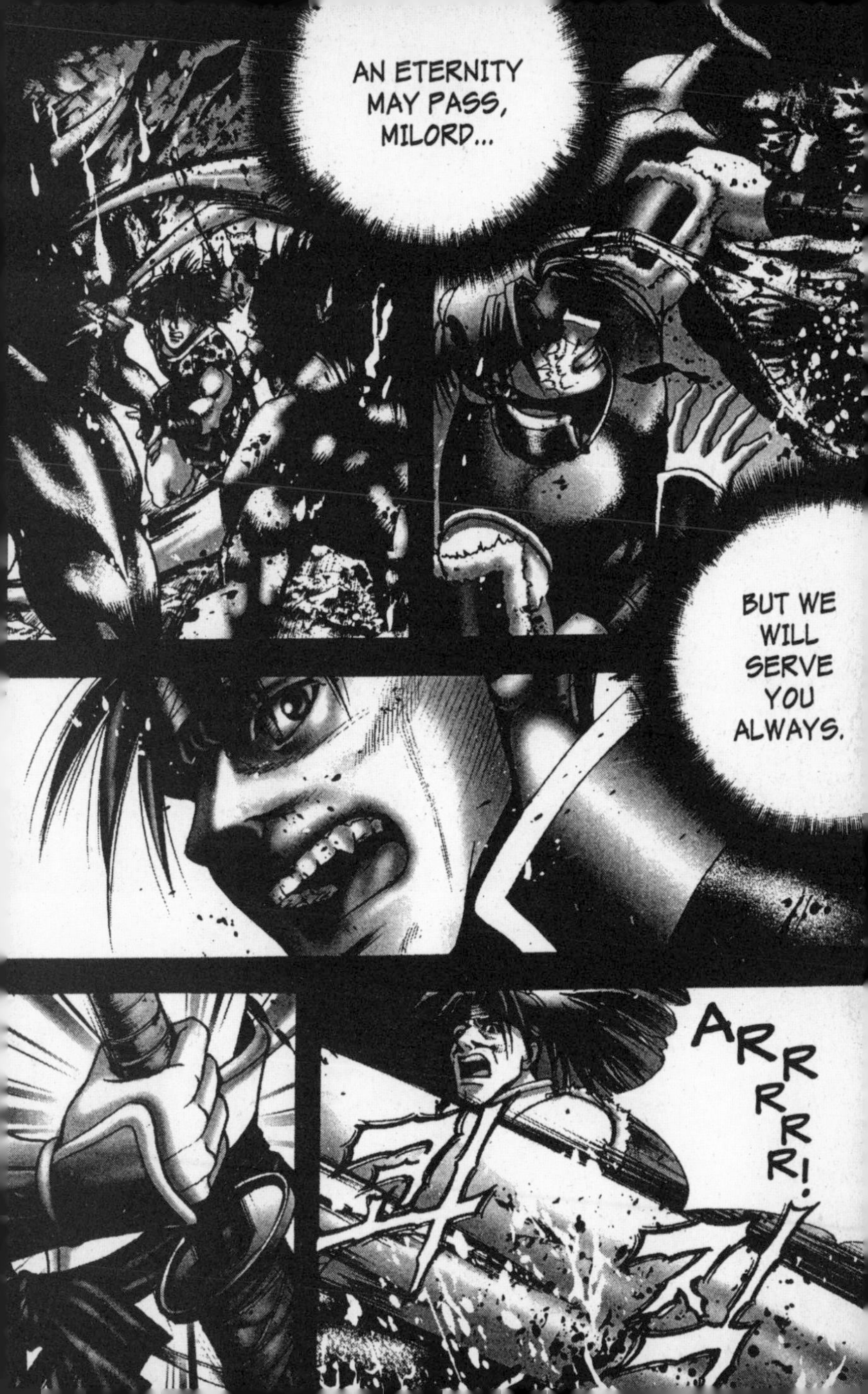
AN ETERNITY MAY PASS, MILORD...
BUT WE WILL SERVE YOU ALWAYS.
ARRRRR!

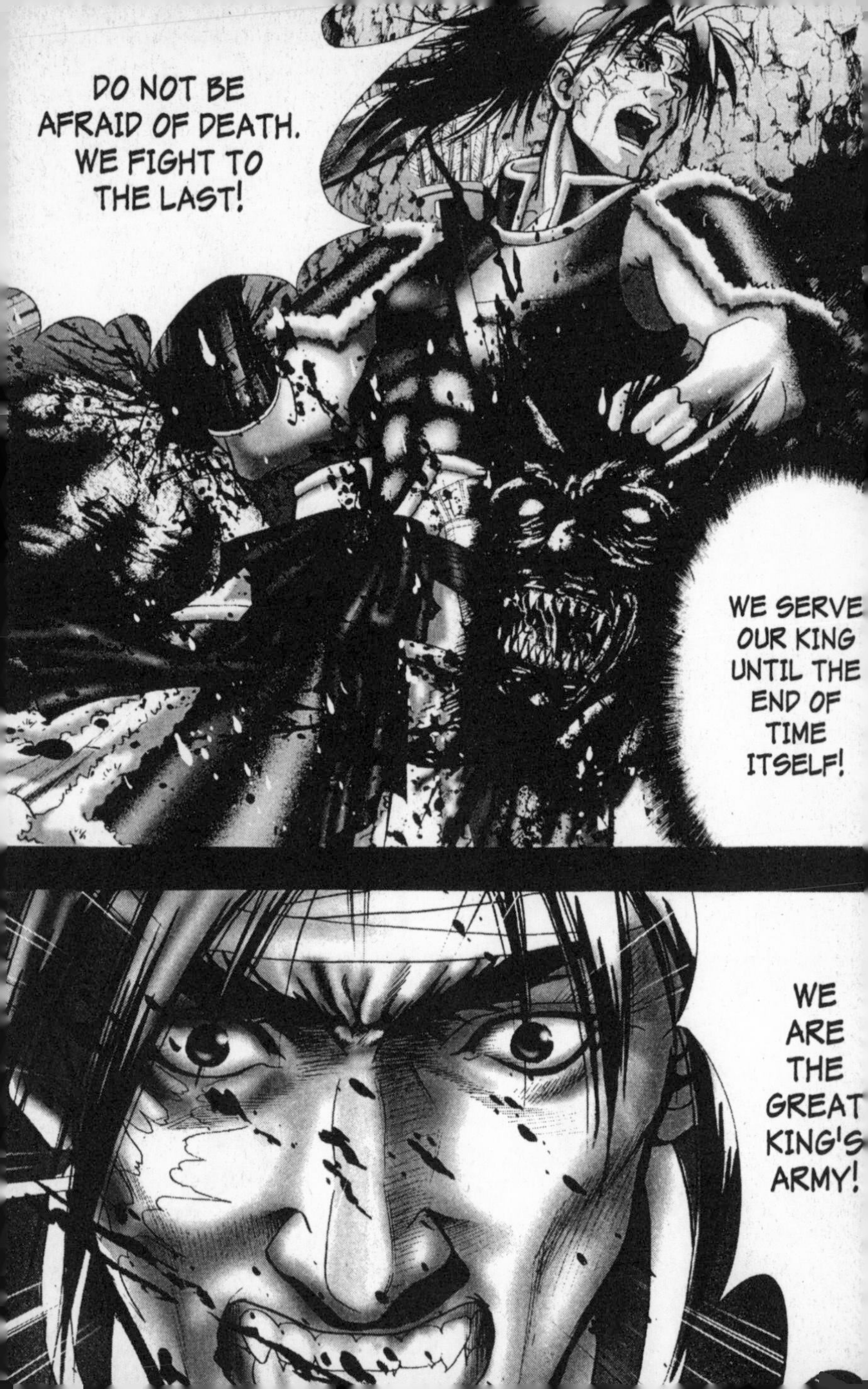
DO NOT BE AFRAID OF DEATH. WE FIGHT TO THE LAST!
WE SERVE OUR KING UNTIL THE END OF TIME ITSELF!
WE ARE THE GREAT KING'S ARMY!

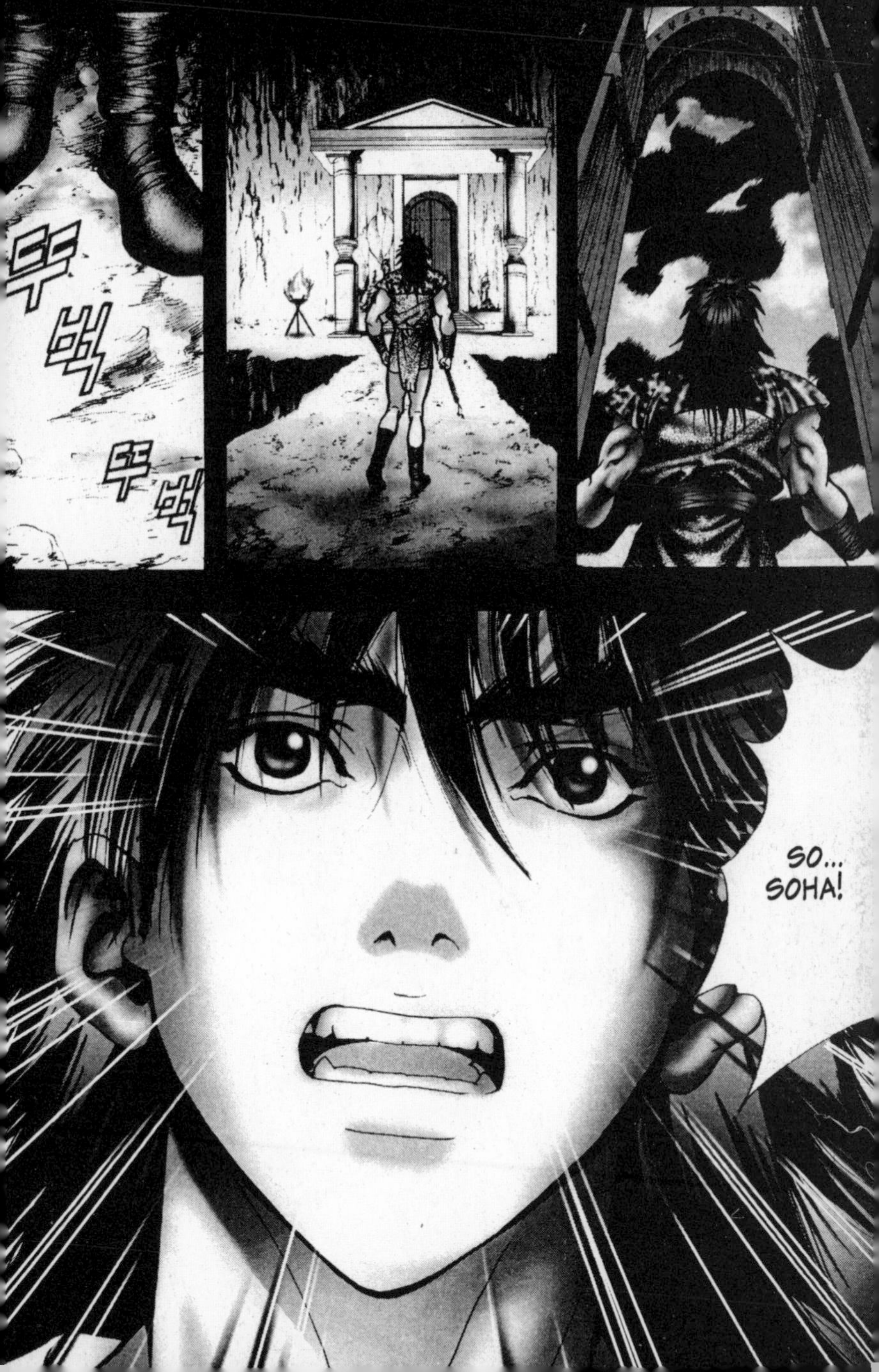

뚜벅
뚜벅
SO...
SOHA!

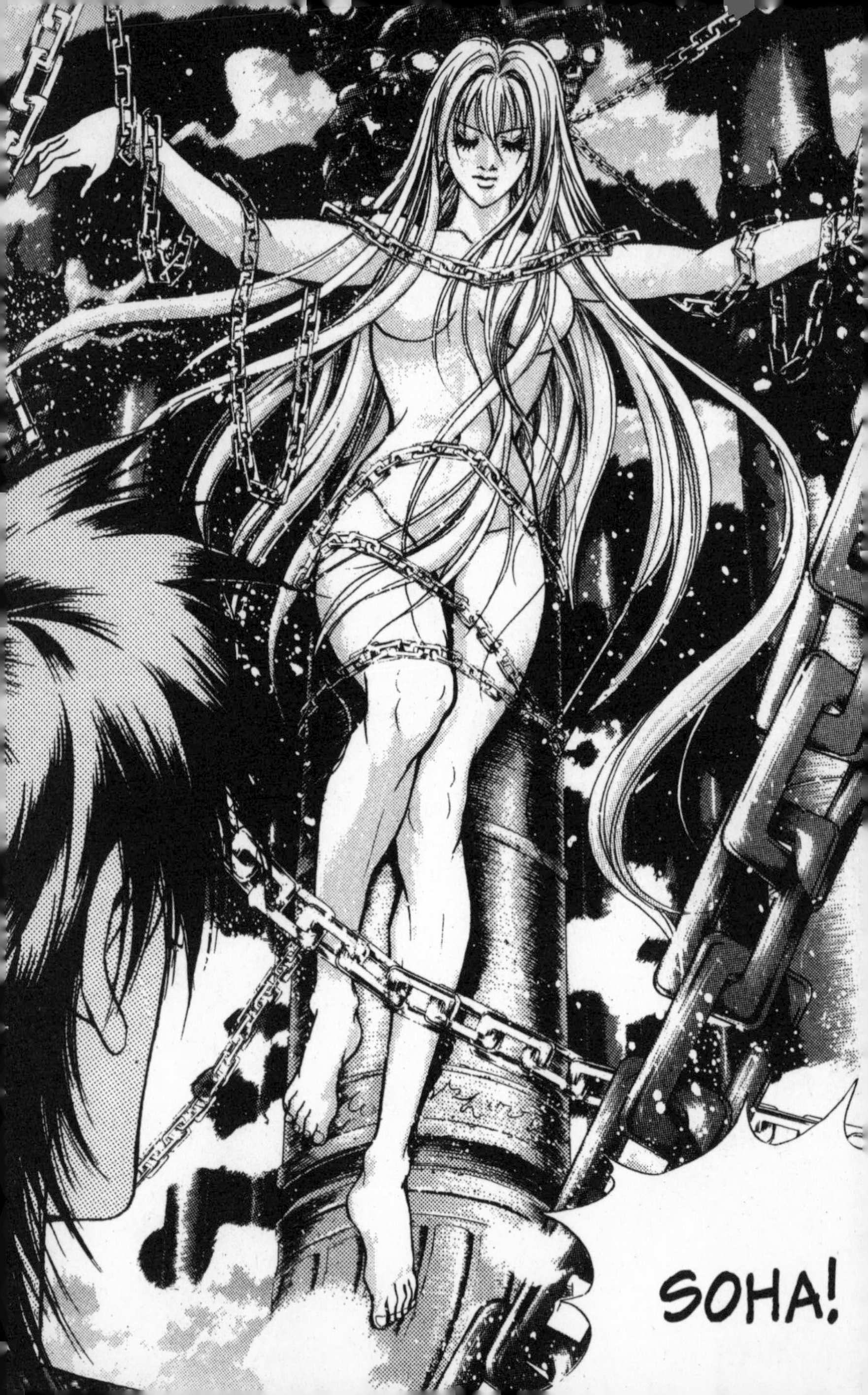
SOHA!

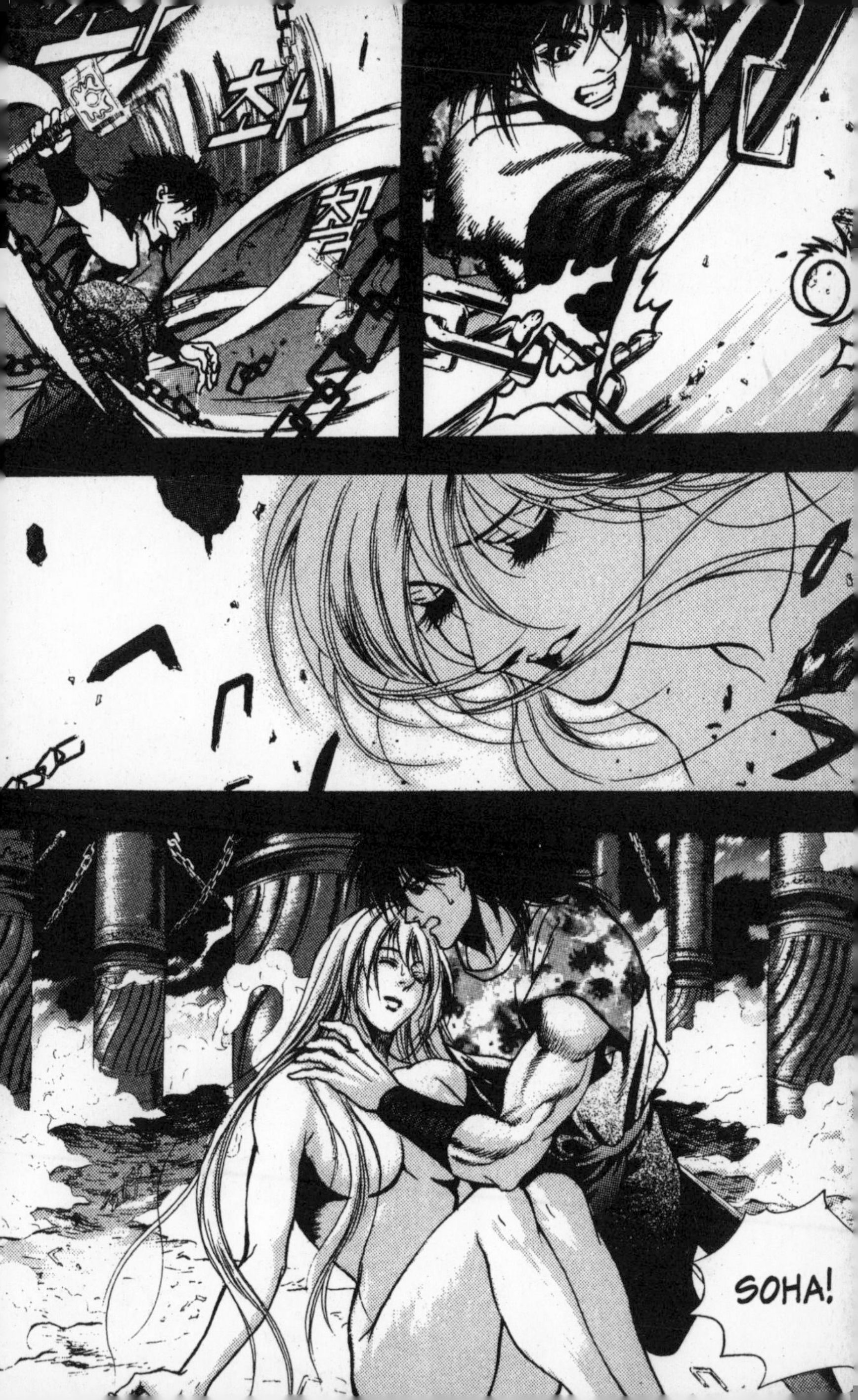

SOHA!

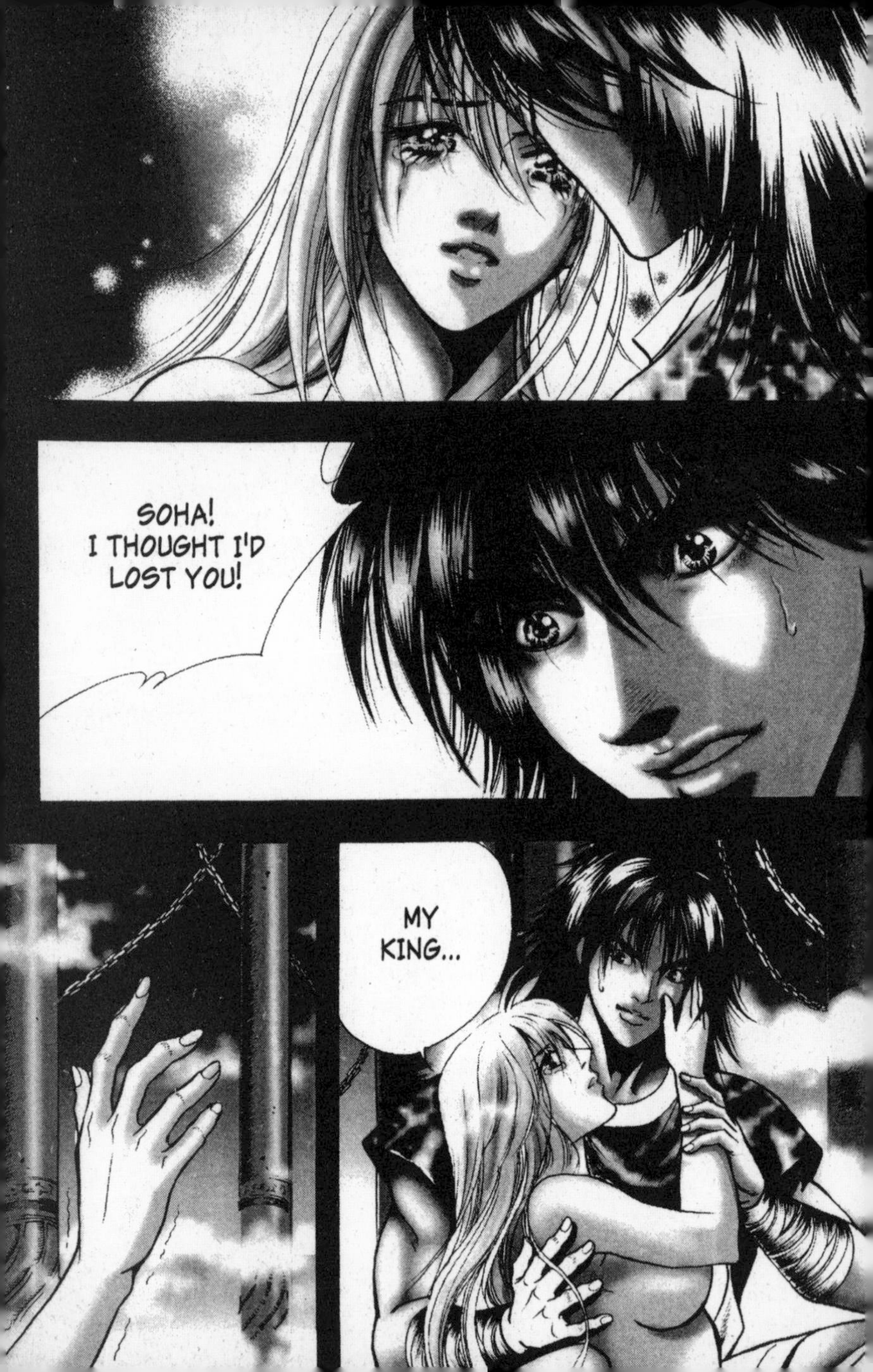
SOHA! I THOUGHT I'D LOST YOU!
MY KING...

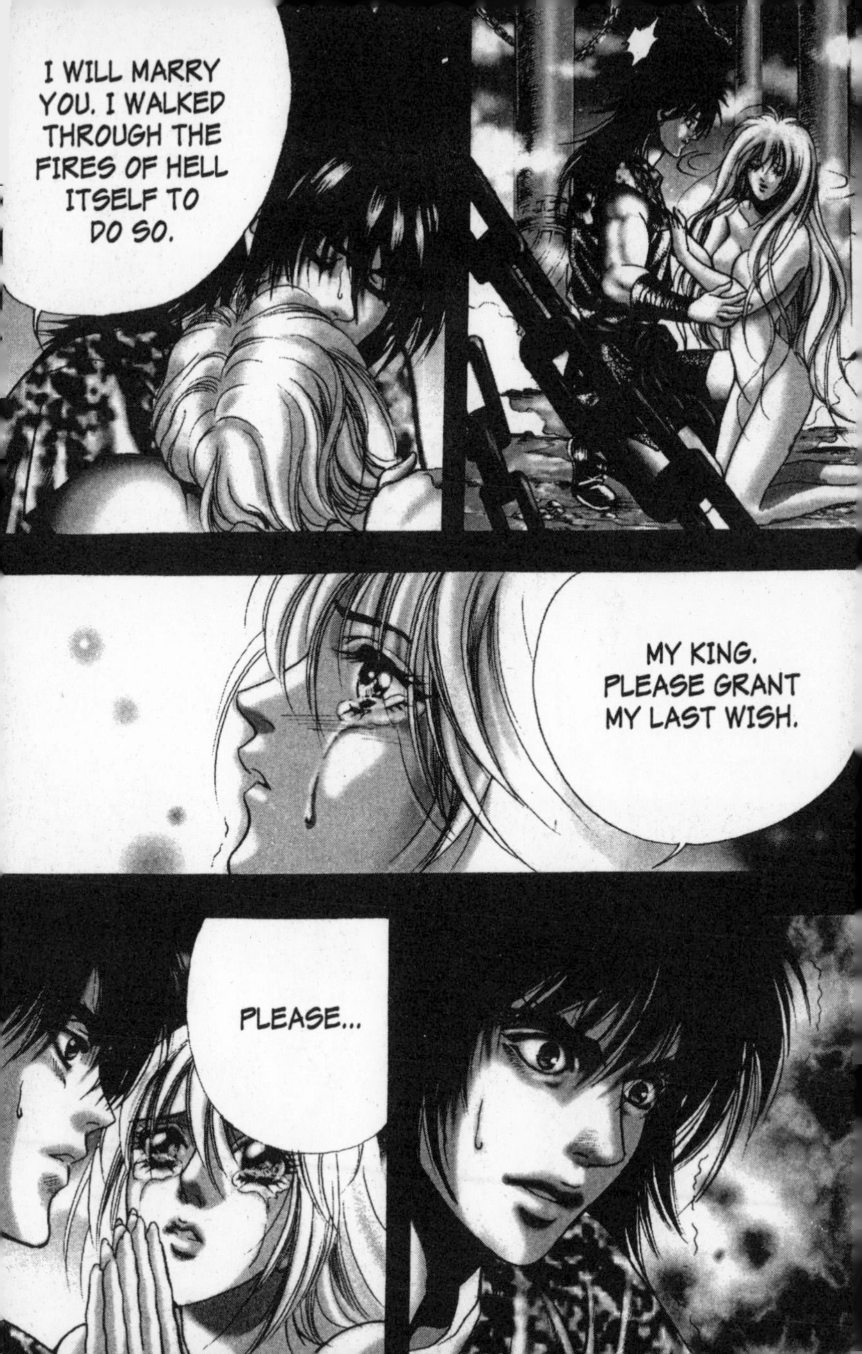
I WILL MARRY YOU. I WALKED THROUGH THE FIRES OF HELL ITSELF TO DO SO.
MY KING. PLEASE GRANT MY LAST WISH.
PLEASE...

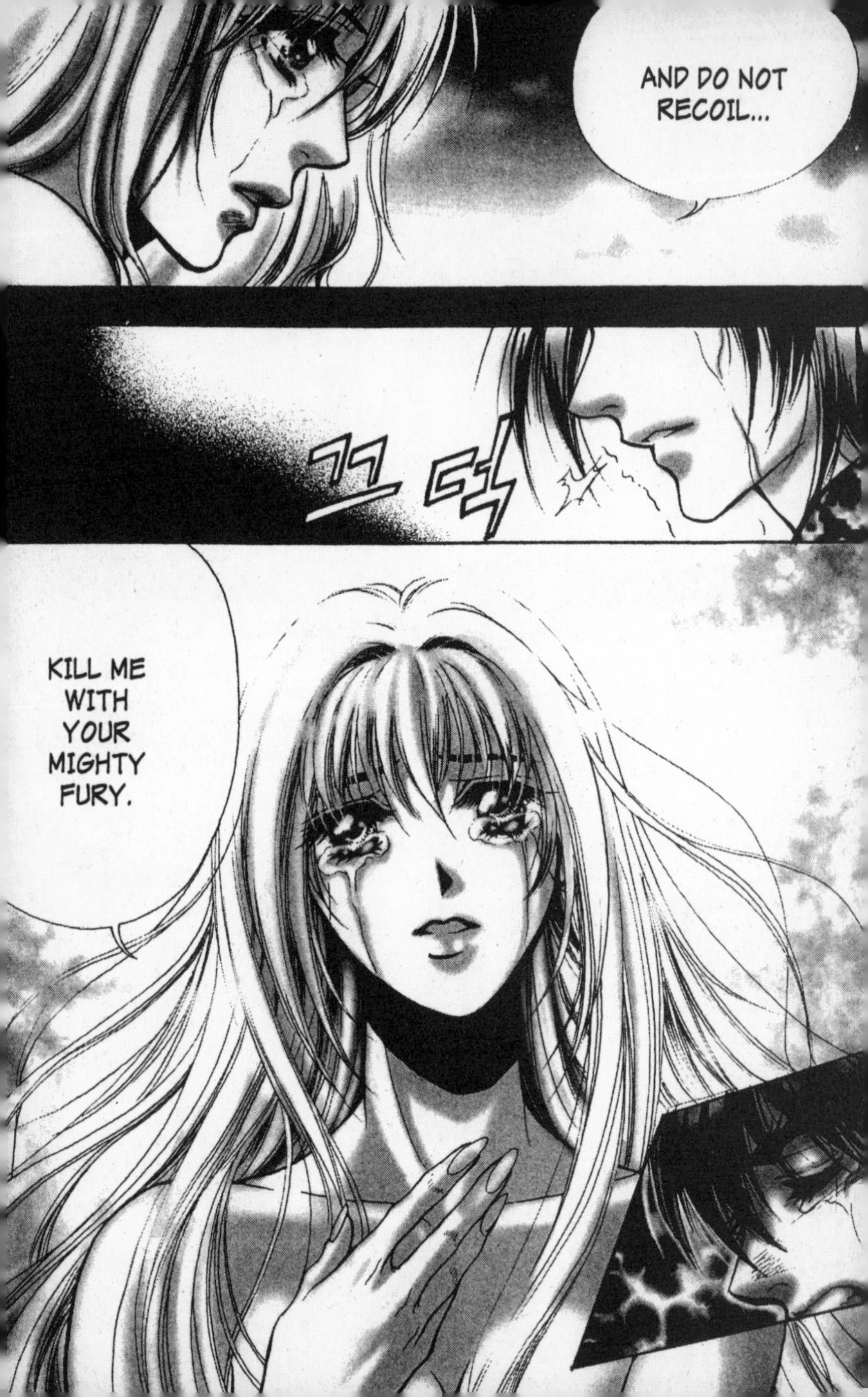
AND DO NOT RECOIL...
KILL ME WITH YOUR MIGHTY FURY.

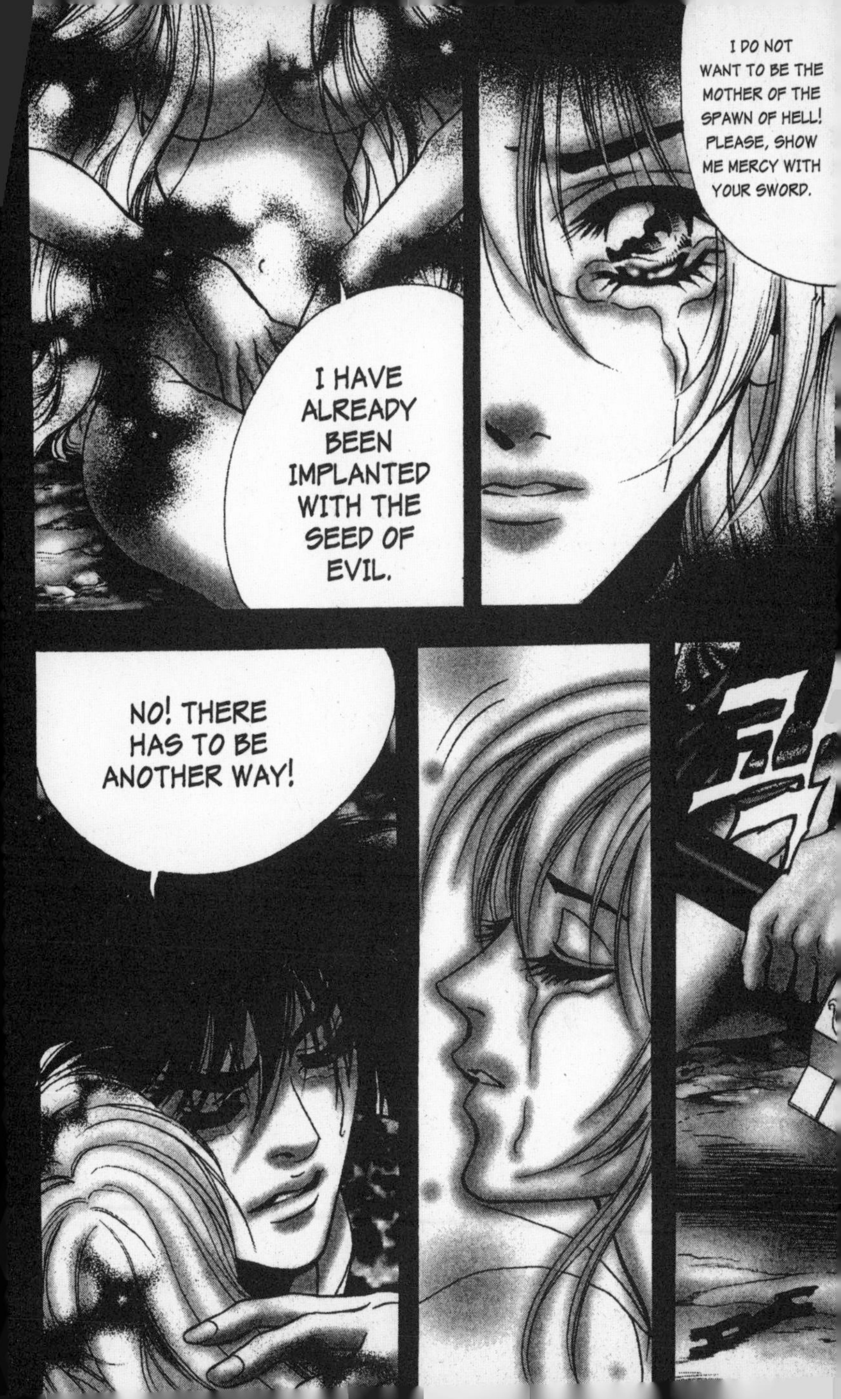
I DO NOT WANT TO BE THE MOTHER OF THE SPAWN OF HELL! PLEASE, SHOW ME MERCY WITH YOUR SWORD.
I HAVE ALREADY BEEN IMPLANTED WITH THE SEED OF EVIL.
NO! THERE HAS TO BE ANOTHER WAY!

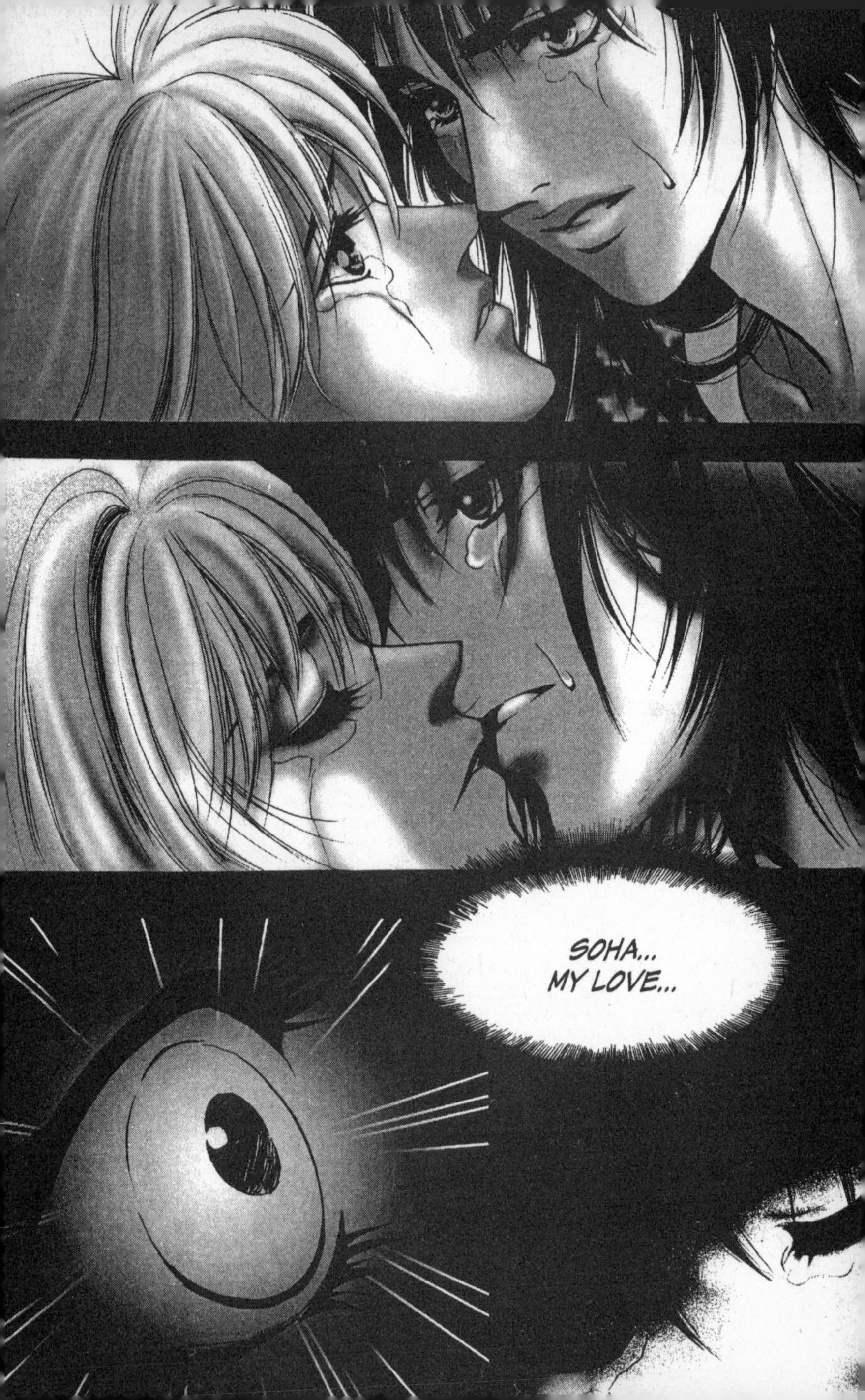
SOHA...
MY LOVE...

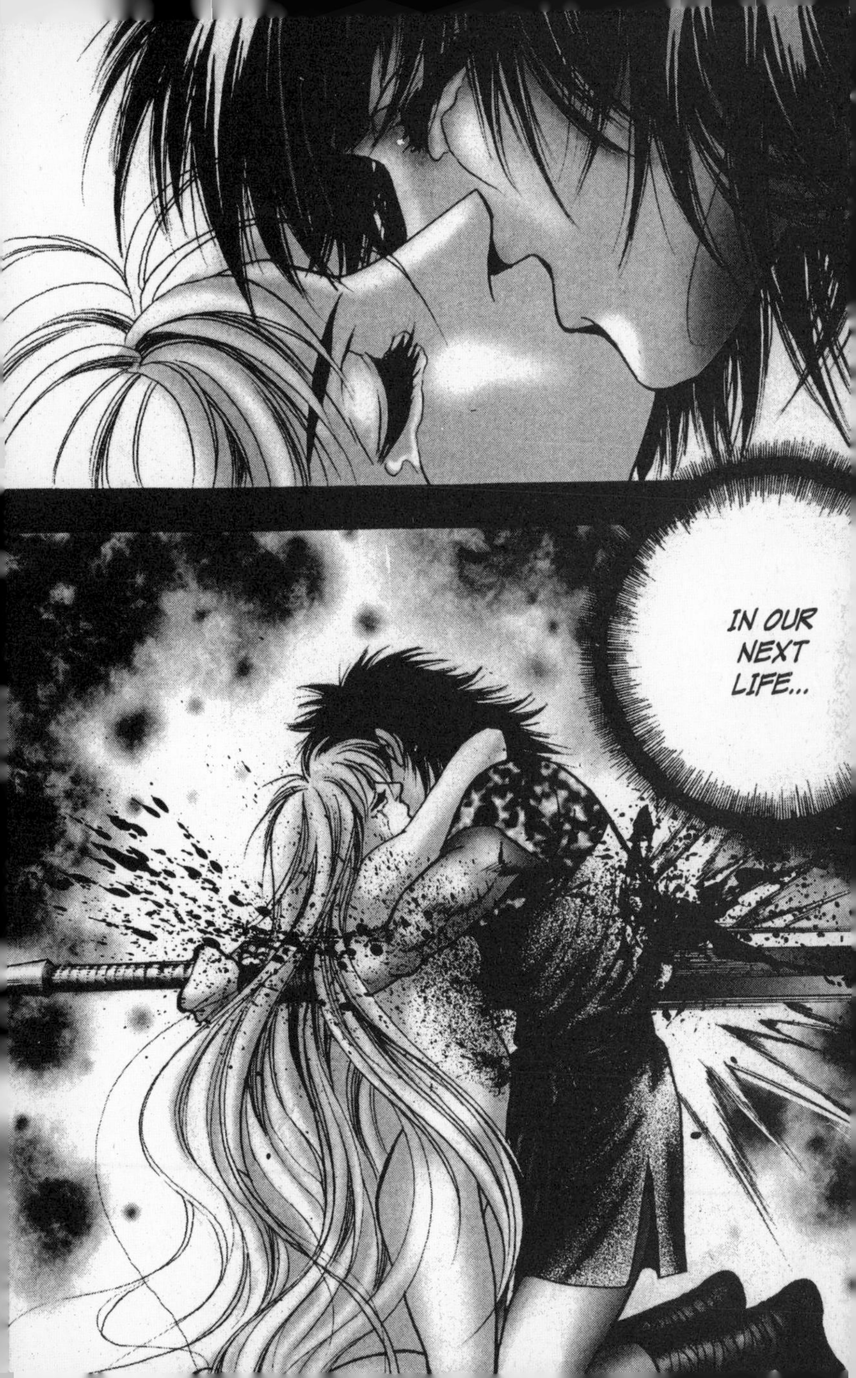
IN OUR NEXT LIFE...

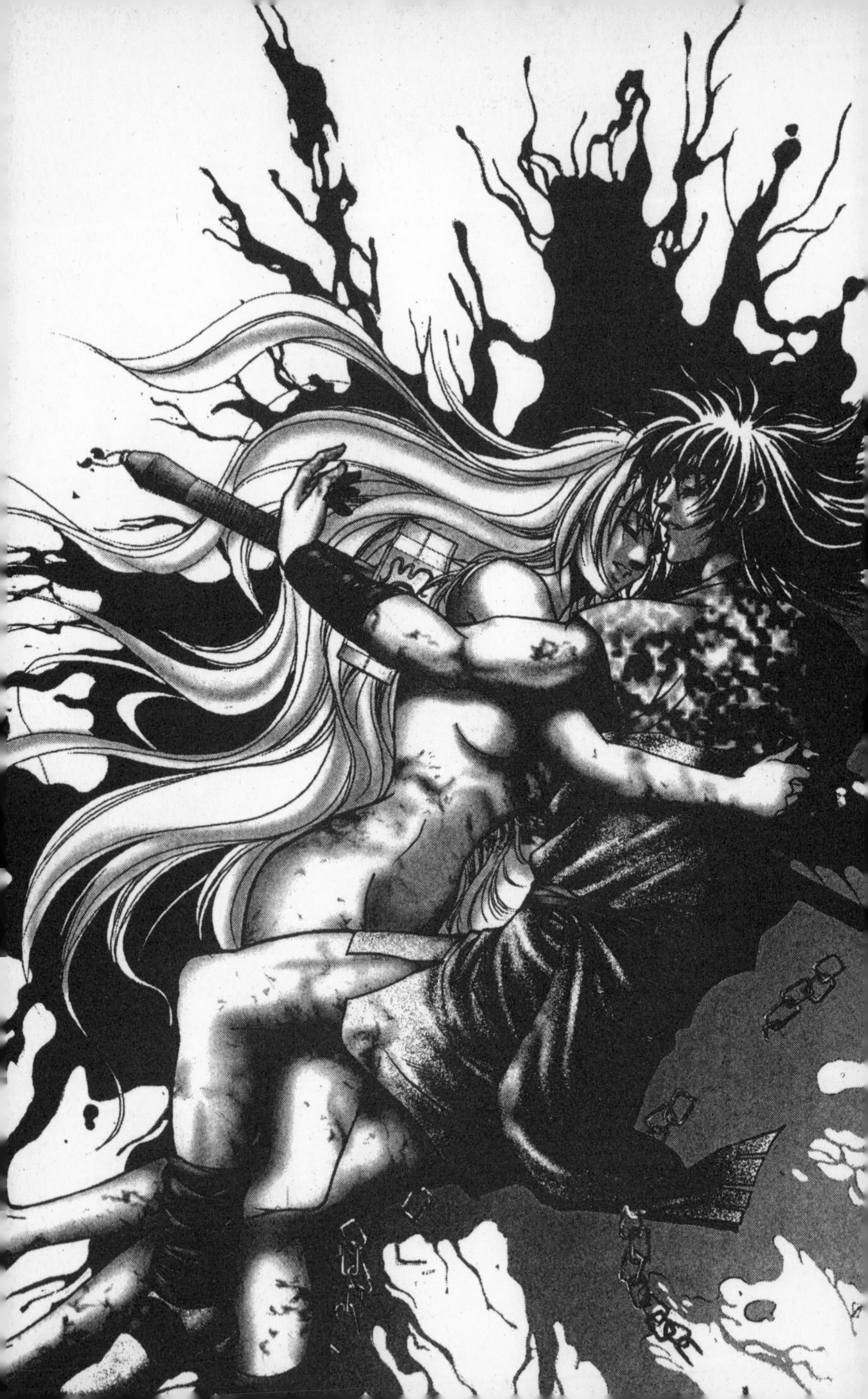

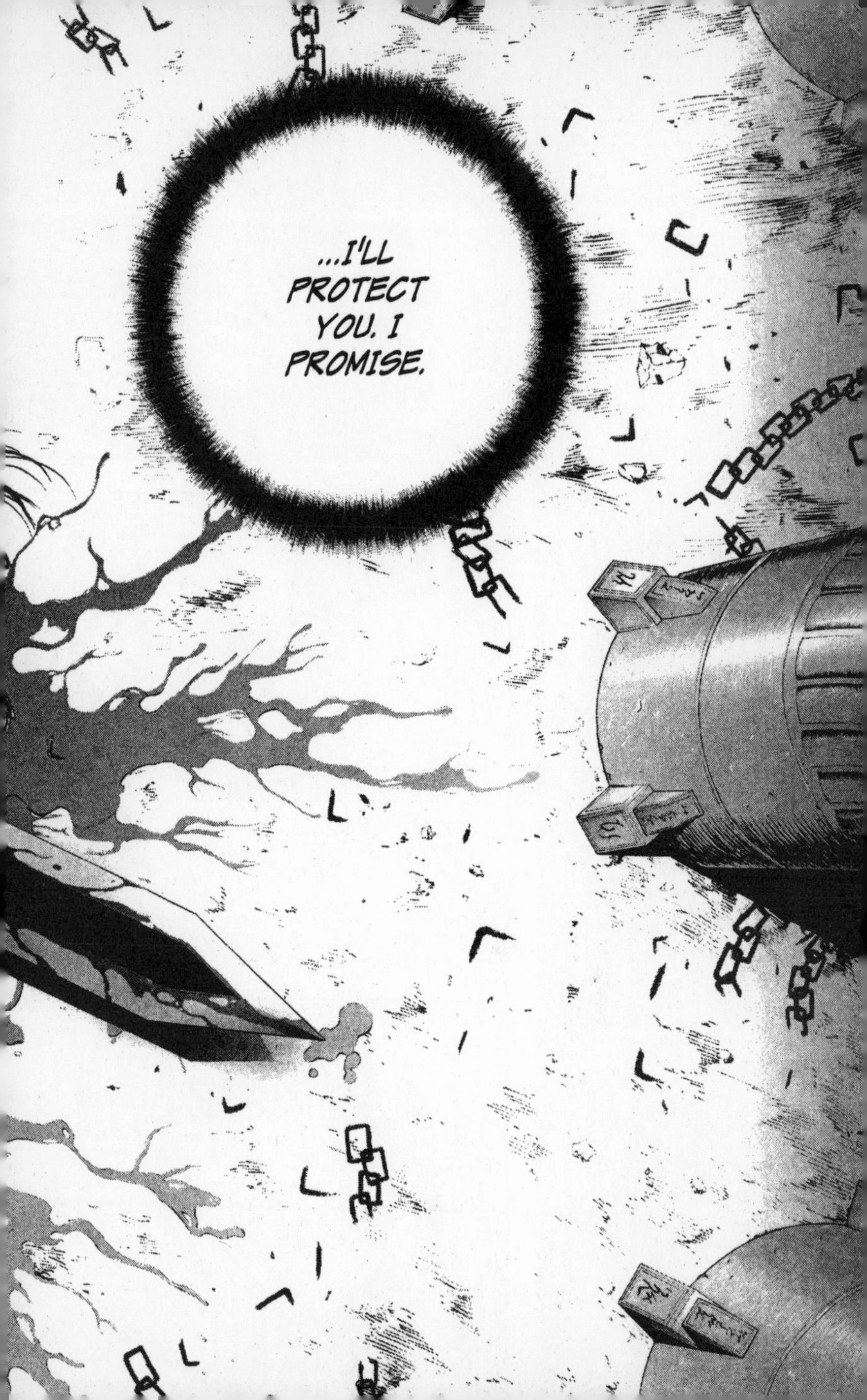
...I'LL PROTECT YOU. I PROMISE.

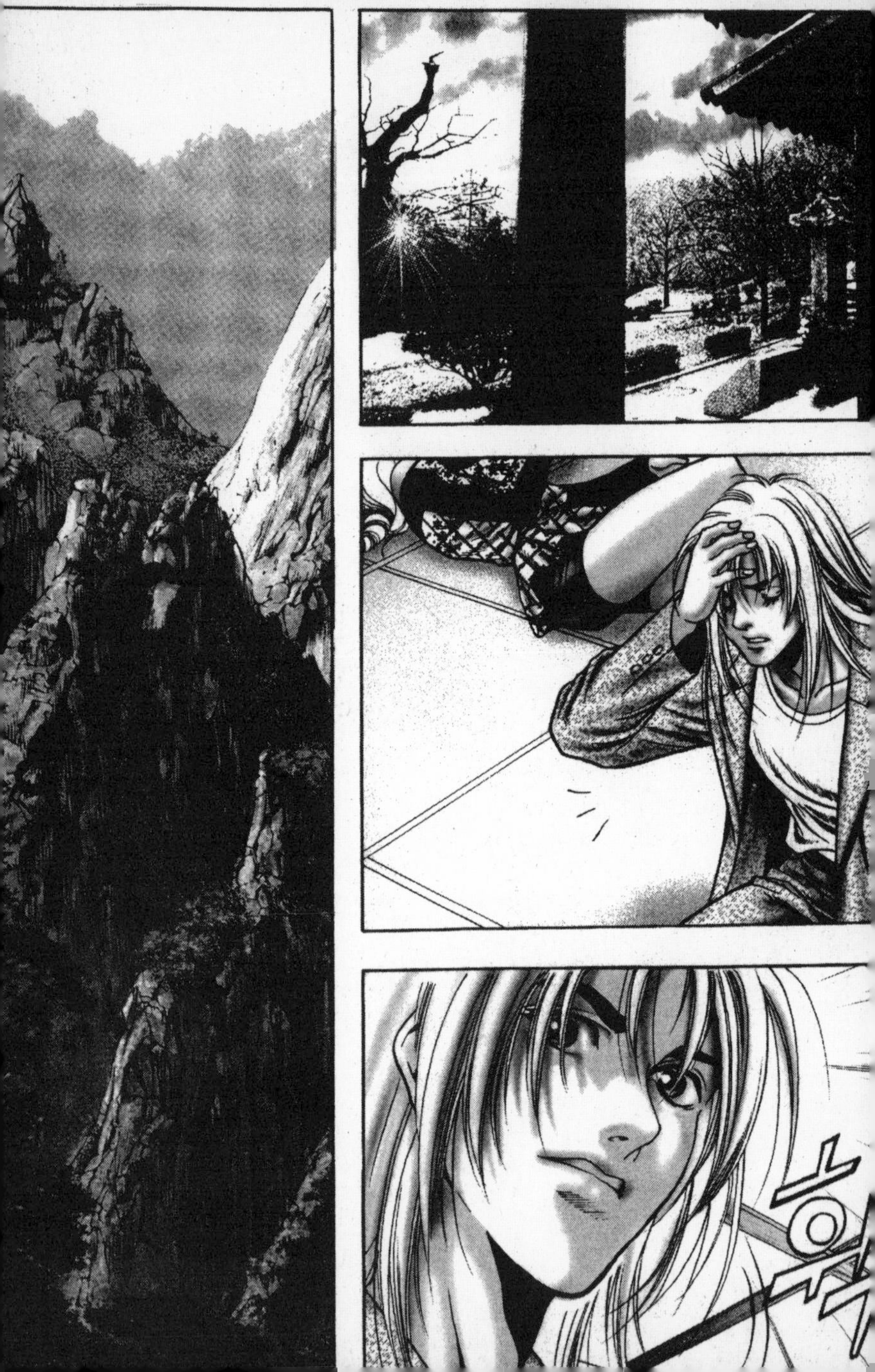

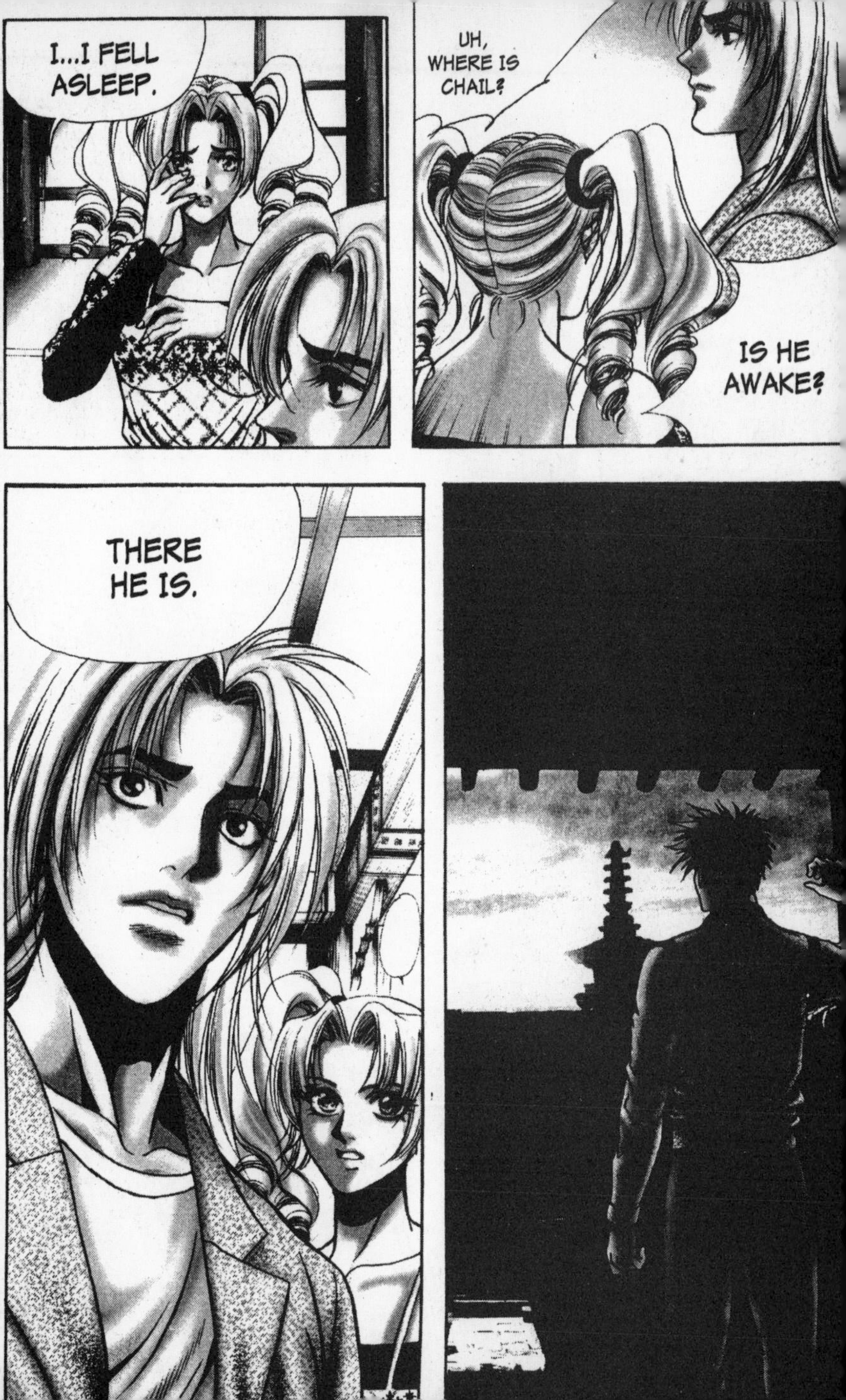
I...I FELL ASLEEP.
UH, WHERE IS CHAIL?
IS HE AWAKE?
THERE HE IS.

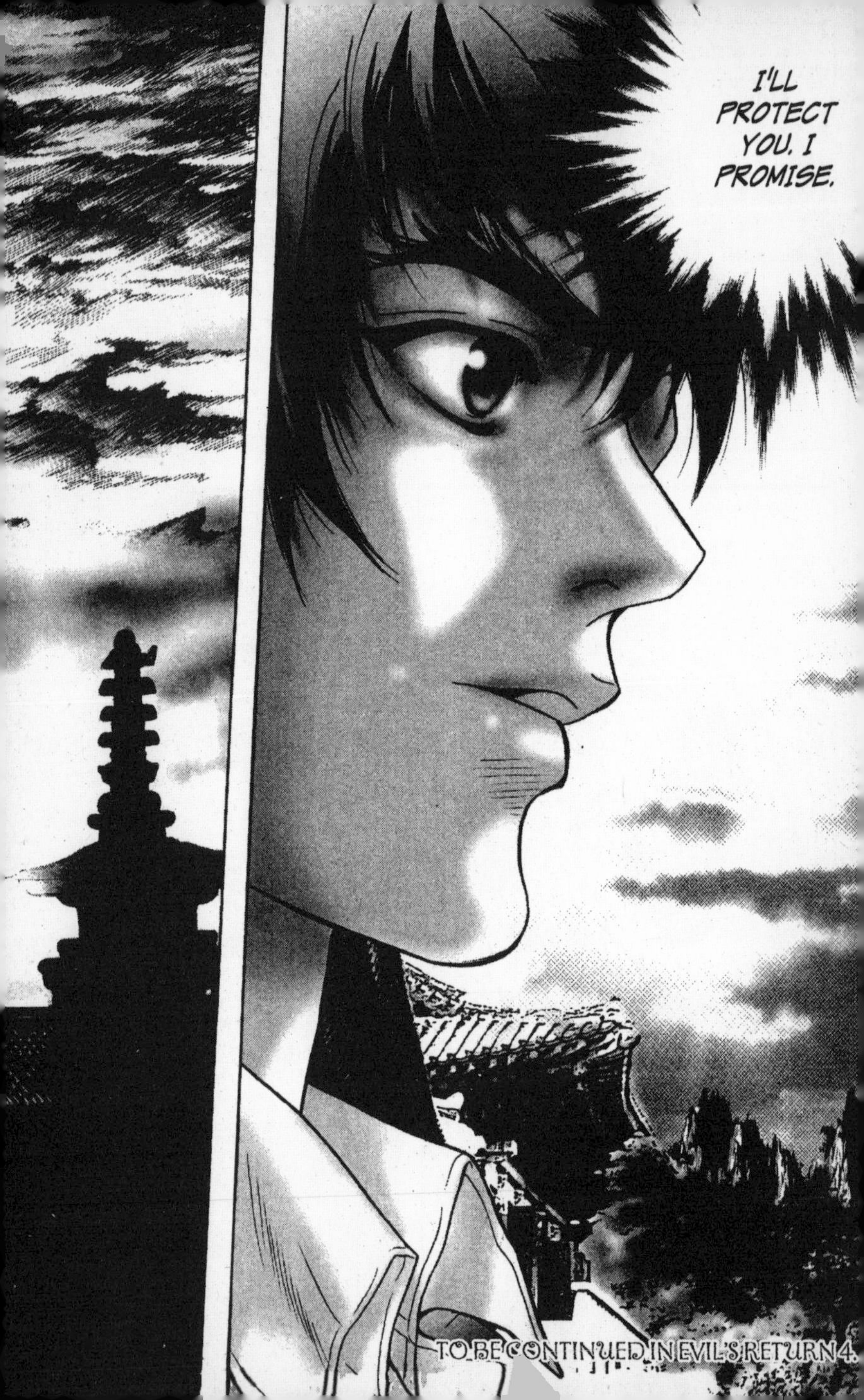
I'LL PROTECT YOU. I PROMISE.
TO BE CONTINUED IN EVIL'S RETURN 4.

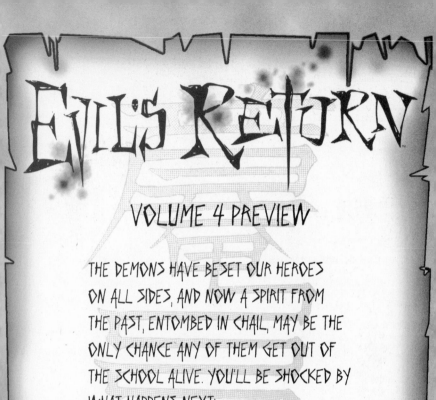

EVIL'S RETURN

VOLUME 4 PREVIEW

THE DEMONS HAVE BESET OUR HEROES ON ALL SIDES, AND NOW A SPIRIT FROM THE PAST, ENTOMBED IN CHALK, MAY BE THE ONLY CHANCE ANY OF THEM GET OUT OF THE SCHOOL ALIVE. YOU'LL BE SHOCKED BY WHAT HAPPENS NEXT!

THE NEXT VOLUME OF EVIL'S RETURN IS ON ITS WAY FROM KOREA AND WILL HIT AMERICAN SHORES SOMETIME NEXT YEAR. VISIT WWW.TOKYOPOP.COM TO KEEP ABREAST OF ALL TOKYOPOP RELEASES.

ALSO AVAILABLE FROM ☯ TOKYOPOP®

MANGA

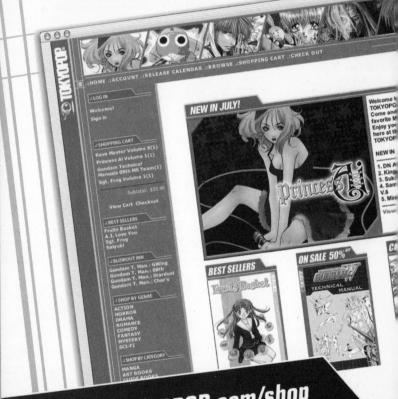

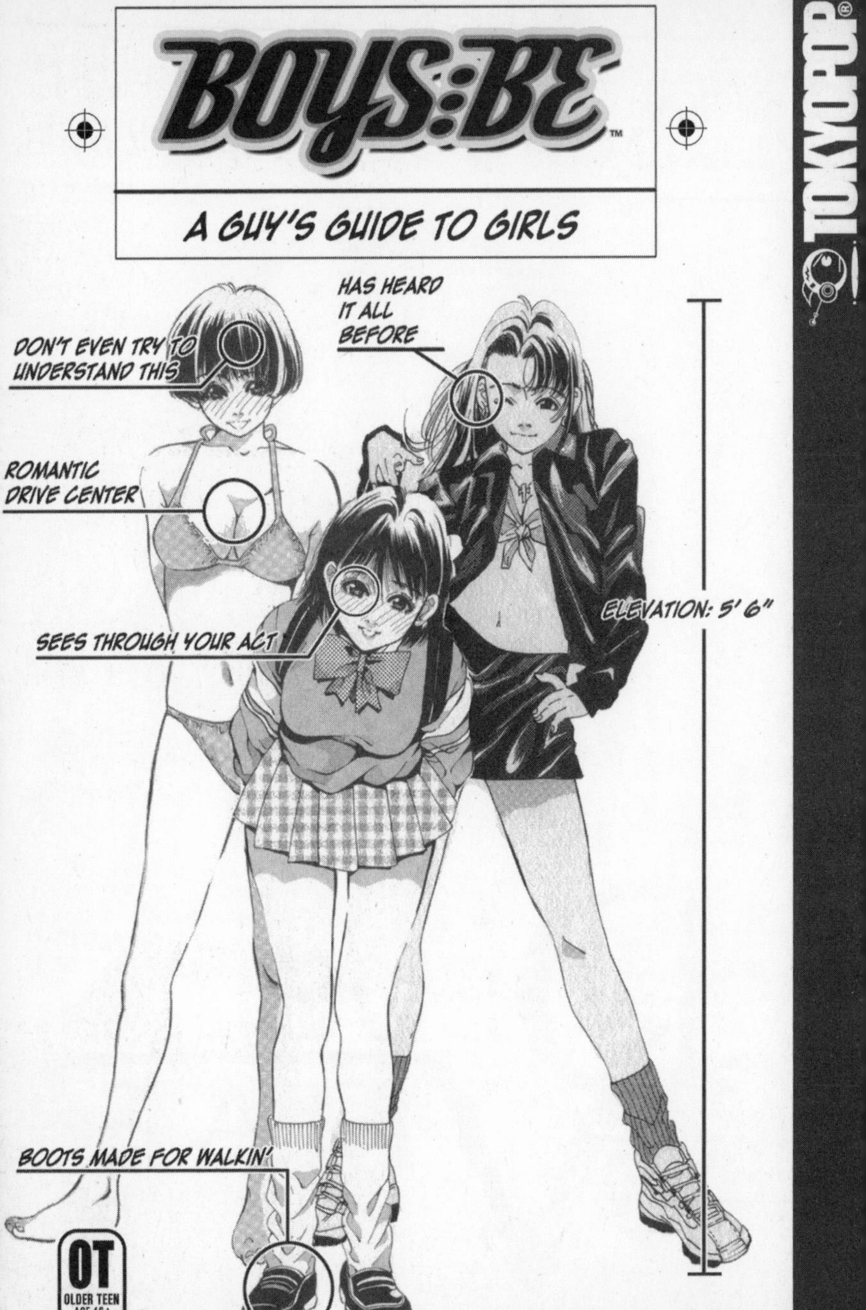
BOYS BE
A GUY'S GUIDE TO GIRLS
TOKYOPOP
HAS HEARD IT ALL BEFORE
DON'T EVEN TRY TO UNDERSTAND THIS
ROMANTIC DRIVE CENTER
SEES THROUGH YOUR ACT
ELEVATION: 5' 6"
BOOTS MADE FOR WALKIN'
OT
OLDER TEEN
AGE 16+

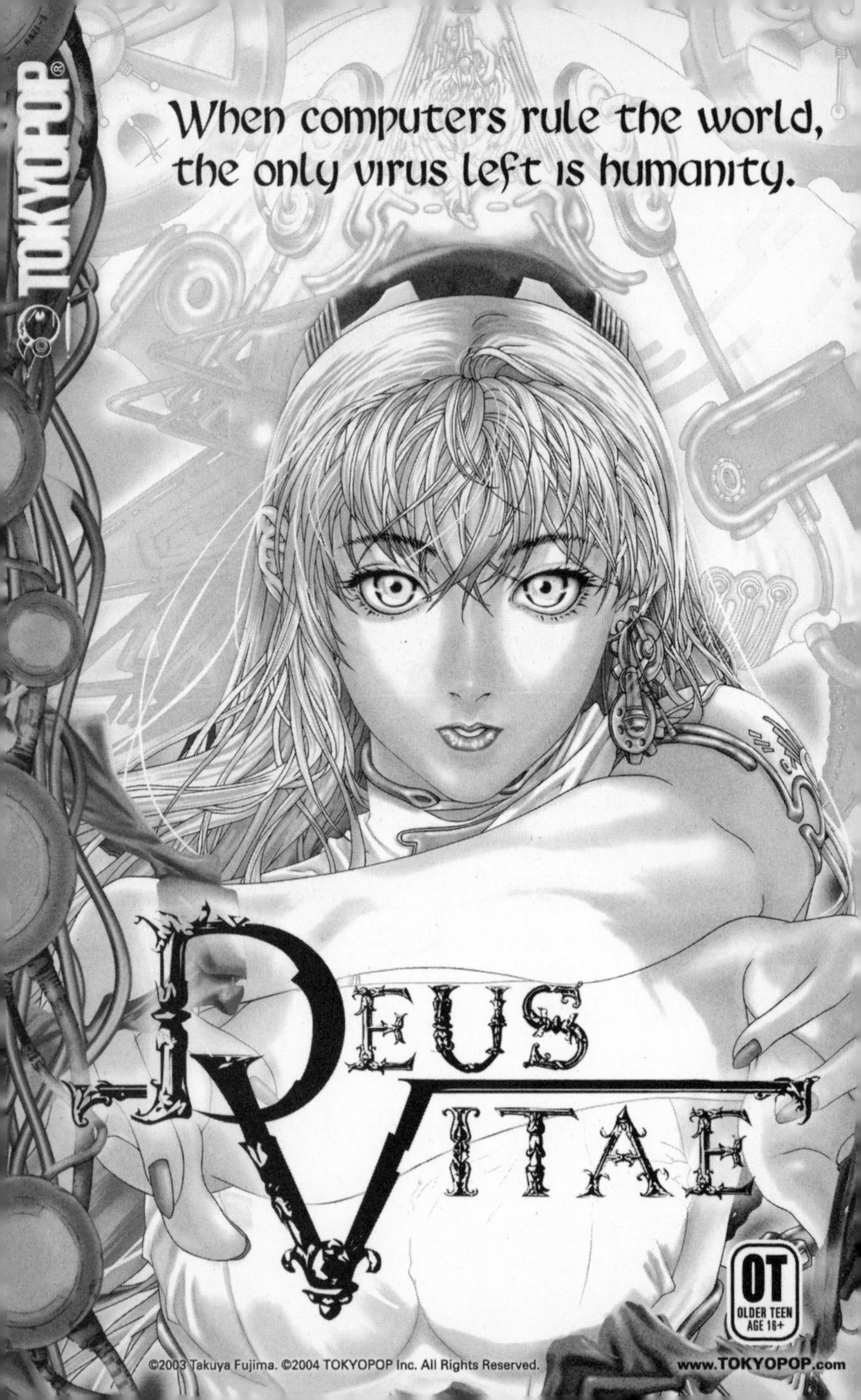
TOKYOPOP®
When computers rule the world,
the only virus left is humanity.
DEUS VITAE
OT
OLDER TEEN
AGE 16+
©2003 Takuya Fujima. ©2004 TOKYOPOP Inc. All Rights Reserved.
www.TOKYOPOP.com

TOKYOPOP®

THE DEMON

OROROON™

Love caught between
HEAVEN
and **HELL.**

www.TOKYOPOP.com

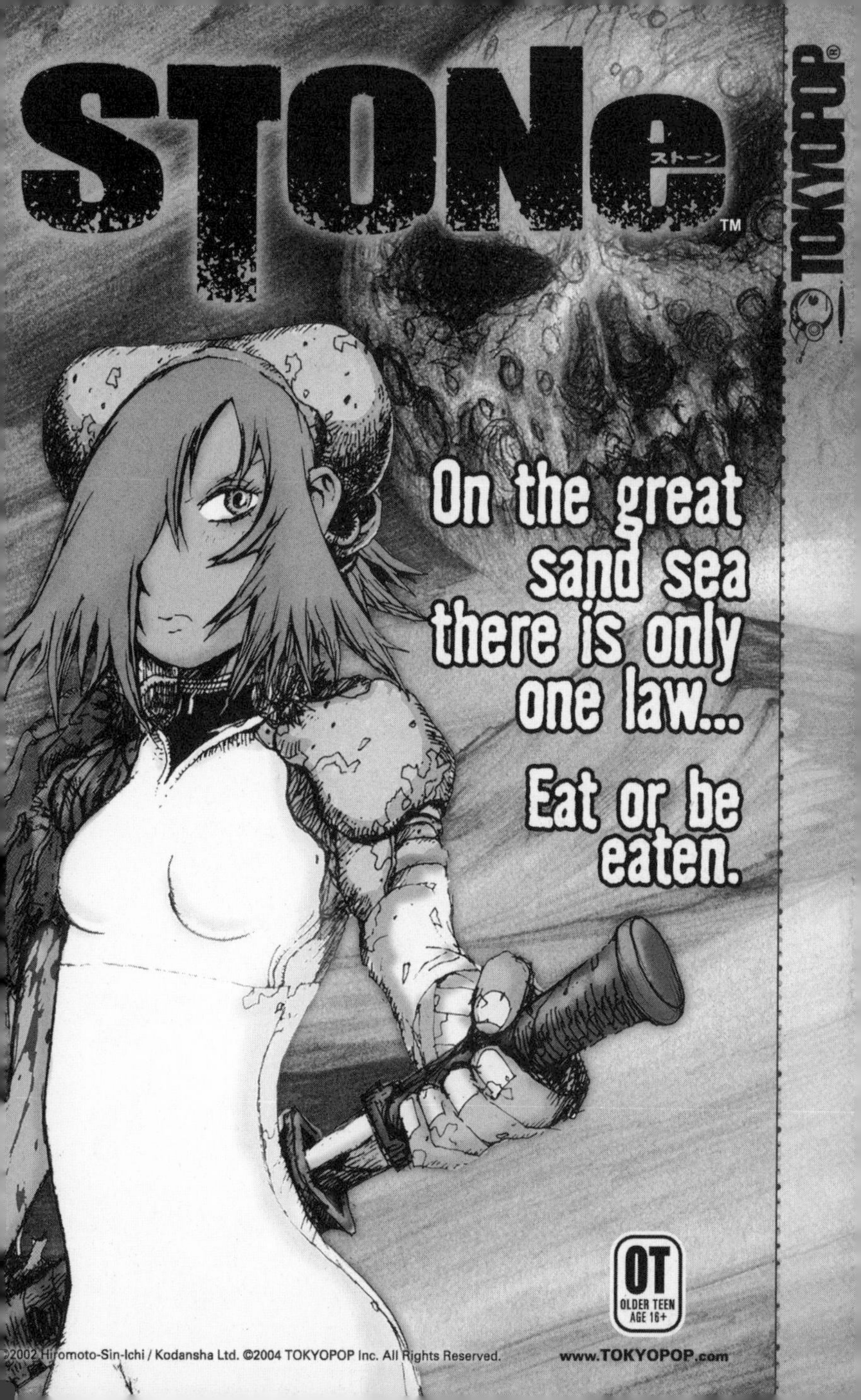
STONe
ストーン
TM
TOKYOPOP®
On the great sand sea there is only one law...
Eat or be eaten.
OT
OLDER TEEN
AGE 16+
©2002 Hiromoto-Sin-Ichi / Kodansha Ltd. ©2004 TOKYOPOP Inc. All Rights Reserved.
www.TOKYOPOP.com

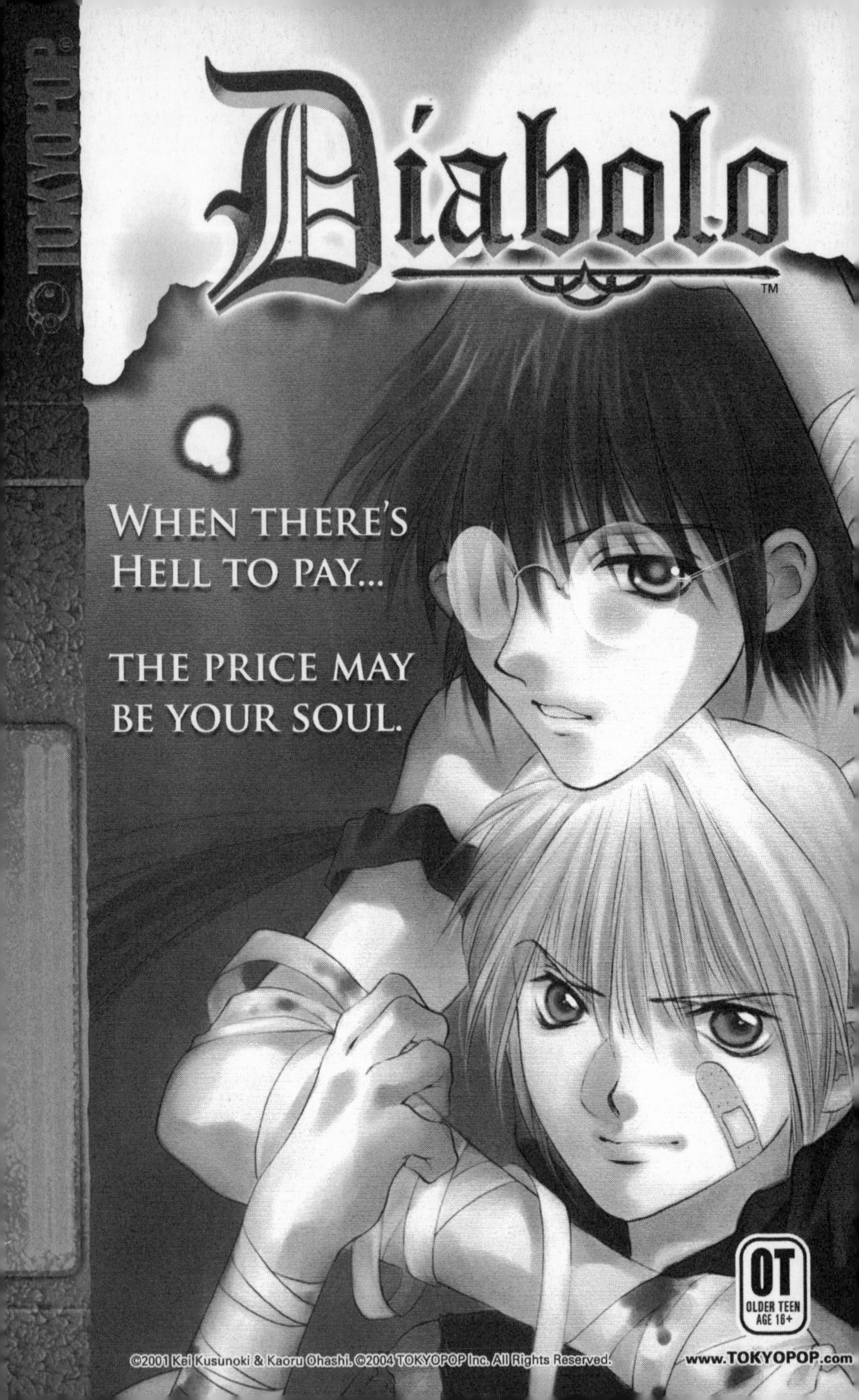

TOKYOPOP
Diabolo
TM
WHEN THERE'S HELL TO PAY...
THE PRICE MAY BE YOUR SOUL.
OT
OLDER TEEN AGE 16+
©2001 Kei Kusunoki & Kaoru Ohashi. ©2004 TOKYOPOP Inc. All Rights Reserved.
www.TOKYOPOP.com

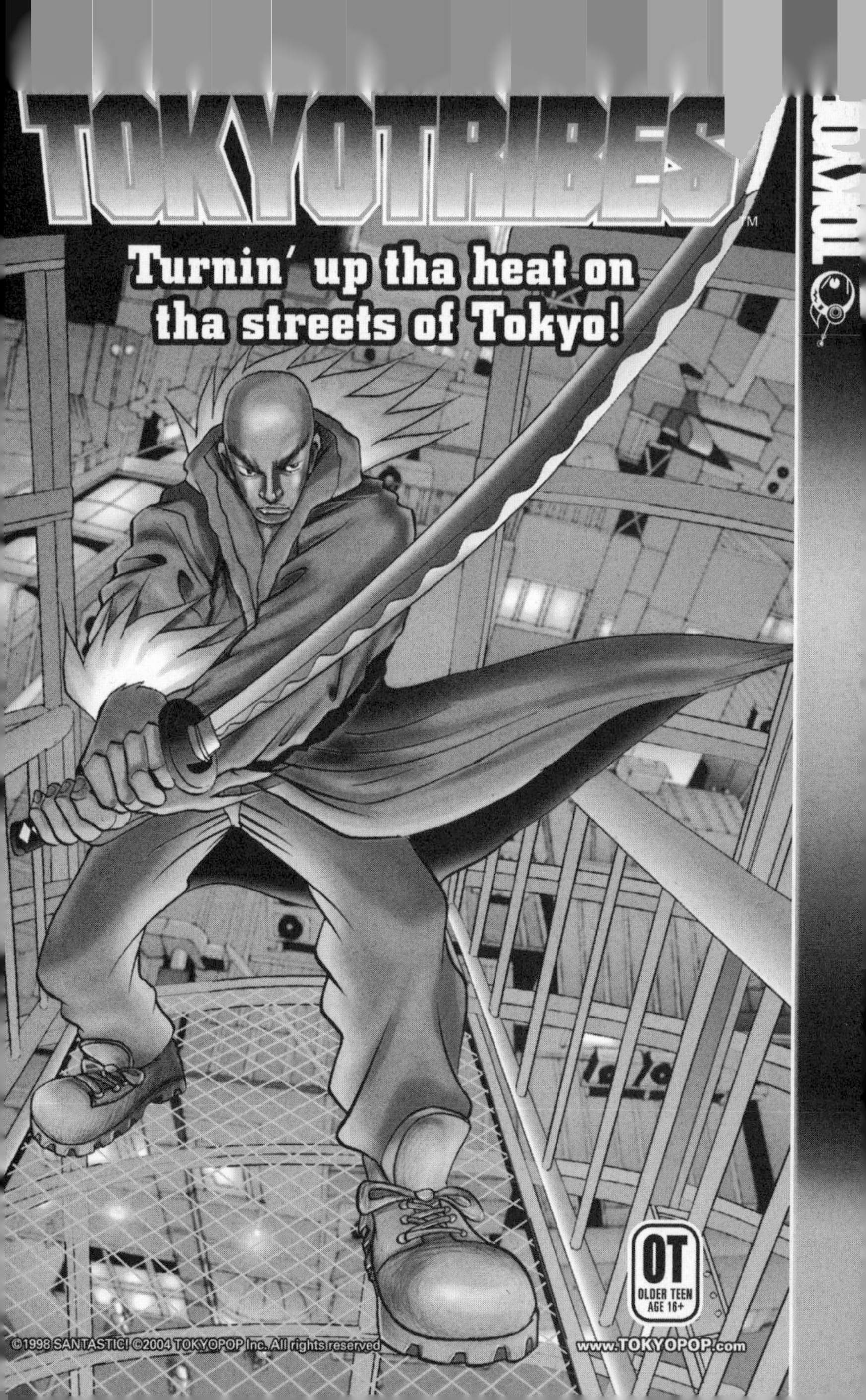
TOKYO TRIBES™
Turnin' up tha heat on
tha streets of Tokyo!
TOKYOPOP
OT
OLDER TEEN
AGE 16+
©1998 SANTASTIC! ©2004 TOKYOPOP Inc. All rights reserved.
www.TOKYOPOP.com

ARM OF KANNON

WHEN EVIL'S LET OUT...
EVERYONE WANTS IN!